BRITAIN ON YOUR OWN

BRITAIN

ON YOUR OWN

A Guide for Single

Mature Travelers

Dorothy Maroncelli

WEST WIND BOOKS

BRITAIN ON YOUR OWN
A Guide for Single Mature Travelers

WEST WIND BOOKS
P.O. Box 246
Dundas, MN 55019

Printed by Thomson-Shore, Dexter, Michigan, in the United States of America.

Cover photo by British Tourist Authority.
Cover design by D. Maroncelli.
Book design by Charles Alexander at Alexander Writing/Design/Publishing
in Tucson, Arizona.

Publisher's Cataloging in Publication
(Prepared by Quality Books, Inc.)

Maroncelli, Dorothy.
    Britain on your own: a guide for single mature travelers /
Dorothy Maroncelli.
    p. cm.
    Includes index.
    Preassigned LCCN: 96- 90538
    ISBN 0-9653652-5-5

    1. Britain--Guidebooks. 2. Single persons—Travel—Britain—
Guidebooks. 3. Aged—Travel—Britain—Guidebooks. I. Title.

DA650.M37 1997   914.104'859
                                   QBI96-40246

To Nick, for all

the days of wine and roses

ACKNOWLEDGMENTS

No book of this kind can be written without the help of many people, and I am grateful for all the incidental help many gave. Very special thanks to Deborah Vajda Johnson, my editor, for her encouragement and for keeping me focused and on the path I wanted to follow. Thanks to Robin Prestage of the British Tourist Authority who, for two years, willingly answered my many questions; to Charles Alexander, my designer, who patiently put up with my nit-picking; to Joan Truax for the lovely illustrations that decorate four of the book's section title pages; and to Barbara Goodman, of Norwest's World Banking Division, who reviewed my section on British currency.

Thanks to Methuen London for permission to use the quotation from H. V. Morton's *In Search of England* and to Ann Kelley for the use of excerpts from *Born and Bred: Portraits of St. Ives*; to *British Heritage* for permission to quote P. D. James from an article in the April/May 1994 issue; and to the National Institute of Adult Continuing Education for allowing me to reproduce a page from its directory *Time to Learn*.

I am grateful for all the help I have received from the Tourist Information Centres in Britain. I especially thank the employees of the Shrewsbury TIC for much help beyond the normal courteous assistance I expected. I appreciate the permission to use photographs from the following: The British Tourist Authority for a number of photographs, including the cover photo; English Wanderer; Forte Hotels; BritRail Travel International; and Bill Kline. And thanks to the companies listed under Resources for their generous offer of assistance to travelers.

AUTHOR'S NOTE

When I look back to my first solo trip, more than a decade ago, I wonder how I set off alone with such ease, such a lack of uncertainty and concern. The state of things in my life at the time was probably the reason that I could take this trip with no misgivings.

My husband of almost forty years had just died, and instead of being half of a couple, I was suddenly single. I remember wanting to be alone to walk on a quiet beach with the sea washing on the sand and to reminisce and think about what lay ahead for me.

So I went to Texas for the winter, and I rented a condo on Corpus Christi Beach. But instead of spending my days in semi-seclusion, I found my time filled with activities. I did walk on the beach, often at sunrise or sunset. But I joined other seniors in classes offered by a local college, and I went to museums, shopped, and had lunch with other snowbirds I met. When I felt like it, I spent the day by myself. I found that traveling solo suited me, and I also discovered what the writer Albert Camus had: "In the depth of winter, I finally learned that within me there lay an invincible summer."

When I returned home that spring, I decided that the next winter I would strike out for a more distant shore, and I chose Britain for obvious reasons—there was no culture shock, no language problem, the transportation system was excellent, and winters there were mild compared with Wisconsin's.

I had no set itinerary that first year; I just roamed for three months. I traveled everywhere by bus and train. Sometimes I lingered longer in a town than I had planned to; sometimes I backtracked to return to a place I'd left too soon. And everywhere I went I stored up paintings of Britain in my mind. I became an Anglophile and continued to spend time in Britain each winter.

I never expected to write a book about these travels, but after wandering through the country for several more winters, I decided that other mature singles, in like situations, should know how enjoyable the experience can be.

Uncommon Gems

    St Ives   163

    Portmeirion   176

    Hay-on-Wye   185

V   TRAVELING SMART

Traveling Smart   197

    Traveling Light   197

    Hotels, Inns, and Cottages   206

    American/British English   215

    On Rails and Back Roads   217

    Dollars and Pounds   225

    Tours and Travel Agents   228

    Staying Healthy—Staying Safe   231

    Restaurants, Picnics, and Pubs   234

    Miscellaneous Notes   236

        Airports   236

        Passports   238

        Insurance   238

        Shopping   239

        Discounts   239

        The Home Front   240

RESOURCES   243

INDEX   246

A COLLAGE OF PLEASURES

A first-time visitor to Britain is unprepared for the intriguing diversity in the towns and villages and in the constantly changing landscape on this island that Oliver Wendell Holmes called "this little speck."

To enjoy carefree travel on your own in Britain, you can design a trip to fit just you. You can trace the history of Britain or follow in the footsteps of kings, writers, craftsmen, and artists of all kinds.

A GLIMPSE OF BRITAIN

I took a vow that . . . I would go home in search of England, I would go through the lanes of England and the little thatched villages of England, and I would lean over English bridges and lie on English grass watching an English sky.

— H. V. Morton, *In Search of England*

When the British writer H. V. Morton made that vow more than seventy years ago, he was ill, in a country far from home, and feared he was dying. When he recovered and was again home in England, he set out to wander the lanes and byways as he had longed to do.

He said that with the road calling him out into England he would see what lay off the beaten track; would, as the mood struck him, go into famous towns and unknown hamlets. He would bring the knights and cavaliers back to the roads; talk with lords and cottagers, tramps, gypsies, and dogs. He would just sit and watch the ducks on the village pond, and would suddenly and light-heartedly do anything that came into his head.

Today there are few unknown hamlets, and it is not easy to find an unbeaten track, but the little thatched villages and the ducks on the village pond are still there, and you can still talk with cottagers and dogs. And at times, in the ruins of medieval castles, echoes of knights and cavaliers seem to linger in the air.

Traveling through Britain today is easier than it was seventy years ago. Buses and trains branch into hidden corners and open up places that in the past were reachable only on foot or horseback. Exploring on your own is an exciting adventure. It stretches your mind; it recharges you. Writer William Zinsser called just stepping off a plane in a foreign country "instant otherness." The "otherness" is not so great in Britain, and this simplifies wandering through the country on your own. You will find similarities to America everywhere. And without the foreignness that might intimidate a solo traveler, you can have a relaxed and memorable experience.

This little island, Shakespeare's "precious stone set in the silver sea," would fit into less than two-thirds of California, but despite its small size,

British towns and villages are suprisingly diverse. There are golden stone cottages in Cotswold villages so mellow that they suggest a life of ease—of tweed and cashmere—while not far away are gray stone hamlets hunkered at the foot of Welsh mountains, where, not long ago, the slate that roofed Britain was laboriously quarried. Nearby are the bustling market towns of Shropshire with their half-timbered black-and-white buildings. In old Cornish fishing villages the sun glints off houses of granite, and farther north along the coast, cottages where Somerset fishermen once lived are still wrapped in whitewashed cob under thatch.

Courtesy of Bill Kline

Today harbors in old fishing villages draw more tourists than fishermen.

These striking differences in regions go back to the days of poor transportation, when towns were built using whatever materials could be found locally. You can still find hardscrabble areas where, earlier in this century, Scottish crofters lived in small stone cots roofed with heather and farmed tiny, mere subsistence, patches of land. In the Southeast, the "Garden of England," houses might be made of brick and timber, hung with clay tiles, or faced with mortar embedded with black cut flint that glistens in the rain. The exterior of some houses in East Anglia are still decorated, as they once were, with intricate ornamental plasterwork known as pargeting. Towns that were once famous for their spas are known today for the parks and gardens that complement their build-ings' elegant Regency and Georgian architecture.

As distinctive as each separate town is, Britain is unified by the ines-capable fact that it is an island. Wherever you go in Britain, you are never more than seventy-five miles from the sea. And Britain's heritage is strongly linked to the sea. England became a sea power after the defeat of the Spanish Armada in 1588; fishing was the livelihood of those in hundreds of villages that dot Britain's coast; artists and poets have long celebrated the sea with their masterworks. The sea still influ-ences life in Britain, but in different ways. Sheltered harbors where fish-ing trawlers once rocked are now scattered with yachts and sailboats; sand beaches that were used in olden days by fishermen mending nets are now filled with bikini-clad swimmers; and North Sea oil rigs speckle the ocean off Scotland. The sea will always have a hold—one way or another—on the British.

Of all the customs and traditions in British culture, the singular institu-tion that most Americans seek out is the pub—the public house. In 1776, Samuel Johnson wrote, "There is nothing which has yet been contrived by man, by which so much happiness is produced as by a good tavern or inn."

When Johnson wrote those words, scattered wayside taverns and inns were places for weary stagecoach passengers to rest and have a meal by fireside. In villages and towns, the public houses were for drinking, socializing, and eating, and on market day tradesmen carried on their business over a pint of ale. Today, many travelers find, as I do, that lunch in a pub is just what suits one after a busy morning. Some pubs still have swinging signs, elaborately painted with pictures depicting the name of the pub—Queen's Head, White Hart, Black Bull, Rose and Crown. Many of these date back to the 14th century when few people could read and Richard II made it compulsory for inns to have pictorial signs that were easily recognizable.

Most pubs have a cozy feel. Old ones have ancient beams, leaded windows, and low ceilings. Many have high-backed wooden settles or benches and chairs upholstered in tapestry or some other sturdy fabric. I found one with snuggeries—little nooks partly walled in for privacy—where I would go during off-hours to have cider and a snack while I made notes on my morning excursion.

In most pubs the hiss and crackle of a log fire will welcome you on a chill day. Or there might be a blazing coal fire with its slightly pungent odor, as my "writing" pub had. It is easy to find the genial hearth, hospitable board, and refined rusticity that Wordsworth wrote of. If you stop after the lunch rush, most bartenders are eager to tell you about their town or to talk about America, and often others join in the conversation.

As hospitable as a pub but more sedate is the hotel lounge, sometimes called the drawing room or the "residents' lounge." Unlike American hotel lobbies, which are often used for meeting or waiting, these inviting sitting rooms are for guests to enjoy and relax in. Some lounges have marshmallow-comfy chintz-covered sofas and chairs grouped around a fireplace. Others have the air of a British men's club, with leather furnishings and walls richly paneled in polished dark wood. And you will find some with lovely rose or spring-green velvet furnishings lit by the glow of wall sconces. Most have a small library and a desk or writing table for guests to use.

This lovely drawing room is a restful oasis in a luxury Forte Hotel.

The hotel lounge is a place where you can meet other guests over coffee, tea, or wine, or simply spend a quiet hour reading or writing. Instead of having this separate room for relaxing, some hotels have an area between the bar and the dining room where you can unwind. Your days in Britain will often be brightened by someone you meet in a hotel lounge.

Two hundred years ago an Englishman wrote, "It must be admitted that the English are in general inhospitable toward foreigners," and that notion seems to persist today. But I have found the British to be open, good-humored, and easy to talk with—and always helpful. Perhaps they are more welcoming to one traveling alone, or to a more mature person. Or maybe wearing a smile makes the difference.

On one trip, I stayed in a town not far from Castle Combe, a village I wanted to visit. It was voted the prettiest village in England in 1962 and was Puddleby-on-the-Marsh in *Doctor Dolittle*. When the woman in the bus office told me there was no service to the village, she could see how disappointed I was. She thought for a moment and then said, "Everyone should see Castle Combe. If you can wait until Saturday—that's my day off—I'll take you." Unfriendly? Hardly.

I remember, with fondness, another "day brightener." From Stroud I was walking to Rodborough Fort, on a hilltop outside of town. As I neared the fort I came to a point where I was on the brow of a hill overlooking the rooftops of Stroud. I stopped to photograph the town and as I concentrated, a voice some way behind me said, "That'll be a good picture."

I turned and saw a lanky young man smiling as he strode up. With him was a little black-and-white dog with a pointy nose and perky ears. We talked for a minute and when I said I was on my way to the fort, he said they were, too, and they'd walk up with me. We followed the path edging the ridge, and below us stretched a broad valley, rumpled with hills and seamed with hedgerows. Towns were scattered as far as we could see. He named the places for me while I photographed them. The little dog dashed ahead and then stopped to wait patiently for us to catch up.

After we had reached the fort, we said good-bye and parted. I started down the hill back toward town while they set off down the other side of the hill. It just happened that after we had walked a short way, we each stopped and looked back at the same time. He waved and I waved, and we each continued down our side of the hill. Day brighteners like these are free gifts, and there are many of them.

Instead of limiting your horizons, maybe it's time to think about spicing up your life with a trip just for you. You might find Morton's England or you might discover your own special corner of Britain. And a solo trip can truly be a carefree trip when you design it to fit just you.

No one can draw a chart for someone else. But perhaps some of the ideas here will kindle your curiosity—will press you to dust off the dream you filed in a cubbyhole in your mind long ago. Maybe it's time to treat yourself, and start planning your trip.

A DESIGN FOR SOLO TRAVEL

Life was meant to be lived, and curiosity must be kept alive. One must never, for whatever reason, turn his back on life.
—Eleanor Roosevelt

When I planned my first trip to Britain, I got an unexpected reaction from friends. "You're going alone? You have no relatives there? No friends? I could never do that." Even after I told them of things I would do—take classes, walk in the mountains, sightsee from buses and trains, sit by the sea and eat my lunch—they were still skeptical.

They said, "Maybe if I were younger," and added, "but not at my age." Age was not a consideration in my decision to go, but my friends' doubts about it brought to mind a story about Oliver Wendell Holmes. Franklin Delano Roosevelt stopped to pay his respects one evening and found Holmes in his library, reading Plato. After visiting awhile Roosevelt asked, "Mr. Justice, may I ask why you are reading Plato?" The ninety-two-year-old Holmes answered, "Why, to improve my mind, Mr. President."

Barring medical problems, age is no reason to fear setting off on your own, to be afraid to gather memories to treasure instead of just collecting birthdays. At the age of eighty-five, political advisor Bernard Baruch said, "To me old age is always fifteen years older than I am." Traveling alone can be intimidating if you're a first-timer, especially if you are newly single after years of being half of a couple. Many British people were as surprised at my going alone as those at home had been. They voiced their approval with comments like "Good on you" and "Marks for you." If you are apprehensive about traveling solo, there are choices you can make to lessen fears you have.

There are three steps you can take to raise your comfort level and increase your chance of having a really special time. *Design your own trip* by choosing the places you want to visit and enthusiasm will replace doubts; *go off-season* to assure an easier, more relaxed trip; and *travel light* and you will have freedom. You can take these three steps with little effort and you will find your optimism growing.

Travelers to Britain often mistakenly refer to the entire island as England, but Wales and Scotland, though united politically with England, are independent countries. The Welsh and the Scottish are proud of their distinct history and traditions and hold their separate identities. Understanding the terms that define Britain and the islands will eliminate confusion in your travels.

Britain (Great Britain): England, Scotland, and Wales

United Kingdom (UK): Britain plus Northern Ireland

British Isles: UK plus the Republic of Ireland and the adjacent islands.

Design Your Own Trip

Part of the romance of travel is seeing, at hand, places you've read about and almost know. And planning "on-your-own" travel to Britain is easier and more enjoyable than you might think.

Britain is a land of soft green hills flecked with sheep and crisscrossed with centuries-old hedges and drystone walls. It is a land of meadows and marshes, of windswept moors, bleak and forbidding in a rain. There are places where rugged crags plunge a hundred feet to an angry sea and then share the ragged coast with white sand beaches edged with waving palm trees. And there are mountain massifs that once sheltered men defending their lands against invaders where today outsiders come to enjoy the solitude.

Ancient forests, once the hunting grounds of kings, are among many places that are designated Areas of Outstanding Natural Beauty. These, together with many splendid National Parks, make up almost a quarter of England's total area. In Wales and Scotland, mountain and coastal stretches are among the regions named for their scenic beauty. When you begin to narrow down the places you'd like to visit, some will probably be in or near these parks and special spots.

Doing research and deciding where to go is part of the pleasure of travel. Singles are often advised to go to a large city because there is more to do there, but I disagree. You will want to spend time in London, one of the world's greatest cities, but it is easier to relax and really enjoy yourself away from the city bustle and rush. City restaurants and pubs are crowded at all hours, as are city-center streets. The press of people in cities and the noise of streets clogged with cars and buses belching exhaust rule out the leisurely vacation most of us want. I like the unhurried atmosphere of a smaller town and find that the people have a warmth not found in big-city dwellers.

More than seventy years ago Frank Tatchell, an English clergyman, said, "The beaten track is often the best track, but devote most of your time to the by-ways. In no other way can you so quickly reach the heart of a country." That statement is even more true today. Although the charm of the original "old town" in most major cities has been preserved, many places have lost their character in the rush toward progress. Miles of housing developments, called "estates" (many just connected row houses), have been built, and as the towns burgeoned they became victims of "placelessness"—look-alikes of other cities.

However, there is still much to attract you to bigger towns and cities— museums, historic treasures, theaters, and the old town centers. So if what you're interested in seeing and doing can be found only in a big city, you can get the best of both by finding a nearby small town to stay in, and taking the train or bus to the city for the day. Edinburgh (pronounced Edin-bur-uh), for example, is an excellent city for a day-trip if you're in that part of the country. Well-groomed, elegant, and dignified, it's one of Europe's most beautiful cities. It is easy to get to by train, and the train station is in the center of the city, so you can touch many of the highlights in one day.

The easiest and most pleasurable way to travel is to pick one place, a "hub," where you can unpack, settle in for a few days, and have a temporary home. Then you can take day-trips to nearby places. Consider three to four days the minimum time to spend in a hub town. On a two-week vacation you can easily visit two or three areas and still have a few days left to spend in London at the beginning or end of your trip.

In even those few days you will get to know people in your hotel and in the restaurants, pubs, and shops that you frequent. When you become acquainted with a few and are greeted by them when you meet on the street it adds a note of cheer to your day. And if you are among those who become true Anglophiles and you return to the town on another trip, some of the people you get to know just in passing will remember you.

If this is the first time you have planned your own trip and done your own research, you might have misgivings, but you will find that as you get into it you will look forward to the time you spend making plans. You can design your trip in easy steps. Because Great Britain is the number-one overseas destination for Americans, there is a wealth of information available to you.

The place to begin is with the **British Tourist Authority** (BTA), one of the best foreign tourist offices in the country. Contact it in person at either the New York or Chicago office or call the toll-free telephone number. (All addresses and telephone numbers referred to are listed under Resources at the back of the book.) Ask the BTA for the annual *Your Vacation Planner* and a map of Britain for travelers. The planner briefly describes every area of Britain and has helpful details on many subjects: climate, currency, traveling around, and special events are just a few. This and the map will quickly give you an overview of Great Britain. Included in the planner are a few pages showing books that you can buy from **BritRail's British Travel Shop** to make your planning easier.

If you have a special interest or hobby ask the BTA for a list called *Forthcoming Events* for the time of year you will be in Britain. It lists fairs, shows, and festivals of special note throughout all of Britain and it might steer you to a particular area for an event you'd enjoy attending. After

you have read the BTA planner and are fairly familiar with the map of
Britain, you can begin to think about areas you'd like to visit. When you
start studying different places in detail, a good atlas becomes important.
Buy one and consider it part of the cost of your trip. Look for an atlas
with a scale of three miles to an inch rather than the more common four
miles to an inch. This magnification makes a real difference in clarity and
detail. If you can't find a 3 mile/1 inch atlas at a bookstore, you can get
an excellent one from BritRail's British Travel Shop. It is called *AA Big
Road Atlas — Britain*. The travel shop is owned by BritRail Travel International, the British railway company. Call the travel shop and ask for its
catalog of maps and books on Britain.

With an enlarged atlas like this you'll find villages too small to be on
some maps—villages with curious names like Piddlehinton, Scrooby,
Blubberhouses, Thimbleby, and Logie Pert. And some with unpro-
nounceable names like Ffawyddog, Myddfai, Plwmp, and the
grandaddy of them all—Llanfairpwllgwyngyllgogerychwyrndrobwlll-
lantysiliogogog och, called just Llanfair P.G. Incidentally, the name
means "the church of St. Mary by the hollow of white aspen, over the
whirlpool and St. Tysilio's Church close to the red cave."

The maps also clearly show railway lines and stations, which will help
in your planning. If you are not used to reading maps, now is the time to
practice. Get one of your familiar home area and use it. You'll enjoy finding your way around towns and following your routes on buses and
trains in Britain if you can easily read a map.

Area divisions in England and Wales are counties, and in Scotland
they are regions. In Anglo-Saxon days counties were called shires and
were often named after an important town. Many counties such as Yorkshire, Warwickshire, and Cambridgeshire still carry those names. The
Old English word for administrative head of a shire was reeve, shire-
reeve, still in use today as sheriff. The map reproduced here shows the
counties as they were revised in the 1970s.

With the great diversity that exists between the counties in Britain,
choosing where to go can become a puzzle. Gwynedd in Wales shares
few similarities with Kent in England, just as Cornwall and Gloucestershire are as different as a harp is from a bagpipe. It takes a few weeks of
reading to comprehend the contrasts between counties, but visiting
places that are distinctly unalike will add interest to your travels.

When you're ready to begin researching seriously, start with your
local library. Some of the popular travel guides cover so many areas that

MAP OF THE ADMINISTRATIVE COUNTIES
AND REGIONS OF BRITAIN

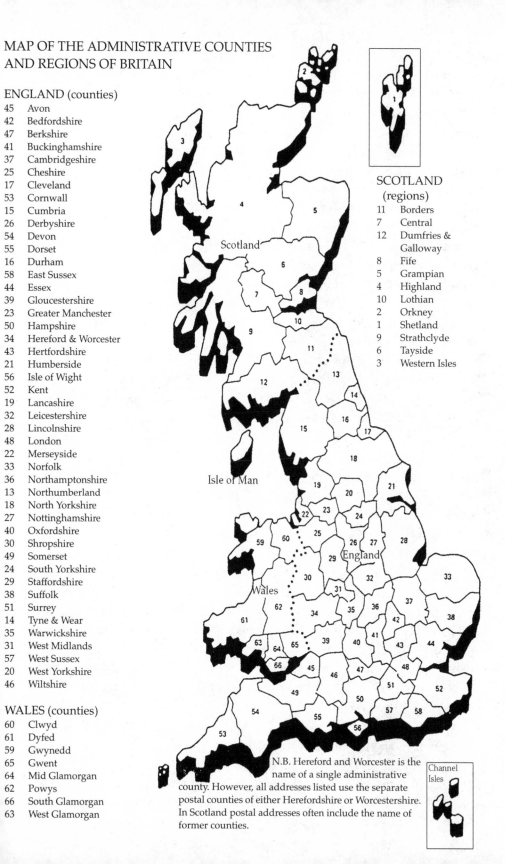

ENGLAND (counties)

45	Avon
42	Bedfordshire
47	Berkshire
41	Buckinghamshire
37	Cambridgeshire
25	Cheshire
17	Cleveland
53	Cornwall
15	Cumbria
26	Derbyshire
54	Devon
55	Dorset
16	Durham
58	East Sussex
44	Essex
39	Gloucestershire
23	Greater Manchester
50	Hampshire
34	Hereford & Worcester
43	Hertfordshire
21	Humberside
56	Isle of Wight
52	Kent
19	Lancashire
32	Leicestershire
28	Lincolnshire
48	London
22	Merseyside
33	Norfolk
36	Northamptonshire
13	Northumberland
18	North Yorkshire
27	Nottinghamshire
40	Oxfordshire
30	Shropshire
49	Somerset
24	South Yorkshire
29	Staffordshire
38	Suffolk
51	Surrey
14	Tyne & Wear
35	Warwickshire
31	West Midlands
57	West Sussex
20	West Yorkshire
46	Wiltshire

WALES (counties)

60	Clwyd
61	Dyfed
59	Gwynedd
65	Gwent
64	Mid Glamorgan
62	Powys
66	South Glamorgan
63	West Glamorgan

SCOTLAND (regions)

11	Borders
7	Central
12	Dumfries & Galloway
8	Fife
5	Grampian
4	Highland
10	Lothian
2	Orkney
1	Shetland
9	Strathclyde
6	Tayside
3	Western Isles

N.B. Hereford and Worcester is the name of a single administrative county. However, all addresses listed use the separate postal counties of either Herefordshire or Worcestershire. In Scotland postal addresses often include the name of former counties.

not much can be written about one place, but you can get basic facts from them, so they're a start.

The best reference books I've seen on Great Britain are those published by the **Automobile Association of Great Britain** (AA). Their chief value is in the specific details they give about places. There are three books in particular that are excellent. Unfortunately they are out of print, but try your library for them. If your local library doesn't have them it might be able to get them for you through its library lending system. One of the books, *AA Illustrated Guide to Britain,* is divided into thirteen "zones" covering all of Britain. Each zone includes physical description, climate, and special points of interest and is then subdivided into smaller sections with brief descriptions of a total of almost 2,000 villages, towns, and cities. This book gives a wonderful overview of all of Britain.

AA Book of British Villages profiles 700 villages and *AA Book of British Towns* includes almost as many towns. All three books are filled with numerous color photos that picture every part of Britain, from isolated lochs and castles in northern Scotland to snug coastal villages in southern Cornwall—and most of the spots in between. Maps in these books are well defined, are easy to use, and will help you focus on specific areas you might be interested in.

I was fortunate in being able to buy all three of these AA books in used book stores on my trips to Britain. If you aren't able to find them at a library, AA publishes many other books that are available from Brit-Rail's British Travel Shop, but I haven't seen any that are as all-inclusive as these. Be sure to go through the travel shop's catalog of all the books, maps, and other helps that are for sale.

In most libraries of any size you can get books on certain regions of Britain. You can probably also check out travel magazines that contain articles on Britain. An excellent magazine to look for is *British Heritage,* published bimonthly. It is self-described as delivering the "best of British pleasures, treasures, travel, traditions, and more," and that is what it does. If your library doesn't subscribe to it, look for it on the newsstand. You can also check with a university or college, if there is one near you, to see if you can use its library.

Another useful publication is *International Travel News,* a monthly newsprint magazine on foreign destinations, with features and columns covering all aspects of overseas travel. Much of the magazine is written for veteran travelers who visit exotic places, but the information on basic planning, accommodations, and sightseeing, with firsthand tips given by readers, makes it a worthwhile magazine for anyone going anywhere. It even has a column called "Tips for the Solo Traveler." For a free sample copy of this "reader-friendly" magazine, just request it from the publisher.

As you read about Britain, certain areas will begin to stand out as appealing to you. Now would be a good time to take advantage of an offer included in BTA's *Your Vacation Planner*. In the booklet is a coupon for ordering a number of brochures, including some on specific interests, such as guides to gardens, antiques, sports, and filming locations of movies. The only cost is a small charge for postage and handling.

Once you have chosen the places you want to visit, you can check your atlas to see where the nearest railway station is and what towns are nearby for possible day-trips. Most towns have local bus service, but you will want to be sure of it. Occasionally I have taken a taxi to a village for a day-trip, but on a daily basis you will want more economical and reliable transportation. The only way to get information on local buses is by contacting the tourist office in or near the town you're interested in. The BTA has a map-directory called *Tourist Information Centres in Britain*. It shows the location of all the centers (TICs) in the country, gives the address and telephone number of each, and tells which ones are open all year. If you have reached the point of zeroing in on a number of towns, find the center nearest your choices and contact it about bus service. One caution: the TICs in Britain have neither the staff nor the funds to answer all letters, especially those from other countries. As a courtesy, send a Postal International Reply Coupon with your inquiry. These coupons are expensive, now over a dollar, and have a value equal to only one first-class British stamp. Not enough if a TIC has to send large brochures or schedules, but still some help. And of course, U.S. stamps cannot be used in Britain. Expect about a two-week wait for a first-class reply. I sometimes make a short telephone call for a bit of information that is holding up my planning.

Most books and brochures you read will include the history of a place, particularly in connection with two events—the Domesday Book and the English Civil War. Domesday Book was a survey of property in England ordered by William the Conqueror in 1086, twenty years after his Norman conquest of Britain. This elaborate detailed record was an accounting of villages, buildings, farmlands, and woodlands—even down to numbers of horses, pigs, ploughs, and serfs.

Domesday (Doomsday) was what the people called the Final Day of Judgment from which there was no escape, so Domesday Book was an appropriate name for this record of searches. Although the survey didn't include all of England, if towns you visit were listed in the Domesday Book, material will probably refer to it and give the name of the town as it was then. For example, York was Euruic and Shrewsbury was Sciropesberie. In many places no records had ever been kept until the Domesday survey, even though some towns and villages were already several hundred years old at the time, so places that are included in the book could well be more than 1,000 years old today. Remembering that roads you walk were trod by people that long ago and imagining how their lives were then enriches your stay anyplace.

The Civil War, sparked by political and religious differences between King Charles I and Parliament, took place in the early 1640s. The king's Royalists eventually lost to the Parliamentarians, led by Oliver Cromwell, and in 1649 Charles I was executed. Perhaps the reason the Civil War is mentioned so often is that some 600 battles were fought during those years. With such widespread combat, the war touched many towns and became an important part of their history.

courtesy of British Tourist Authority

Caernervon Castle in northern Wales is one of Europe's greatest medieval fortresses.

Many places of historic interest are being preserved by an organization called the National Trust, founded 100 years ago to protect Britain's heritage. The trust is a private charity, not a department of the British government. It cares for more than 500 miles of coastline and almost 600,000 acres of countryside. The National Trust has thousands of properties, including medieval manors, massive castles, and great houses where the famous once lived. Not all of its properties are of such a grand scale, however; it also has some as small as a dovecote or a cottage garden. Canals, windmills, even islands and entire villages are under its protection. The trust is now the biggest private landowner in the country. Most of its holdings have been gifts or legacies.

Fortunately, people of all ages volunteer to help with the tremendous task of maintaining all these treasures. By welcoming children's help the trust is, in a way, educating future adults to conserve their heritage. Today there are about 28,000 volunteers who do the work of 800 full-time employees.

Because of the overcrowding and heavy tourism on this small island, the trust, in an attempt to protect the countryside, does not publicize some of its lands. Writer John J. Norwich wrote in the *National Trust Guide*, "Of all the qualities of landscape that this country can boast, solitude is already one of the rarest and consequently one of the most vitally important to preserve where it exists."

Wherever you are in Britain you will be near some gorgeous National Trust property. Most of the trust's houses are closed in midwinter, when trained staff check every object in the buildings for needed repairs, but you can still visit many of their other properties. And there are some 200 National Trust Shops scattered throughout the country where you can buy British gifts.

Sometimes working with the trust is a fledgling charity that only recently celebrated its twenty-fifth anniversary—the Landmark Trust. It rescues and revives derelict buildings of all kinds. Some of its buildings were abandoned and so overgrown with brush and weeds that they could hardly be reached; others were partly roofless—their original timber beams rotted, walls decayed, and floors fallen away. In one room of a restored building most of the exquisite plasterwork that originally decorated the ceiling and walls had crumbled away. Skilled plasterers worked for 6,000 hours to restore it to its former beauty. In a Landmark Trust account of its work it was noted that "to repair these ruins of wood and plaster, eaten away by English weather, is like patching a cobweb." Visitors to Britain are fortunate that these two trust organizations, along with others, are caring for many of the properties that we come to see.

When you get to the point of deciding on dates for your trip be sure to note any holidays that fall during the time you'll be there. On many holidays, banks and some businesses are closed and public transportation is reduced. On Christmas Day and on Boxing Day, December 26, there are no trains or local buses. The BTA's *Your Vacation Planner* shows the dates of all holidays, including "bank holidays." Most of these dates change each year just as some of ours do. You won't want to plan on moving from one place to another when service is sharply reduced or nonexistent.

Go Off-Season

When traveling on your own you'll want a carefree trip, and going in the off-season, usually November through March, offers a relaxing and easy vacation. And, of course, it usually costs less. There are normally three "seasons" of airfares—peak, shoulder, and off-peak, or off-season. Depending on which city you fly out of, it is possible to save several hundred dollars by going in the off-season. In all the years I have traveled to Britain I have always been able to get a "sale" fare that is the lowest one of the year. Usually these fares are offered for a short time in the early fall and are good for travel between November and March or early April, with blackouts over the Christmas holidays. To reserve these fares you must, of course, know your exact dates of travel, and there are restrictions and sometimes charges on changes, cancellations, and so forth.

You'll also save on hotel costs by traveling during these months. Most hotels not only lower their rates, but they also have more rooms available. Everyone likes saving money and you will save during the off-season, but there are other unthought-of benefits.

The real reward of traveling in the off-season is that you can have the memorable trip you want. The hordes of tourists are gone. There is no jostling or elbowing by throngs of rushing sightseers. You can get a seat in a pub or restaurant; walk on a beach that in summer would be peopled like Coney Island; linger in a museum and ask questions of unoccupied guides. And queues are shorter. The British "queue" up (stand in line) everywhere—in banks, at bus stops, at taxi stands (called taxi ranks), in shops, wherever more than one waits for something. And, of course, you wait in line with them. The queue is such a fact of life in Britain that the writer George Mikes wrote, "An Englishman, even if he is alone, forms an orderly queue of one."

This beach, deserted in the off-season, is crowded with tourists the rest of the year.

With the high season finally over, the British get back to their daily lives. A sense of peace returns, with an almost audible sigh, and the casual neighborliness found in small towns is back. This is the Britain you came to see.

You might have reservations about vacationing in the winter, about rain and snow and cold, but don't let that deter you. Although Britain's weather can be as unpredictable as ours, the climate is generally moderate with few extremes of temperature. If you live in our warm southern states, you might find some days damp and chilling. But you might find that a light snow adds a Dickensian touch to a village square and is a picturesque plus to your stay.

On the other hand, if you are from our icicled deep-snow country, you will appreciate how green everything is in normally mild British winters. On a rainy day you will be sure to find a chair by a crackling fire where you can watch flames flicker and rise, then disappear, while you write letters or make plans for the next day. The often nippy air is ideal for a brisk walk. I have traveled in Britain during every month from September through March and on every trip there have been days or weeks of sunny, windless, mild days—sweater weather.

My favorite off-season months are February and March. The air is soft with the scent of spring fields, and flowers and trees are fuzzy with buds. There is an almost expectant hush except for the sparkle of birdsong. Of course, there are rainy days, but there are rainy days at home. I remember days in Oregon with a rain so light it was only a mist, and many of the rainy days in Britain are these same mizzly days.

In Britain the southern and eastern areas are the driest. The western regions, being on higher ground, get more rain, and gales off the Atlantic and the Irish Sea bring windy days. Then there are the fogs of Britain. I loved foggy days as a child and I still get great pleasure from walking in the snug intimacy of fog. "This island of ours is and always has been covered with a kind of beautiful cloud," wrote the British author G. K. Chesterton. "No one can be a good critic of England who does not understand fogs. And no one can be a really patriotic Englishman who does not like fogs."

Whatever weather you find on your trip, you can adjust to it as you do at home. Spending a day in unplanned browsing in shops near your hotel or reading a book about the area in the hotel lounge, or writing letters you haven't gotten to yet can be a welcome break on a rainy day, and if you've been rushing for several days it can revitalize you.

Of course, for some there are disadvantages in traveling in the off-season. Museums, castles, and historic sites may be closed or open only on weekends. Many of the gardens that decorate Britain are closed until March or April. There are few winter festivals, and many B&Bs and small hotels are not open. But, for me, this is the only time to go to Britain. I asked a bus driver in the Lake District when the tourist season really begins there. He answered, "Easter, but we sort of gear up at the back end of March."

The British calendar lists only two seasonal dates. "British summertime" starts the fourth Sunday of March and ends the fourth Sunday of October. That's seven months of summertime. And with the five off-season months being mild compared with winter in our northern states, even a sudden cold snap or snow can't ruin my trips to Britain.

Travel Light

Traveling light is the most important and maybe the most difficult thing to do to make your trip carefree. But it can make the difference between having a wonderful time and dreading every exhausting move you make with your luggage. Because it is absolutely critical to your happiness, a lengthy section in the final chapter, Traveling Smart, is devoted to the easy way to travel light.

Travel is about a change of pace, about new and interesting things and places, and if you plan your trip well you can set off on your own with a sense of adventure—and with confidence and élan.

NICHES FOR SPECIAL INTERESTS

Our story centres in an island, not widely sundered from the Continent,
and so tilted that its mountains lie all to the west and north, while south
and east is a gently undulating landscape of wooded valleys, open downs,
and slow rivers. It is very accessible to the invader, whether he comes in
peace or war, as pirate or merchant, conqueror or missionary.

—Winston S. Churchill, *A History of the English Speaking Peoples*

When you're making final decisions about where to go, you'll probably find that you have too many "first choices." So many places invite you that it's like trying to decide what to buy in a candy store. Nut fudge? Licorice twists? Peanut brittle? Lemon drops? Peppermints? When you go through Britain's candy store of towns and villages, you will probably pick many more than you'll have time to see, so you'll have to narrow down the list. One way is to choose the places that most closely correspond to interests you have, or interests you would like to develop. If you have a keen interest in a particular subject, such as history, literature, art, or music, it's easy to plan your trip around it.

History

Across the channel they came—the invaders—the Romans, the Angles, the Saxons, the Vikings, the Normans. It lasted for more than a thousand years. They came to plunder and conquer, and they stayed to settle.

Most often they attacked along the island's southern or eastern shores, then charged inland. Thus England, assaulted first, was always subdued more easily than Scotland or Wales. In fact, none of these invaders could bring Scotland to its knees or completely subjugate Wales. Gradually, the Celts who had immigrated to Britain centuries earlier were driven south and west to Cornwall and Wales.

In the second century, the Roman emperor Hadrian built a wall that stretched from sea to sea across Northern England as a defense against raids by tribes from what is now Scotland. Six centuries later, Saxon King Offa had a giant ditch and rampart earthwork laid, again from sea to sea, to fix a border between England and Wales and as a barrier against the marauding Welsh. Five hundred years after Offa, King Edward I ringed northern Wales with castles to contain the Welsh, whose stronghold was the mountains of Snowdonia.

Fragments of Hadrian's Wall still stand; miles of Offa's Dyke are now a long-distance walking path; Edward's fortresses, now ruins, still tower in grandeur from clifftops and on sea fronts where they guarded against attack. Today you can stand in the shadow of the wall, walk the path on the dyke, or linger on a castle wall where sentinels of old kept watch. And you'll find the trail of Vikings in York, where you can ride through a reconstructed Viking street and see workers and families as they were when the Vikings lived on the site centuries ago.

It is easy to ralize history while standing on the ruins of a 13th-century castle wall.

The date 1066 is famous to all historians. It was the year that William, Duke of Normandy, sailed from France with almost 5,000 knights and, at the Battle of Hastings where King Harold was killed, routed the English army and became King William I of England. The Normans changed the face of England and left their prints throughout the country. They founded new religious houses and built great churches and castles.

Although Henry VIII dissolved the monasteries and let many be destroyed, you can still see ruins of many once-magnificent abbeys.

John L. Stoddard, in his Lectures of 1898, wrote of seeing "a massive bridge built, by King Edward I two hundred years before Columbus gazed upon the shores of the New World. . . . It was my first sight, then, of any genuine relic of past centuries; and the mere thought that these old arches had supported Queen Elizabeth, Charles I, and Cromwell . . . gave me my first experience in realizing history, which is, perhaps, the greatest charm of foreign travel." If you want to realize history you will find the opportunity everywhere you go in Britain.

You can look down on the remains of a Roman amphitheater in Chester and imagine legionnaires from a warm Mediterranean clime shivering in the chill winter air of this outpost far from home.

At the harbor in Plymouth, plaques tell the story of the *Mayflower* and of the Pilgrims departing on their perilous sixty-six-day voyage to America.

In every town you visit, the tourist office will have details about how historical events affected that area. The events might have taken place in Roman times, in the days of the Normans, or during the many wars the British fought among themselves. And modern history is very much alive in Britain. At the Swan Hotel in Lavenham, signatures left on a pub wall by young American Air Force men are preserved under glass. The men often waited there, sometimes uneasily, for orders during World War II. At 4:15 A.M. on June 5, 1944, General Dwight Eisenhower said, "O.K. Let's go," and launched the greatest military operation ever known—the Allied invasion of Europe. "Operation Overlord," as it was called, is remembered in every hamlet, village, town, and city in Britain. This story of "D-Day" is preserved in the *Overlord Embroidery*, which hangs in a museum in Portsmouth. The needlework memorial contains thirty-four panels of "patchwork" embroidery measuring a total of 272 feet long. It took students at London's Royal School of Needlework five years to complete it.

Overlord Embroidery conveys the emotion of this great event in its heart-rending scenes and depictions of devastated villages. It pictures some of the more than 2,000 ships that carried one million men from England's shores to battle at Juno, Omaha, Sword, and the other beaches, as well as some of the 10,000 planes that left in wave after wave before dawn that morning of June 6. It is said that as Eisenhower watched the planes circle and turn toward France tears filled his eyes. With pieces of fabric from actual battle uniforms in it, the needlework is a touching reminder to Americans who see it.

Literature

The history of Britain is only a part of its heritage. The tangibles are found in the prints left by writers, musicians, and artists of all kinds. Their marks are still seen and felt in galleries, in bridges, and in great country halls. Touches of greatness are in quiet country churches, in castles, and in places easily reached by anyone who looks for them.

Every part of Britain, from the northern tip of Scotland to farthest Cornwall, from the coast of Wales to the eastern shores of England, has had its share of the great describers of Britain. The works of these writers and poets not only are moving accounts of the times in which they lived, but can be used as maps for us to follow in visiting the places where these authors and their characters lived.

Jane Austen, born in 1775 into a large fun-loving family in the south of England, wrote about the easy middle-class life of her time. She told of the social whirl in Bath; the frivolous goings-on in the Pump Room and in the Upper Rooms; the theater and the shopping; and the importance of "being seen." She called it all "busy idleness." Her house in the Hampshire village of Chawton is now a museum filled with mementos of her life.

Thirty years after Austen's novel *Northanger Abbey* was published, a life different in the extreme was portrayed by Emily and Charlotte Brontë. The darkly brooding moors of Yorkshire that Emily loved were the setting for her novel *Wuthering Heights.* To her the glens that she wandered and the slopes where the north wind raved were beloved. The cheerless scenes of misery in Charlotte's *Jane Eyre* were taken from childhood memories. Both novels were published in the same year, 1847.

Of the six Brontë children, Charlotte was the only one to live past thirty years of age. Left alone with her father, she married the curate Arthur Bell Nicholls, but died just nine months later. Most of the Brontës' brief and often unhappy years were spent in the Haworth parsonage, now a museum. The museum has a leaflet that maps the sisters' favorite walks and it's worthwhile to follow one.

Thomas Hardy's footprints cover the countryside and towns of West Dorset, a part of old Wessex, which often provided the setting for his novels. In Dorchester (Casterbridge in his stories), the County Museum has a collection of Hardy memorabilia including a reproduction of the study from his home at Max Gate. Three miles from Dorchester is the thatched cottage where Hardy was born and lived for many years. The garden can be seen from the lane, but you need an appointment to see the house.

Charles Dickens, who placed his many characters in settings he knew personally, is associated with more locales that any other British writer or poet. Dickens and his characters, and the places they lived in and visited, are mentioned in the dozens of towns and pubs and inns that he used in his books. There is a Dickens museum in London and one in Portsmouth, his birthplace.

You might choose to visit places that favorite modern writers loved. Daphne du Maurier's beloved Cornwall inspired stories of romance and mystery, of smugglers and shipwrecks. You can wander in her part of Cornwall in search of some of the landscapes in her books—Frenchman's Creek, near the village of Helford, and Jamaica Inn on Bodmin Moor. DuMaurier's house Menabilly became Manderley in *Rebecca*.

In *How Green Was My Valley* Richard LLewellyn portrayed the struggles and the often bleak life in a coal-mining town in the mountains of southern Wales, where the black dust and the slag heap were moving and pressing on down toward the cottages that lined the street. He wrote about the hardships and the troubles that beset families, but then he brought out the beauty of their mountains. "The quiet troubling of the river, and the clean, washed stones, and the green all about, and the trees trying to drown their shadows, and the mountain going up and up behind, there is beautiful it was." Today most of the mines are closed, and the mining villages are gone, and grass grows on the slag heaps, but you can take a train from Cardiff and ride through the Rhondda Valley, which was the setting for the book and for the TV series *How Green Was My Valley*.

You can visit Thirsk, which became Darrowby in James Herriot's homespun tales of the life of a veterinarian in the moors and dales of Yorkshire. The late James Alfred Wight, the real James Herriot, called work as a vet "happy work." In Lyme Regis you can walk the Cobb where John Fowles's *French Lieutenant's Woman* waited, cloaked and hooded against the wind.

The homes of many poets—Wordsworth, Burns, Milton and others— are open. You can walk the roads and seaside, the hills and countryside that inspired them to sing their songs. All of Britain is a library of centuries of books and stories and poems.

Courtesy of British Tourist Authority

Willy Lott's cottage, featured in John Constable's paintings, is now a learning center.

Art

Just as Britain's great writers left narratives of centuries of life, the country's artists left visual records in paintings, stained-glass windows, fabrics, pottery, sculpture, gardens, and every other art form.

The East Anglian counties have been famous in the art world for more than 200 years. Two of the country's most celebrated artists—Thomas Gainsborough and John Constable—were both born in Suffolk County. Gainsborough, known for his portraits, often toured Britain to paint what he loved most and had little time for—landscapes. His house in Sudbury is now a museum that, with both permanent and temporary collections, covers his entire career.

The valley of the Stour River is called "Constable Country." Constable, who rejoiced in being a countryman, is most famous for his paintings of this area where he lived for most of his life. His famous "Constable clouds" dominate many of his landscapes. He has been called the most genuine painter of English landscapes, and it is said that to look at a Constable painting is to see England. You can walk the lanes of his Suffolk and see Flatford Mill and Willy Lott's cottage, featured in some of his paintings. They are now part of a center of learning where weekend classes are offered.

In 1803, while Constable was painting in the Stour Valley, a short way north, in Norwich, an art school came into being. The Norwich School was made up of artists who, like Constable, preferred country land-scapes. John Crome, the "father" of the school, used quiet colors to paint the wide-open country that he loved. He had a special reverence for trees, and his gnarled oaks have been called portraits. John Sell Cotman and Crome were the artists most representative of the school. Cotman's watercolors captured the atmosphere of his subject, whether it was a townscape or country scene. The Castle Museum in Norwich has collec-tions of paintings by the artists of the school.

Most painters of the so-called Romantic period of the late 18th century traveled to areas of Britain endowed with some particular beauty. The Wye Valley, North Wales, the Lake District, and the Scottish Highlands were all painted by many artists. And seaside scenes were done of most of Britain's shores. Thomas Girtin and J. M. W. Turner both made many sketching and painting tours and often painted the same scenes. It was said that these two "brought the poetry of landscape to their paintings." The spirit in some of Girtin's paintings has been likened to the poetry of William Wordsworth. Many of Turner's paintings have a shimmering, incandescent radiance—a luminous haze. He once said of Girtin, who died at twenty-seven, that if Girtin had lived, he, Turner, would have starved.

Another way to experience art is to visit one of the great cathedrals. Many have medieval masterpieces of illuminated manuscripts on dis-play. On these handwritten pages, the initial capital letters were embel-lished with gold or silver that spilled over into the painted borders, making them seem lighted. Hereford Cathedral has the world's largest library of chained books, still secured as they were in medieval days when books could not be removed from the premises. Many of these 1,500 books are exquisitely illuminated manuscripts done by monks as long ago as the 8th century. The cathedral also has the Mappa Mundi, a priceless 13th-century map of the world.

It takes some time to really see the works of art in most cathedrals. Stained-glass windows from the Middle Ages and those by 19th-century artist Edward Burne-Jones are a study in themselves. Fine stone tracery adorns windows, and figures carved in stone decorate arches and pillars and fill niches and alcoves. Woodworker's lace is in the filigree of wooden canopies and cathedral screens and choir stalls. Attached to the undersides of hinged seats in the choir stalls are ledges that supported monks or others who stood during long services. These misericords, meaning "merciful things," often have elaborately carved figures, even scenes, on them. You will find paintings on walls and pillars and covering ceilings. If you want to seriously study a cathedral, it's a good idea to bring a pair of binoculars so that you can see the marvelously detailed carvings and designs on the soaring roofs.

Potters might want to spend time at the Potteries, as the six towns of Stoke-on-Trent are called. This is where some of the world's finest china is made. Bone china was invented by Josiah Spode in the late 18th century. Spode has a museum and factory that are open to the public, as do Minton and Royal Doulton. Wedgwood has a visitor's center with a video presentation and museum gallery, where you can watch craftspeople using traditional and modern methods of making dinnerware. And the Gladstone Pottery Museum has displays and workers demonstrating their skills.

For anyone with an interest in weaving and with the fortitude to pursue this adventure, a real treat awaits in Scotland. In the Western Isles, known as the Outer Hebrides, is the island of Lewis and Harris, home of world-famous Harris Tweed, called Clo Mor (the "Big Cloth"), in ancient days. Many handcrafting skills died out with the advent of machines, but the art of hand weaving Harris Tweed is growing. An act passed in 1993 specified that a Harris Tweed must have been "handwoven by the Islanders at their homes in the Outer Hebrides and made from virgin wool dyed and spun in the Outer Hebrides."

For centuries the island crofters wove the thick wool of the Scottish sheep into cloth for their own use. Then, just over 150 years ago, the wife of the then-owner of Harris introduced the cloth to well-to-do Englishmen, and the outside world began to value this traditional tweed of vibrant colors and beautiful designs.

It is said that the imagination of the designer is shaped by just looking out his window. In the past the islanders used natural dyes from plants and lichens on the island. Today they use man-made dyes in colors inspired by the landscape: the sea, sometimes brilliant aqua, sometimes stormy pewter; the grasses, bright green or straw-colored or sometimes heather gray; the flowers, colors of maize, of a damson plum, or of a sunset; and the sky, always changing. These are the colors of Harris Tweed.

Today you can tour a mill on Lewis or go to Lewis Castle College to see an exhibit that tells the story of how Harris Tweed is made and how the crofters live. Then, most exciting if you're a weaver, you can visit a weaver's cottage and can watch the weaver work.

It takes some effort to get to Lewis and Harris. You can fly in from Glasgow or Inverness or take a ferry from several points to either Lewis or Harris, often referred to as two islands. You can get up-to-date information from Caledonian MacBrayne Ltd, the ferry operator. There is local bus service between most villages on the island.

Don't plan on a Sunday arrival, as most shops, restaurants, and pubs are closed and there is no public transportation. For information on the many things to do on the island write to the Western Isles Tourist Board in Stornaway. Specific questions on Harris Tweed should be sent to the Harris Tweed Authority.

On the mainland you will find fabric designs by famous artists in museums, hotels, and in manors you visit. The fabrics and wallpapers of the well-known Arts and Crafts designer William Morris will almost always be pointed out to you. His bold designs in rich subdued colors are often idealized versions of medieval decorative arts. In stark contrast to Morris is Laura Ashley, who thought the more faded and mellow an interior was, the more beautiful it was. Her delicate pastel designs are in shops in many countries today. In Paisley, Scotland (just southwest of Glasgow), there is a museum and art gallery with more than 700 paisley shawls in different styles and types on display.

Music

If you feel as the philosopher Friedrich Nietzsche did, that "without music life would be a mistake," then you will want to find places that fit your taste in music. The sound of Britain's music is as varied as the patterns in a kaleidoscope. The spectrum takes in the chilling skirl of Scottish bagpipes that once brought dread to the enemy in battle; the sometimes soft and sometimes resounding voices of male choirs born in the Welsh mountains; the "Mersey sound" beat of the Beatles that changed pop music forever; and the modern musical. Gilbert and Sullivan's lively operettas—*Pirates of Penzance, The Mikado,* and *H.M.S. Pin-*

afore—are as popular today as they were 100 years ago. And Andrew Lloyd Webber's musicals—*Evita, Phantom of the Opera,* and *Cats*—will probably continue to seduce people for another 100 years.

In the preface to John Burke's *Musical Landscapes,* Yehudi Menuhin wrote, "I am drawn to English music because I love the way it reflects the climate and the vegetation which knows no sharp edges, . . . where different hues of green melt into each other and where the line between sea and land is always joined and changing, sometimes gradually, sometimes dramatically." Nature is an inextricable part of the music of British composers. After Gustav Holst walked with Thomas Hardy over Winfrith Heath, he composed *Egdon Heath* to describe the brooding heath and the fretting of the wind. Ralph Vaughan Williams interpreted A. E. Housman's poem *On Wenlock Edge* with the peal of bells on Bredon Hill and the stormy rustling in the woods. Edward Elgar revealed his lifelong love of nature when he wrote of squatting on the banks of the Severn River as a child, trying to fix on paper "what the reeds were singing." In his best-known work, *Enigma Variations,* each variation represents a cherished friend and portrays that friend's character and personality in what has been called a "musical character sketch."

Always in Britain, there is the sea. Composers showed the raging of a tempestuous sea and the serenity of the wash in moonlight. They composed the screech of sea birds and the crash of waves on sea cliffs. Elgar, Vaughan Williams, John Ireland, Frederick Delius, and others set the sea to music. And Frank Bridge, born on the coast in Brighton, brought the sea to people in four movements—"Seascape," "Sea-foam," "Moonlight," and "The Storm." Bridge built a house at Friston that could still be found a few years ago—perhaps it still can.

Composers from other countries were drawn to Britain over the years. Bach, Haydn, Handel, and Mozart all lived and worked there for a time. Mendelssohn, after crossing a stormy sea to get to the island of Staffa in Western Scotland, wrote the *Hebrides Overture,* usually referred to as *Fingal's Cave.* After hearing it, Richard Wagner referred to the composer as a "great landscape painter in music." Years after his tours of Scotland, Mendelssohn completed the *Scottish Symphony.* In 1981 Vangelis, transplanted from Greece, won the Academy Award for best musical score for *Chariots of Fire.*

Unfortunately, Britain has few museums dedicated to musicians outside of London. Elgar's cottage in Lower Broadheath, near Worcester, is now a small museum. You might need an appointment to visit there. The

Gustav Holst Birthplace Museum in Cheltenham has exhibits of his life and career in a part of his house.

Edinburgh and Oxford both have museums of historical instruments. The University of Edinburgh's collection has more than 1,000 instruments covering the period from the Renaissance to the present. The Bate Collection of Historic Instruments in Oxford includes European woodwind, brass, and percussion instruments and a display of bows and bow-making equipment.

Musical festivals are held throughout Britain, and there are concerts, symphonies, and operas to attend. The location and dates vary each year. The BTA has listings of these events. Welsh male choirs rehearse in towns and villages in Wales, and you are usually welcome to be at these practice sessions. The Overseas Marketing Department of the Wales Tourist Board will send information on where and when the choirs rehearse. The great gathering of poets and musicians that takes place in Wales is called the Eisteddfod. Many towns and villages hold their own, but the LLangollen International Musical Eisteddfod and the Royal National Eisteddfod, which is entirely in the Welsh language, are the two big events. They are both held in the summer.

It is easy to arrange to hear one of Britain's highly trained church choirs. Services are sung in more than seventy abbeys, cathedrals, and chapels. A brochure listing them is available from the Friends of Cathedral Music.

Although the national orchestras, ballets, and operas all tour the country, a serious music-lover will want to spend some time in London, where there are five symphony orchestras.

Theater

Not far removed from the world of music is the world of the stage. Theater is the performing art for which Britain is best known. Until 1576, when the first playhouse was built in London, actors had performed on platforms in inn yards. Today there are more than fifty theaters in London's West End alone, making it the undisputed theater capital of the world. And those seriously interested in theater will have to spend time here.

You will find first-class theater in most cities and larger towns in Britain; Bath, Birmingham, Coventry, Brighton, Chichester, Oxford, and Bristol are just a few offering top productions. Cardiff in Wales and

Edinburgh and Glasgow in Scotland are all famous for their theater. The world's best-known theater company, the Royal Shakespeare Company (RSC), is in Stratford-upon-Avon. There are three RSC theaters in Stratford; the Royal Shakespeare Theatre and the Swan Theatre are on the bank of the River Avon, and the Other Place is across the street.

The season begins in late March and runs through the following January. The Royal Shakespeare Company will send you a schedule of performances. It publishes two brochures—spring/summer and fall/winter—so specify which one you want. Crowds fill the town in summer, but in the off-season months you can wander and sightsee at ease. Stratford has taken advantage of all connections with Shakespeare, and the well-maintained properties related to him are of interest. A favorite way to spend a few hours is to take the footpath to Anne Hathaway's cottage in Shottery. A little over a mile from the town center, it is a "must" walk on a nice day.

Dublin-born George Bernard Shaw, considered one of the great playwrights, is probably best known to Americans for his play *Pygmalion,* which was adapted into the musical and movie *My Fair Lady.* In 1925 Shaw was awarded the Nobel Prize for *Saint Joan* but refused to accept it. Shaw's Corner in Ayot St. Lawrence, his home for more than forty years, is now a museum. It usually is open only from April to October. If you are interested in visiting it in the off-season check to see if it will be open.

Playwright and actor Noel Coward is familiar to many through his play *Private Lives,* revived and often presented here. *Still Life,* rewritten as the film *Brief Encounter,* is also frequently shown. Agatha Christie's *Mousetrap* has the distinction of being London's longest-running play; it has been onstage for more than forty years.

Many of the theater's finest actors were British—Maurice Evans, John Gielgud, Alec Guinness, Peggy Ashcroft, Laurence Olivier. Theatrical director Peter Hall, on the death of Olivier, called him "perhaps the greatest man of the theater ever," and Hall was not alone in his opinion.

In 1994 a promotion for the London Arts Season was launched. Visitors can get a free London Arts card at the British Travel Centre near Piccadilly Circus. With the card they can take advantage of discounted theater tickets, backstage tours, and other offers. If you are interested, check with the center to get a card.

You can get half-price theater tickets at the Society of West End Theatres ticket booth in Leicester Square. There is a small service charge, and tickets to the most popular shows are usually not available. You can also buy theater tickets before you leave home. Edwards & Edwards and Keith Prowse, both in New York, sell tickets. Your travel agent can get them for you.

If you visit Britain in late December or January you can take part in another British tradition—the pantomime. I say take part in, because this is audience participation theater. These hilarious slapstick "pantos" are based on fairy tales and adventure yarns; Cinderella, Aladdin, and Peter Pan are just a few. The leading male is usually played by a beautiful young lady, and some of the female roles are taken by big strapping men. Throughout the performance, the children in the audience, as well as most adults (particularly fathers), shout and scream at the characters who rush about onstage doing nonsensical things. Pantomimes are usually offered only in larger towns, but if there is a matinee performance in a nearby easy-to-get-to place, it is a fun way to spend an afternoon. Although December and January are the usual pantomime months, a few companies perform them into February.

Those interested in ghosts might like to know that many theaters are said to be haunted. London claims the most ghosts, but Margate, Bath, Winchester, and Bristol are just a few outlying cities with theaters that have apparitions. People have heard footsteps, heard doors slam, and even heard clear whispers. Backstage rooms are said to become ice cold while the spirit is in the room. In one cinema, later converted to a bingo hall, the manager received numerous complaints from nearby residents about the loud organ music in the wee hours of the night. The organ had been removed several months before the music was heard.

You probably will not meet any ghosts because they usually seem to be seen or heard when the theater is almost empty, although a few have been seen watching performances. Most of the ghosts are spirits of people who had a part in stage production—actors, backstage workers, or managers.

Gardens

Dedicated gardeners will surely want to visit some of the hundreds of gardens that decorate Britain. There are formal gardens and informal gardens, grand ones and small ones, castle gardens, abbey gardens, and cottage plots. There are botanical gardens, herb gardens, and water gardens. And you will find some designed by the famous Lancelot "Capability" Brown, so nicknamed for his habit of saying a place had "capabilities."

Some gardens are open all year, but many close from November to February or March. If your trip to Britain must include visits to gardens, get the BTA's brochure *Your Guide to Britain's Gardens.* Almost half of the gardens listed are open year-round. The brochure shows the locations of each one so you can tell how to reach it. If a garden is listed as being near a town, you might have to take a taxi to reach it unless there is local bus service nearby. You might also decide to plan your trip for April or May for peak spring flowers.

Legends and Myths

If the romance of legends and myths intrigues you, Britain is the place to find some. The origins of the story of King Arthur and his knights of the Round Table are not as simple to trace as it might seem. There are hundreds of sites with a claim to Arthur, including Wales. The earliest written references to Arthur were found in Welsh literature of the 6th century, and some of the best-known Arthurian legends can be found in the *Mabinogion,* a collection of eleven medieval Welsh tales passed down orally from generation to generation. And Merlyn has a Welsh connection; he was said to have been born in Wales.

Tintagel on the rocky crags of the Cornish coast is where tourists go to see Arthur's birthplace. Dozmary Pool on the Cornish moors is believed to hold King Arthur's mighty sword, Excalibur. Ogwen, a lake in northern Wales, is another lake said to guard Excalibur. And many places claim Camelot. Some tales of Arthur put him in Scotland where he was in battles at Loch Lomond.

The Round Table on display in Winchester is said to be the legendary king's famous Round Table and King Arthur and Queen Guinevere are said to have been buried in the ruins of Glastonbury Abbey. Visiting sites linked to King Arthur will keep you busy.

Robin Hood's story is easier to trace. It centers in Nottinghamshire. The world's most famous outlaw lived with his band in Sherwood Forest during the Middle Ages. The legend of Robin Hood and his followers Friar Tuck, Little John, Maid Marian, and the others is told in many ways in Nottingham. There is a visitor center in Sherwood Forest with marked paths to guide you past places associated with them. The Tales of Robin

Hood Center takes you on an outing to experience the sights, sounds, and smells of his day. You can also try your hand at archery there. Streets are named after members of the band, there is a statue of Robin Hood, and plaques detailing important events that took place help guide you. Recently uncovered documents seem to authenticate Robin Hood's adventures.

Remember, if you do plan to trace a legend, the towns you go to will offer much more than just sites connected to the story.

Automobiles

An annual event that car enthusiasts will be interested in is the London to Brighton Veteran Car Run, always held the first Sunday in November. The first run was in 1896 and was called the "Emancipation Run" in celebration of a new speed limit allowing cars to travel at 12 miles per hour, without a man walking in front of the vehicle carrying a red flag. The instructions for that first run were "Owners and drivers should remember that motor cars are on trial in England and that any rashnes or carelessness might injure the industry in this country."

Run by the Royal Automobile Club (RAC) since 1930, it now draws crowds of more than a million each year. Only vehicles built before January 1, 1905, are eligible to take part in the run. This is not a race, but a sixty-mile drive from Hyde Park in London to Brighton on the coast. For details write to the RAC Motor Sports Association.

There are a number of automobile museums to visit, and one of the largest and most comprehensive is the National Motor Museum at Beaulieu, Hampshire. With 250 historic cars, commercial vehicles, and motorcycles in seven galleries, it is one of the finest museums of its kind in the world. Coventry has the Museum of British Road Transport, which has 200 bicycles, 75 motorcycles, and more than 150 vehicles from the 1940s, '50s, and '60s.

Photography

Photographers will find a challenge in the misty days and overcast skies of Britain. My favorite photo of Salisbury Cathedral was taken early on a morning opaque with fog so dense that I could only hear, rather than see, the few others who walked in the close. The soaring spire was shrouded from sight. My first glimpse of the cathedral's "walking Madonna," veiled in fog, is still impressed on my mind.

Sheep-dotted hills crisscrossed with rock walls, mountain passes with ribbons of rivers sparkling in the sun, and islands that pepper the ragged coast all make postcard pictures. But don't forget the medieval villages. The beauty of these ages-old streets and buildings offers you a "must-have" picture wherever you look.

Photographers can record subjects like this ancient Roman mosaic.

If you're interested in photographing locations of famous films or scenes from TV series, get the movie map from the BTA. There are two outstanding photography museums worth visiting. One is the Fox Talbot Museum of Photography in the village of Lacock in Wiltshire. The museum is housed in a 16th-century barn at the gates of Lacock Abbey. It commemorates William Henry Fox Talbot, the pioneer photographer who is recognized as the inventor of photography as we know it.

The other is the National Museum of Photography, Film, and Television in Bradford, West Yorkshire. The museum is open year-round. It explores the past, present, and future of these industries with models and exhibits that include everything from photojournalism to satellites.

Antiques

Britain has so many places for one interested in antiques that it might be hard to choose which ones to visit. Of course, London, with antique shops, markets, fairs, and auctions, is the major antique center. But the rest of Britain has many areas where you might unexpectedly come across that rare find. The BTA has a brochure called "Lockson's Guide to Antiques in Britain," which has a map listing villages and towns that would be of interest.

Golf

Golfers might want to play at St. Andrews in Scotland. You can get information on the courses from the St. Andrews & N.E. Fife Tourist Board. Advance reservations for the five 18-hole courses and the one 9-hole course can be made through the Links Management Committee in St. Andrews. You must meet a number of requirements to play the famous Old Course. If golfing here is on your list of things to do, send for the details as early as you can. The Old Course is always heavily booked and there are some times that are never open for reservations. The British Golf Museum in St. Andrews is a must for golfers. It has galleries and a video theater that trace golf's 500-year history, as well as much golf memorabilia.

Britain has a rich store of museums of all kinds, and you will find some for any special interest you might have. You don't need a hobby to ensure an exciting vacation. Perhaps your interests are more general than specific. If you are open to new ideas, you might find a fascinating hobby while you are browsing through Britain. With a curiosity about the world, about things new to you and things ages old, you can have a rare experience to remember—and maybe to repeat.

BRIEF ENCOUNTERS

When Henry David Thoreau stayed in his cabin on the shore of Walden Pond he lived, as much as possible, the life of a hermit in "undisturbed solitude and stillness," and said, "I love to be alone." But you won't want the isolation that Thoreau sought. As you travel you are constantly in touch with others—the British or other travelers—and you won't feel alone. If you travel for a month, or for even two weeks, you might find a mid-trip break a welcome diversion. You can join a British group in some activity that interests you. It could be a rewarding experience that might become one of your most cherished memories.

GET A CABIN ON A CANAL

Imagine floating under a leafy canopy on still water dappled with a moving pattern of sun. The only sounds are country whispers—the swish of a bird flashing overhead; a murmur of leaves as a breeze passes; the plash of a duck settling on the water. You could be cruising on the Mon and Brec Canal in the Brecon Beacons National Park in South Wales.

Sometimes the canal meanders through green meadows where sheep nuzzle a canalside fence and the Brecon Beacon foothills rise in the distance. In places it clings to a hillside above the Usk Valley, following the river winding silver in the sun far below. Often the canal slips through woods of beech and sycamore maple. Old trees edge the banks and reach branches across the water, spreading a parasol of deep shade. Boughs, mirrored in the water, become a tunnel of leaves to glide through.

Our canal boat floated under a nature-made bower where country whispers were all we could hear.

The idyllic peace found today was missing when the canal's story began. Built as the Brecknock and Abergavenny Canal, it was later joined with the Monmouthshire Canal to the south and is known today as the Mon and Brec.

At the peak of their use, more than 4,000 miles of interconnected canals ran throughout Britain. Winston Churchill called these inland waterways "liquid history" and they helped make Great Britain the world leader of the Industrial Revolution. Built 200 years ago, the Mon and Brec was needed as a highway for barges carrying coal, lime, and iron brought down from mountain quarries on tramways. The men who built the canals were called "navigators" or "navvies"; they had only picks, shovels, and wheelbarrows to cut through the mountain hillsides. An old drawing shows a navvy carrying his pick and shovel with his wheelbarrow strapped to his back—the wheel, at the top, faced out away from his head. The life of activity on the canals didn't last long. Instead of the laden barges plying the canals in both directions as they once had, railways began carrying the goods. As traffic declined, many canals were abandoned, some never to be used again. Then in the 1960s people started to walk on the towpaths that had been laid beside the canals for the horses that towed the barges. And many canals were restored. Today there are 2,000 miles of canals being used for recreation.

My October cruise was with Willow Wren Cruising Holidays. There were seven of us on the cruise, all women, mostly retired, and all with similar interests. Five were British and two of us were American. We had a crew of three—Mark, who captained the boats; Jenny, who kept us happy with her cooking; and Simon, who did a little of everything. Each morning there was a soft knock on the cabin door and a smiling Simon would peek in and set down a cup of hot coffee or tea. I usually had my coffee while standing at the window watching the day begin. On some mornings a heavy mist closed in the quiet; on others the sun burst over the countryside; and always there was birdsong.

Canal boats are built narrow to go under bridges and through locks that are just over seven feet wide. On our cruise we had two hotel boats—the *Abergavenny Castle* was the cabin boat and the *Rose of Brecon* was the day boat. Replicas of the old craft that were both home and workplace in the 19th century, these boats have all the modern comforts to make this a delightful pause in a trip. Each boat was fifty feet long and only seven feet wide. With space on the cabin boat taken up with a passageway, a shower, and a toilet, the cabins were postage-stamp size. Each one had a bunk or bunks, a sink with hot and cold water, and space for a small suitcase, leaving little room to walk. But we had everything we needed and were rarely in our cabins except to sleep.

The *Rose* had a dining room and a windowed lounge of polished wood with comfortable seating for eight. It had a supply of games and a case of books to use on a rainy day. A small self-service bar, always open, was used on the honor system. We kept our own tabs and paid at the end of the cruise.

The day boat had the engine and pulled the *Abergavenny Castle*, called the "butty," or buddy. Most nights we moored in a broad section of the canal so we could be "breasted up," tied side by side. It was an easy step from one boat to the other through doors that met in the middle of each boat. The doors were painted with brilliant blue, yellow, and red pictures of roses and castles. In long-ago days when families lived on board the barges, these popular designs decorated the small living quarters.

Meals were delicious—baked Scottish salmon, roast Welsh lamb, trout, homemade soups, mouth-watering desserts, and freshly baked breads and cakes. We had coffee or tea and biscuits midmorning and again in the afternoon. It might seem as though we had little time for anything except eating, but we did.

We walked the towpaths at a slow easy pace that kept us ahead of the boats. After a rain the path could be slick with mud, and I found that having to watch my step kept me from seeing the views, so I would join those sitting on our small well-deck at the front of the *Rose*. We talked, took pictures, greeted those on boats we met, and just soaked up the beauty around us. The maples, now turned scarlet, were reflected in the water and were doubly gorgeous. Holly and mountain ash covered with red berries grew on the banks alongside dark evergreens. Anna, one of two who were from London, identified trees and birds for us. We fed ducks on the canal from a bag of bread kept on the deck; ripples circling out from them were the only movement on the water.

We passed old stone barns and wondered about them. How old were they? Who had built them? There were neat cottages and stables once used for the towboat horses. We went under more than fifty bridges, mostly old stone arches built low over the water, used by farmers crossing the canal with cattle and horses. There were drawbridges and locks and we crossed the River Usk on an old stone aqueduct. In Ashford Tunnel there was no towpath, so horses used to be walked around it. To get through the 375-yard tunnel, men sometimes lay on their backs and "legged" the boats through by "walking" the tunnel walls. There were also spaces in the walls where building stones had been left out, leaving a place for men to grab and shove the boats through.

When we reached Talybont we all watched as the electric drawbridge was raised so our boat could pass.

When we got to Talybont, once a busy canal village, we wandered along the streets, mailed letters at the post office, and stopped at the White Hart Inn for a cider. It was an ancient coaching inn with low ceilings and heavy beams. Logs burned in a huge smoke-blackened fireplace. It was the kind of pub you'd like to linger in.

One afternoon we were taken on a half-day road trip high in the Brecon Beacons. Our Land Rover, an all-terrain vehicle, followed an old trail once used by drovers to take sheep and horses to England. We stopped at a 17th-century mansion that had a number of interesting out-buildings and a church with 300-year-old yew trees standing in the yard. Our driver told us about the old woman who had owned the estate. She lived to be 103 years old. When she decided to make a will she invited her three cousins to lunch so she could choose the heirs to her property. Only two cousins were able to come and the sharp-eared old lady heard them whispering about what they would sell and how much they could get for it. She left everything to the third cousin who had not come to lunch.

We drove high up a narrow winding track through bracken-covered hills onto the largest sheep farm in Wales. The entire 13,000 acres was enclosed by a stone wall. These mountains were named the Brecon Beacons after the huge fires that were once set on the mountaintops as a signal to ships.

We took pictures of breathtaking views in the high moorlands and then drove back down to the lower green hills where we had our afternoon tea and cakes at a picnic table in the shade of a spreading beech tree.

Most canal cruises have side-trips like this or have half-day stops at famous towns. Cruises usually last seven days, but I took Willow Wren's four-day "Country Break Cruise" because it fit my schedule best. Many companies have cruises on canals or rivers and each one offers something different. Some are luxury cruises where you dine by candlelight with fine linens and crystal. Others travel on "wide" boats with large cabins and private baths. With so many choices, you will be sure to find one that fits you. I chose my cruise because I wanted a casual atmosphere and I knew I'd enjoy the tranquility of this isolated part of Wales. The cruise began in Abergavenny, a Welsh Marcher town with a fine museum in the remains of a Norman castle. The group met at the Angel Hotel, which is a good place to stay for a day or two before the cruise begins. Costs for a cruise vary widely. A seven-day cruise can be anywhere from under $600 to more than $2,000. Canal and river cruises usually run from early April through late October, which would be at either end of the normal off-season travel months. Your travel agent can tell you about most of the cruises offered in Britain. For information on Willow Wren cruises you can call the U.S. representative, Wilson & Lake International.

I found that the four-day cruise was a nice break in the middle of my one-month trip. And I enjoyed the luxury of having someone else take care of details for a few days and of sharing the days with a companionable group.

TRY A TOUCH OF CLASS

When Thomas Carlyle said, "Silence is deep as Eternity," he could have been describing the spot where I stood—at the top of a mountain in Snowdonia, in northwestern Wales. There was no sound, not even of wind. Nothing moved; only the shadow of a cloud crossing a snow-filled hollow near the jagged peak of the next mountain.

Snowdonia, known by the Welsh as Eryri, "Land of Eagles," is the great heart of Wales. A natural fastness against invaders, it was the fortress of Welsh princes—Llywelyn ap Gruffydd, Owain Glyndwr, and others who led the fight for the independence of Wales. In this silent place, among crags that have stood for millions of years, the myths and legends, the epic poems of wizards and dragons passed on by Celtic bards somehow seem almost true.

With six others I was taking a class in photography here in the Snowdonia National Park, and we had walked up this mountain to take pictures. The others had gone behind a broad spur of rock to get a different view. I lagged behind to be alone in this immense stillness.

It was in these mountains that climbers trained for their ascent of Mount Everest with Sir Edmund Hillary. When writer George Borrow reached Snowdonia on his trek through Wales in 1854 he wrote, "Perhaps in the whole world there is no region more picturesquely beautiful than Snowdon, a region of mountains, lakes, cataracts and groves, in which Nature shows herself in her most grand and beautiful forms." Since then Snowdonia has been a destination for walkers and hikers and sightseers.

On this February afternoon we had the mountain to ourselves. We took time snapping photographs and then set off down the mountain the way we had come up—on old tracks used by slate miners in the last century.

Near the mountaintop the path was just piles of slate chips, now dusted with snow. I kept a chip—it now shares space with a piece of the Berlin Wall in a small glass box on my desk. On the way up I had been uneasy walking on these slick hills of slate, especially where the narrow track dropped off on each side, but going down seemed easier.

Slate buildings that had once been dormitories for the miners were now roofless ruins. Each had once been crowded with bunks and heated with only a small fireplace. The men lived in these dismal places six days a week and went down the mountain to their families in the valley only on Saturday. There was a small chapel on a bare open hillside where Sunday services were held for the miners in those days. One spindling fir stood beside the chapel, probably planted to give a soft touch to their place of worship. On our way up the mountain we had sat on rocks from a broken wall behind the tiny chapel and had eaten our packed lunch. Warmed by the sun, we sat on the rocks like contented lizards basking in the sun and had almost hated to move.

A fence of split slates wired together edged the path near the old miner's chapel where we sat in the sun and ate our lunch.

Farther below we looked down on a small clear lake. Whipped cream clouds that drifted above made it a mirror of blue and white. As we neared the lake the reflection changed to a copy of the other side. A few buildings were scattered on a narrow strip of land beside the water. Just behind them was an enormous long hill of waste slates four times as high as the buildings. A whiff of breeze sighed through the valley, trembled the image on the water, and riffled the amber grass. Then it was still again.

It was late afternoon before we left the mountain and climbed into our van. With time for one more stop, we went to Criccieth. The town curves along Tremadog Bay and castle ruins stand guard from a hilltop. In a few months this would be a crowded resort, but now it was just another quiet Welsh town. A classmate pointed across the bay to the mountain we had just been on.

We took our last photos of the day and then headed home. Home was Plas Tan-y-Bwlch, a lovely 18th-century country manor standing in more than 100 acres of woodlands and gardens. Inside, polished wood gleams and touches of the original grandeur are seen in carved wood, stained glass, and beams in vaulted ceilings.

There are lounges, a library, classrooms, and a bar, where we met before dinner. While I was there another group was experimenting with reproducing techniques of iron smelting that had been used in prehistoric ironworks discovered nearby. It was when we met in the bar that I kept up with this class's progress.

Guest rooms at Plas Tan-y-Bwlch are simply furnished doubles or singles. All have washbasins and some have private baths. I had a single room overlooking the centuries-old village of Maentwrog in the valley below. In the early morning a mist usually hung low over the huddle of houses. Wisps of chimney smoke wafted up and disappeared in the mist.

In my three-day class we were kept busy all day. We started out after breakfast and our last lecture followed dinner. Every day we visited several different places to get a variety of photos. One day we visited Llanystumdwy, the boyhood home of David Lloyd George, Britain's first prime minister from Wales. He was a remarkable statesman often called the Welsh Wizard. A giant boulder on a wooded bank of the River Dwyfor, which he had loved as a boy, was inscribed simply DLG.

Another day we spent several hours in the fantasy village of Portmeirion. It was my introduction to the village where I stayed several years later. We wandered through villages and walked in the hills. We photographed placid lakes, waterfalls plummeting down bouldered courses, and green hills webbed with gray stone walls hemming in sheep. The walls often ran high up the hillsides, and I imagined what arduous labor it had been to build what seemed to be miles of walls up the mountains.

Wales—*Cymru* to the Welsh—is part of Great Britain, but it is distinctly apart. Especially here in the northwest you can feel the separateness, the Welshness. Everyone speaks English, but many speak the old Celtic language as well. It is now being taught in schools, and signs on the roadsides and in towns are in both languages.

The influence of Wales can be seen throughout American history. A National Welsh American Foundation publication records seventeen signers of our Declaration of Independence, four signers of our Constitution, and eleven of our presidents with Welsh ancestry. Architect Frank Lloyd Wright's homes in Wisconsin and Arizona were named after a 6th-century Welsh bard—*Taliesen*, which means "shining brow." Some Welsh societies in our eastern states were founded more than 250 years ago.

I was introduced to Wales in that photography class in Snowdonia. It became a favorite part of Britain for me and I have returned to some part of Wales every year since that class. Some time ago actor Sir Anthony Hopkins, who is president of the National Trust's Snowdonia Appeal, spoke of the "need for places like Snowdonia that help replenish the human spirit." And Snowdonia will surely replenish your spirit.

Courses that let you slow down and see Britain and meet British people are offered in all parts of the country—from Scotland to Cornwall. Classes might be held in a medieval hall, an Elizabethan manor, an old abbey, or the former home of a prime minister. You might go to a mansion listed in the Domesday Book, to a former brewery, or to a simple farmhouse. You can even take a course at one of the ancient universities—Oxford or Cambridge. Many of the classes are held on country estates that border a river or lake and have woodlands or parklands to saunter in.

One of the first courses I took was held on a farm near Stratford-upon-Avon. It was a class in carving walking sticks. The old manor had a large light room with oversized tables to work on. We each chose the materials for our canes, and no two were alike. I picked a stick of blackthorn, said to make the best walking sticks, with a collar of red deer antler and a handle of buffalo horn. It stands in a corner of my living room.

Everyone in the class was interested in the different canes being made, and we followed the progress of each one. During breaks for tea or coffee in a comfortable fire-lit room, we met students from a class in writing poetry. I bought a lovely chapbook of poems written by one of the poets. Unfortunately, this farm center no longer offers classes.

One year I spent five delightful days at the Old Rectory in Fittleworth, a village near the South Downs in Sussex. Parts of the Old Rectory date back to the 16th century. Two acres of gardens back up to the town's old stone church. Rooms are double or single and have been furnished and decorated with care. I had a large corner room with a private bath on the second floor (first floor to the British.) Large windows on each wall looked out on the gardens and one framed the sunset each evening. The twin beds had white bedskirts sprigged with pink flowers and green vines and matching ruffled duvets and pillow shams. I had requested a single room with bath and was charged only the single rate for this lovely twin room.

The course I took was on writing. I was interested in seeing what differences there might be in writing classes in Britain and those offered at home. Our group was made up of poets and writers with a wide range of experience—from near-beginners to well-published authors. The class was held in a large sunny room with French doors that opened onto the gardens. Classroom seating was in sofas and chairs that were arranged in a semicircle that made for friendly discussions.

We had morning, afternoon, and evening classes, and we each had a private session with the instructor, who was a former publisher turned writer. Morning and afternoon breaks were in a small coffee room with an alcove filled with secondhand books that were for sale. I bought several books that I mailed home. There was a small counter-bar that was open before lunch and dinner and in the evening for those who wanted to relax with a drink.

We did have free time to enjoy other things. One afternoon I went to Arundel with a young man from the class. Arundel is a town that climbs from the River Arun up a hill to an 11th-century castle. In ruins after the Civil War, the castle was rebuilt in the 18th century, but still has a restored Norman keep and gatehouse. The view of the town from the river, with the beautiful castle towering over all, is breathtaking. We browsed in a bookstore and then had tea in a tiny shop with old beams and a crackling fire. On the way back to Fittleworth we stopped at Bignor, the site of a Roman villa where mosaics of extraordinary beauty have been uncovered.

On another day a classmate and I spent the afternoon together. She was a poet who had lived in Illinois for many years. Although she was a Londoner now, she was eager for firsthand news from the States. We walked through Fittleworth, along shady paths, past old stone cottages and attractive newer houses of classical design. We spent a couple of hours in the pub in the famous Swan Inn, a 14th-century tile-hung building with a heavily timbered interior. The warm glow from the soft light of wall sconces and the blaze of logs in the hooded fireplace kept us longer than we had planned to stay.

Back at the Old Rectory we had time to spend in the well-landscaped garden before dinner. A walled sunken spot had benches edging the lawn. Pieces of sculpture stood in planted borders and urns of flowers were set beside paths that led to more flower beds beyond a row of shrubs.

Meals, not gourmet, at the Old Rectory are served family style in adjoining dining rooms. To lower costs, students help with certain chores. You make your own bed and take care of your room. On the last morning you strip the bed and remake it with fresh bedding. After meals you help clear the tables and reset them for the next meal. Those who make coffee or tea for themselves during the day wash their cups and saucers. At the first meal you sign your name on a label and press it on a cloth napkin at your place. That is your napkin for the rest of your stay.

There is a large lounge with a fireplace and sofas covered in bright flowered fabric where you can meet students taking other classes or just read the daily papers that are provided. In another class held while I was there, machine-knitters fashioned jackets and vests from fabric they had knit at home. There was an air of excitement in the room as they slipped on sleeveless jackets and the instructors and classmates offered advice on getting that perfect fit.

The Old Rectory is family run, and though children are seldom seen, I found telltale signs of them—a pair of tiny patent leather Mary Jane shoes in the middle of a hallway or a child-sized caned chair left standing in a doorway where it was last used. It is all a part of the friendly atmosphere of the place.

The center is one of many that have added pleasure to my travels in Britain. Throughout Britain classes such as these are held year-round and are as short as just a weekend or as long as a full week. A directory called *Time to Learn* is published by the National Institute of Adult Continuing Education (NIACE). It lists courses offered in more than fifty colleges and other centers. Two directories are published each year; the winter issue covers October through March, and the summer issue has April through September. You can get a directory by sending a payment to NIACE. Rates are shown in British pounds. At press time the cost of the directory was eight pounds (about $13). You can get a draft in British pounds at your bank, or send U.S. dollar bills. NIACE is one of the few places that will accept dollars in payment. If you send a personal check, there is an additional charge of five pounds to cover the cost of cashing it in Britain.

Prints, cleaning and restoring 567
Psychology 616, 1379
Public enquiries 309, 311, 1952

Quilling 1312
Quilting 125, 450, 660, 661, 787, 962, 1338, 1438, 2026, 2045, 2173

Rachmaninov 784
Rag rugs 76, 499, 502, 521, 918, 1137, 1469, 1816, 1914
Railways 461, 1435, 1441, 2067
Rakes and rogues, 18th century 1118
Rambling 1108, 2139, 2147, 2185
Ravel's piano music 13, 1216
Reading 1287
Reading, music and reflection 1177
Recorder weekend 601, 1272
Recorders 132, 316, 438, 476, 625, 1191, 1279, 1383, 1937, 2009, 2165, 2202
Relaxation 1415, 1524, 1611, 1695
Religion 1626
Religion and science 1033
Renaissance art 595, 1252, 1605, 1629
Renaissance music 343, 1451
Retirement 1362
Retreat 1189, 1332
Rhythmic images 2157
Roaring twenties, the 773, 1227
Rock and roll 1554
Rocks and fossils weekend 905
Rocks and minerals 1960
Romanesque and Gothic illustration 1783
Romantic concerto 157
Rome 626
Rome and the Etruscans 2174
Rush and cane seating 103, 405, 548, 889, 945, 1164, 1306, 1496, 1645, 1843, 2092
Rushcraft 238
Ruskin linen work 1281
Russell, Bertrand 1386, 1806, 2190
Russia 348, 987, 1455, 1529
Russian 591, 1422, 1614
Russian art 170
Russian culture 1223
Russian weekend 781

Salt dough weekend 1920
Sampleri Cymreig 58, 880, 1301
Santorini 129
Saxophone 1459
Schubert 270, 568, 1350, 1671, 1734, 1804
Schumann 1288
Scotch malt whiskey 1762
Scottish country dancing 248, 1286
Scraper board art 1198
Scroll work and branch welding 1450
Sculpture 1765, 2023
Second half of life, the 232, 464, 1515
Senior citizens – autumn break 215
Seychelles 2216
Shakespeare 203, 280, 345, 479, 1181
Shelley, P.B. 1028

Sherlock Holmes, the world of 333
Shiatsu 251
Ships in bottles 799
Shipwrights' workshop 809, 1647
Shores of Caria and western Lycia, the 124
Short story, the 453
Sibelius 420
Silent weekend 881
Silk painting 101, 254, 317, 460, 546, 566, 618, 943, 983, 1068, 1162, 1229, 1404, 1494, 1560, 1841, 2035, 2201
Silk workshop 1021
Silversmithing 128, 514, 561, 875, 1173, 1228, 1391, 1570, 1951
Singing 323, 360, 393, 1025, 1452, 1701, 2090, 2111
Singing for the tone deaf 874, 1996
Singing weekend 777, 1805
Sketching and drawing (see also painting and sketching) 152, 1401
Skirts, making 34
Slate, jewel of Snowdonia 1561
Small mammals weekend 457, 851
Smugglers and seamen 662
Social change 834
Social research 1387, 1728, 2191
Socrates 681
Soft furnishing 1547, 1933
Soft furnishing (C & G) 659, 961, 1337, 2044
Somerset churches 249
Song, 20th century 27, 1694
Song for Cecilia, a 1733
Song recital 1361
Song, solo 71
Songwriting 2154
Space to create 252
Spain 168, 553, 950, 1170, 1501, 1698, 1848
Spain, music and painting 2171
Spanish 108, 168, 355, 459, 487, 553, 584, 843, 950, 1049, 1111, 1170, 1385, 1431, 1501, 1584, 1697, 1848, 2081, 2129
Spanish literature 859, 1772
Spanish weekend 454, 1001, 1209
Spark, Muriel 2071
Spinning 1, 80, 286, 525, 922, 1141, 1263, 1473, 1808, 1820, 2117
Spinning and weaving 737, 2042
Spires, squires and scutcheons 258
Sport and leisure 115, 560, 1855
Spreadsheets 441, 1408, 1423
Spring ideas and colour workshop 2213
Sri Lanka 1564
Stained glass 31, 66, 180, 229, 241, 378, 1005, 1275, 1509, 1535, 1634, 1732, 2031, 2083, 2088
Stencilling (see also paint finishes; marbling and decorative techniques) 102, 547, 944, 1163, 1495, 1653, 1842
Still life painting 391, 455, 485, 990, 1012, 1547, 1658, 2156, 2179
Stock market, the 192
Stoicism 1375

The page of a recent *Time to Learn* directory reproduced here will give you an idea of the variety of courses available. This issue lists over 2,000 classes in more than 700 different subjects. You will probably find seventy or more courses offered every weekend between October and March. The center you choose to go to will be partly determined by the course you're interested in. For example, if beekeeping, blacksmithing, or belly dancing interest you, you'll have to go to the one place that has these classes. But if bridge, painting, or lacemaking is your choice, you'll find it offered at dozens of places. And classes in almost every imaginable craft are available.

There is a music center where more than 100 classes are given during the year, including choir, chamber music, and jazz. The Shakespeare Centre in Stratford-upon-Avon has a six-day course in connection with the Royal Shakespeare Theatre. This center is one of a few where you find your own accommodations in town.

If you get an NIACE directory and find a course you'd like to know more about, write for details to the specific center offering the class. The director or administrator (sometimes called the warden) will send information on the class as well as on accommodations.

One of the organizations listed in the directory is the Field Studies Council (FSC). It has eleven centers scattered throughout England and Wales that offer many courses for those with an interest in the outdoors—bird watching, signs of spring, woodland plants, even the study of mosses. It also has painting classes at its Flatford Mill Centre. The buildings and grounds include the 18th-century Flatford Mill and Willy Lott's Cottage, both made famous by the paintings of John Constable, who lived in the area. In the painting classes given here you can paint from the exact viewpoint Constable used in his works. The FSC brochure listing courses offered is sent free on request.

If you plan a trip to Cornwall, send for a brochure from the Creative Activity Network (CAN). Classes are described in some detail and listings include the person and address to write to about a course. You will have to inquire about transportation and accommodations if you find a class you're interested in, as some of these centers offer day classes without room facilities.

I found that classes in which each student works individually or where everyone takes part in some group activity afford better opportunities to become acquainted with fellow students than classes based mainly on lectures, which leave less time to meet and talk with others.

Group activity classes usually have a more casual atmosphere where everyone mixes during class. It is also easier to get to know other students when you're on a field trip; many courses include visits to places related to the class subject.

On a class field trip we visited this 15th-century house that still has many of its original features.

In one course I took we studied the growth of an 8th-century village and we spent an afternoon there. The village consisted of a long strip following the main road and, except for a small addition, was much the same as shown on a map drawn in 1764. We stopped at the only 15th-century house left in the village. The house was built of stone and still had a 16th-century thatched roof. The main room of the house was a two-story hall with a timbered ceiling blackened with smoke from the original central hearth that had heated the hall. The kitchen and service area were at one end of the house and bedrooms were at the other end. We stopped at other places on our walk through the village as the teacher pointed out things of interest from the past. Our tour ended in a quiet spot overlooking fields at the edge of the village. We had cakes and tea or coffee there and had time to stop in a little country store up the road.

Some learning centers are not in a town, but most of them arrange to meet a certain bus or train in the nearest town. You might have to take a taxi a short way if you arrive at off-hours.

I like to spend a couple of days in the place that's closest to the center before the classes begin. Then I can see a bit of Britain that I might not get to otherwise.

Many organizations, including some hotel chains, have activity weekends of various kinds. If you are interested in taking short courses, get another directory that has so many tempting classes you'll find it hard to pick just one. It is HF Holiday's brochure called *Special Interests: Holidays and Short Breaks in Britain*. The brochure lists more than 150 classes on fun things, covering everything from all kinds of dancing—folk, square, ballroom, Scottish, and more—to card games and sightseeing. Some include short walks to interesting places. Many are three or four nights, which makes a nice mid-trip break. You can get this beautifully illustrated brochure by calling the U.S. representative, Wilson and Lake International. Just looking through this brochure will help ease doubts you might have about traveling solo.

Rates for courses vary widely. Centers that employ dining-room waitresses usually charge more. Where meals are self-service or buffet style the cost is kept down. Field trips, entrance fees, and materials increase the rates. A single room or one with a private bath will also be higher. Overall, even in the centers with higher rates, I find costs to be very reasonable. The daily cost is often about the same as what I would spend for a hotel and meals on my own, and these rates include the courses.

The British "dress" for dinner, but in the learning centers this can be just changing a blouse or shirt or wearing a skirt instead of pants.

On my trips to Britain I generally stay for a month or more and welcome one or two of these breaks where I can meet Britons of all ages and backgrounds. If you haven't taken any kind of class for years and hesitate to commit to one, then get your feet wet first at home. Find a class that appeals to you at a community center near your home and try it. Most classes in crafts are good icebreakers.

If you decide to take a class on your trip you will want to set the dates and your itinerary around this activity. You can probably find one of the colleges or centers near the towns you've chosen to visit. If not, a short bus or train ride will take you to one. It will be an experience you will long remember. Those you meet will be Britons who share your interests.

If you have no special hobby, pick a subject that sounds intriguing, and it might turn into a hobby.

Learning is fun—it's addictive. You might go home with a new interest to pursue-and your time will have been well spent meeting others with like interests.

TAKE A HIKE

If you are one of the 155 million Americans who walk for pleasure, you will find Britain a paradise. There are 140,000 miles of footpaths through woodlands, valleys, moorland, farmlands, and pastures. You can stroll along canal towpaths, follow creeks through steep-sided gorges, or walk atop crags on a coastal path and hear the Atlantic crashing on the rocks below; amble beside a glassy lake or go around it; roam down country lanes lined with dry-stone walls. The easiest walking of all is on the side-walks that connect villages in many parts of the country. Whether you are a long-distance hiker or a sometimes walker, to fully appreciate Britain, plan to do as the British do—walk.

On weekends, even in midwinter, it seems that everyone in the country is on the trails. They stroll the paths with infants in carriages or dogs on leashes. Booted backpackers hike the hills, and others with walking sticks stride along with purpose.

If walking or hiking interests you, hours or days of your time can be devoted to seeing Britain on foot. If you want to leave the sidewalks and roads and follow some special path or trail, you will find that most are well maintained and posted with signs to follow.

However, you should not leave the frequented paths, especially in isolated or hill country, where even an experienced hiker can run into trouble. In high country the weather can change unexpectedly and a sunny day can suddenly become stormy and closed in by rain or fog. Check with a tourist office for details on area walks. Tell someone at your hotel where you plan to walk if you're going far afield and check in again on your return.

More than a third of the coastline of England and Wales is included in forty-four stretches defined as Heritage Coasts. Footpaths extend along much of these coastlands, including the 598-mile South West Coast Path. It begins in Minehead, Somerset, and links Poole Harbor in Dorset, following the often rugged sea coast. Many paths wind through National Parks and regions designated Areas of Outstanding Natural Beauty (AONB). Foresters in National Forest Parks describe the forest trails as offering "Peace and Quiet," sometimes shortened to just "P & Q."

Many British towns and villages have local walking clubs with organized day-walks, and often visitors are welcome to join these short walks. Notices of dates, times, and destinations of the walks are sometimes posted on outdoor bulletin boards. Tourist Information Centres and sometimes the town library also have details on available walks.

Serious walkers and hikers might be interested in joining a tour group where leaders guide the walks. There are dozens of companies in Britain that offer walks of two to seven days for all levels. Some are for beginners who want easy walking and others are for experienced hikers who like the challenge of a tough hill climb. And there are walks for those who fit somewhere in between.

The tour company HF Holidays has more than eighty years of experience in guiding walks throughout Britain. It handpicks its leaders and has received a national award for its training program. On some of its walks you might explore Cotswold villages or the thatched cottages and historic manor houses on the Isle of Wight. Its rambles include moorland walking on Exmoor and in the North York Moors National Park and walks in the mountains of Wales or Scotland. For experienced hikers there are hard-paced long-distance walks covering as many as 109 miles in six days. The hardy might choose winter mountaineering in Scotland, where instructions are given on ice axe and crampon techniques.

HF groups stay in a variety of houses, usually in the countryside, and each is described in the company's brochure. It offers programs of three to seven nights and has special theme walks with some time spent on special interests such as bridge, sketching, and barn dancing. There is even a theme program on learning to prepare and give a talk to a group. HF Holidays has more than 100 special-interest breaks in the off-season, including holiday house parties. Its representative in the U.S. is the same Wilson and Lake International mentioned earlier.

Another company with a variety of walks is 100-year-old Countrywide Holidays. Its country guest houses include manor houses that were once homes for the gentry and lodges specially built for walking groups. Countrywide also has many special-interest combinations, often with afternoon walks and morning and evening sessions in the special classes you've chosen. Themes include Scottish country dancing, singing for pleasure, calligraphy, canal towpaths, even bird watching. Countrywide also has four-night "house parties." The full-day walk programs offer a range of organized evening activities—card and board games, dancing, singing, and treasure hunts.

Countrywide does not have a U.S. representative, but it will mail a brochure to you without charge. When you write ask for both the general tour brochure and the *Autumn, Winter, Spring Brochure* if you're going off-season.

English Wanderer, established in 1978, calls itself "The Walking Folk." It specializes in walking tours and, except for mountain biking weekends, does not include other interests. Groups on its tours stay in small, friendly country inns and hotels on the walking route, in rooms that often have private baths. It offers a number of off-season walking weekends and four and five-day walks. Some old friends of English Wanderer have been on ten or fifteen of the company's walks, which is high praise for any company. English Wanderer also arranges independent walks for people who would like to strike out on a planned tour of their own. Batavia Custom Travel, Inc., the U.S. representative, will send a brochure and answer any questions you might have.

courtesy of English Wanderer

Walkers on a hike with English Wanderer *pause and look out over Trebarwith Strand in Cornwall.*

If guided walks appeal to you, begin by getting Britain for Walkers from the BTA. This map-brochure has excellent information on the many major walking paths in the country.

All tour companies grade their walks according to difficulty, and though each company uses a different rating system, it always provides information on the approximate number of miles walked and the ascents you can expect each day. Walks described as "easy" or "gentle" can be anywhere from three to eight miles a day on the lower slopes of hills. Walks graded as "strenuous" might be ten to fifteen miles per day but with difficult walking conditions.

Britain is generally hilly, so there will usually be some uphill walking even on the easiest walks. Well-broken-in boots are a must, as paths can be rocky or muddy and your walking shoes will probably not be stout enough for most walks. Some walking tour companies offer a "support" system where a van will pick up tired walkers who are ready to quit for

LAND FEATURES IN BRITAIN

Beck	stream/brook
Ben	mountain peak in Scotland
Broads	flat low area of shallow lakes and marshlands
Burn	small stream
Combe	deep wooded valley
Dale	large valley, usually without trees or shrubs
Dell	small deep hollow
Dingle	a dell
Downs	open hilly treeless land, grass-covered chalk ridges
Fell	hill, mountain
Fens	flat, low marshland
Force	waterfall
Ghyll/gill	narrow ravine with stream running through it
Heath	open land covered with heather or gorse/moor
How	hill
Llyn	lake in Wales
Loch	lake in Scotland
Mere	small lake
Moor	desolate open wasteland, usually heather-covered
Pike	high treeless area
Tarn	small mountain lake
Weald	large mostly wooded area

the day. Rather than depend on this, choose a walk that would be easy enough to finish with your group.

Although I walk miles when in Britain, I have not taken a walking tour. However, the companies mentioned above come recommended and are listed in the BTA brochure on walking. Remember that most brochures printed in Britain will give prices in British pounds and dates in the British style. For example, in Britain, the date 5/12 is December 5, not May 12.

As with most tours, there might be a supplemental charge for a single room or for a private bath. You will also need information on transportation to the starting point of the tour. Be sure to read all the fine print in any brochures you get.

None of these walks is meant to be an introduction to a walking program. If you're a mall-walker or take half-hour walks on sidewalks at home you might not be in condition for even the easy walks. If you're not sure whether you should join a group or not, the tour companies prefer that you ask their advice. They are in the business of offering pleasurable vacations and they want to be sure you'll have one. If you are fit and enjoy the outdoors, a weekend ramble is an excellent choice for a mid-trip break.

The many guided tours available in Britain follow paths that range from centuries-old tracks to newly opened trails. If you're interested in getting off the beaten track and leaving footprints in still forests, on isolated uplands, or on rugged sea cliffs, you might find a guided walk with a small group to be a delightful escape and a highlight of your trip.

BE A GUEST OF THE GRAND OLD MAN

Almost a century ago William Ewart Gladstone, Britain's "Grand Old Man," balanced an ungainly, book-laden barrow and trundled down a rough winding path to a wood-and-iron building perched on the brow of a hill. With great care the four-time prime minister of Britain carried his treasured books into St. Deiniol's Library—his gift to the nation.

Overlooking the Dee Valley and the rolling hills of Clwyd, the library is in the Welsh border village of Hawarden, where Gladstone lived for more than fifty years.

The building where Gladstone shelved his books so long ago is gone now, replaced by an impressive Gothic manor built of red sandstone with olive-green slates and stone-mullioned windows. The front of the building has four niches, in which were placed statues of the great masters of thought that Gladstone credited most with teaching him over the years—Aristotle, St. Augustine, Dante, and Bishop Joseph Butler. A bronze statue of Gladstone stands in an enclosure at the street edge of the broad green lawn. It's as if he is watching over his library.

Today St. Deiniol's Library, the only residential library in the world, welcomes writers, students, book lovers, and anyone who wants a quiet place to work, study, or read. If you've gone back to school and have studying to do or if you just keep learning to stay young, a few days at St. Deiniol's can really enhance your trip.

I spent six weeks at the library studying for a course I was taking at home. There were ten other long-term guests, called readers, while I was there and many others who came for two or three days. Among those I met were a young man from Ghana who taught at the university in Accra and another from Sudan, both studying electronics at a nearby school. A priest from Borneo was spending most of a year at the library. A number of writers worked on books; one guest compiled his lecture notes; a professor from a California university read Gothic novels; and students from Britain's Open University regularly studied for exams on weekends. The library, once also a theological college, drew priests and bishops from many countries. One retired priest, who seemed to be in his eighties, came to continue his study of theology.

Although we each worked on our own projects, there were many opportunities to get acquainted with other guests. We all gathered in the Common Room several times a day for tea or coffee—morning, afternoon, and evening breaks and after meals.

It was a large room with window seats and sofas and chairs grouped for visiting or just relaxing. There were tables and chairs arranged for playing cards or games. Cases of books and an upright piano lined one wall.

There always seemed to be an accomplished pianist in the group. Music coming from the Common Room ranged from Beethoven to nostalgic Irish ballads to American jazz. One guest, a village vicar who resembled the actor Hume Cronyn, began each day by playing Mozart before breakfast, just as he did at home. While he was there I started each day by sitting in the quiet of the Common Room listening to Mozart. I missed him after he went home.

Often a group gathered in the Common Room for late evening coffee. The readers were of all ages, with diverse interests and varied backgrounds, and topics of conversation might include philosophy, American politics, capital punishment, or simply light-hearted small talk. Late one night when a gale roared in from the Irish Sea and the windows were pelted with rain and slapped by branches, we made up a mystery story to fit the Gothic manor and the wild night.

This red sandstone Gothic manor replaced the old wood-and-iron building that was Gladstone's original library.

I usually spent mornings in the library, a stately hall with galleries of carved golden oak rising almost thirty-five feet to an arched timbered roof. A narrow, creaky spiral stairway led to the balcony where lofty book-stacks formed study carrels. The little alcove where I worked had a small table, chair, and lamp, and on arrival I was told that I could leave my books and work there throughout my stay. The library's collection of more than 200,000 printed items includes clippings old from magazines and newspapers, books on history, Victorian literature, and theology, as well as rare volumes dating back to the 16th century. Links with Gladstone are everywhere—in statues and portraits, in worn leather-bound books with his notes in the margins, and in gifts he received from grateful foreign countries that he had helped during his long political career.

The library has room for forty-six guests in single and double studybedrooms. I was originally assigned a third-floor bedroom, which someone told me was much too cold for an American. It was. I was then moved to the warm second floor. Comfortably furnished, the rooms have a desk and an easy chair and a basin with hot and cold water. A number of common bathrooms provide good facilities. My room had a deep sill under tall leaded casement windows that swung wide to bring the outside in. On the sill I kept a cluster of pots with red, yellow, and purple primroses that I bought in nearby Chester and Mold.

Once or twice a week I took the bus to Chester, just seven miles away, to shop or walk the medieval walls or visit museums. Sometimes guests were driving to Chester and we'd go together. One afternoon a reader who was working on a book took a couple of us sightseeing through northern Wales. We stopped in Betws-y-coed and took pictures, drove through the valleys to Conwy, and then had tea in Llandudno in a hotel with a solarium that opened to the sea.

The professor from California and I rented a car for a couple of days to tour northern Wales. We walked among the ruins of castles—Caernarfon, Conwy, and Beaumaris—built by Edward I during his campaigns against the Welsh. We ate in old pubs, stopped to photograph mountain lakes and ancient stone bridges, and knew that two days were not long enough to see even this small part of Wales.

Hawarden, recorded in the Domesday Book as Haordine, was not always the tranquil country village it is today. On the Cheshire side of Offa's Dyke, it was the center of skirmishes and sieges in the border wars between Wales and England. Listed as an English lordship, it was held alternately by the two countries during centuries of warfare.

The village seems to have changed little in the last hundred years. Some of the old buildings are gone, including a thatched cottage on the main street where Emma Hamilton, mistress of England's naval hero Lord Nelson, spent time as a child. As in most places, there are no more wheelwrights or coopers or shoemakers. The saddler and harness-maker's shop is now a private home, the Shambles that housed three butchers is now a bus shelter, and the village stocks have been removed. Still, pictures of the main street that were published in 1881 show Hawarden much as it is today.

A short way from the library is an elaborate memorial fountain that was a gift from the villagers to the Gladstones on their golden wedding anniversary. Behind it is the gateway to the castle grounds. Guests at St. Deiniol's can get an entrance permit to the castle park. I often walked there, either alone or with another reader. My favorite time in the park was early morning, when the only sounds were birdsong and the burble of a rock-strewn brook in a ravine that edged the park.

The winding path leads to the ruins of a 13th-century castle—its round stone keep crowning a steep mound and fragments of the fortified inner tower, which were a staggering fifteen feet thick at the base and sixty-one feet in diameter. The original castle, mentioned in the Domesday Book, was probably a motte (mound) and bailey (courtyard enclosed by a wall) castle built of timber.

Farther along in the park is today's castle, the Gladstones' home. Originally a large house called Broadlane Hall, it was remodeled and romanticized by adding turrets and castle features in 1810.

Today St. Deiniol's seems to be what Gladstone had in mind when he built the old iron building. It is a place where everyone is welcome to come to study or read with complete freedom. Living is casual in the library, and you are truly a guest here; there are no locks on the bedroom doors. A bell is rung midmorning and midafternoon to remind guests of coffee breaks and again before meals. During the week we ate at a long family table in the spacious dining room. On weekends, when there were always more guests, we filled several tables. Waitresses served the meals, which were varied and always good British food.

Hawarden has three pubs—the Blue Bell, the Fox and Grapes, and the Glynn Arms—respectively called the "chapel," the "church," and the "cathedral." If you're invited to join someone for "choir practice" after dinner, you will spend the evening in one of these pubs.

The library is named after St. Deiniol, a 6th-century abbot. The parish church next to the library was originally established by the abbot and also bears his name. Much of the church was destroyed in a fire, but there is still a part that dates from the 13th century. There are memorials to the Gladstones, who were always active in the church, and there is a splendid stained-glass window by the English painter and designer Edward Burne-Jones.

Gladstone, who said, "All the world over, I will back the masses against the classes," was called the "people's William." It is said that a picture of him hung on the wall of every home in the village and countryside. Writer James Capes said of him, "He who knew more of Greek than most professors, more of finance than most bankers, more of politics than most politicians, also knew more of theology than most bishops."

He was happiest just being the squire of Hawarden, but as Britain's Grand Old Man, hundreds of visitors came to hear him speak and pay their respects. Among them were princes, kings and queens, prime ministers, and archbishops. And many of the guests spent time at the library.

On my last day there I took a final walk around Hawarden. Even though it was February, it was a mild and sunny day. I came to a yard enclosed by a low brick wall. The lady of the house was kneeling in the dirt tending her flowers. I commented on what a lovely day it was for gardening and we talked about her flowers and about Hawarden and St. Deiniol's for a while. She invited me in for tea. We were both widows and about the same age and had much in common. She told me that she had lived in Hawarden all her life and had never been inside St. Deiniol's Library, so I said I was sure she'd be welcome to visit and I'd mention it when I got back. I told the parish priest, who said he'd call her and take her and her daughter through the library. I'm sure she finally did get her tour.

If you decide to go to St. Deiniol's for even a few days, you must file an application. As a part of that application, all first-time visitors are required to submit a "testimonial," which is simply a statement made by a teacher, doctor, clergyman, or some authority vouching that you are a "suitable" person to be a guest.

You can reach Hawarden by train in a roundabout way, but taking a bus from Chester is easier. The local bus leaves from Chester's main bus station and stops near the library. You might want to stay in beautiful medieval Chester for a few days.

You can get information on the library from the Rev. Peter Jagger at St. Deiniol's. I have fond memories of my stay in this "almost English" town in Wales, and staying at the library was a different and enriching experience.

BRITAIN AT LEISURE

Philosopher George Santayana wrote of travel, "To drink in the spirit of a place you should be not only alone but not hurried." And you can enjoy Britain fully if you take your camera and your notebook and slow down and savor everything you discover each day.

CAREFREE ON YOUR OWN

There is a special feeling of excitement at the start of a new experience that you have long anticipated. On your solo trip to Britain the adventure really begins when you arrive in your first hub town. Much of it will seem familiar to you from your research. You'll see streets that were pictured in books and recognize buildings, bridges, and harbors. Maybe you chose an island fishing village to start your trip, or maybe it is a castle town, or a little gray stone village in the mountains. Whatever it is, the town you read about is suddenly a place.

You will probably arrive early in the day, and after you're settled in your hotel you can wander along the streets for the first time. You'll find the restaurants and pubs, the banks, shops, and post office. Plan to spend some time in the Tourist Information Centre. Pick up maps and information on the town and area. Find out about bus schedules and taxis. I like to have the taxi telephone number in case I need one for some reason.

Many towns and villages have an "Early-closing Day," when most shops close for the afternoon. Ask about that. Maybe the town has a market day, when stalls topped with colorful awnings line the square. Markets today still have the same twofold reasons for being popular that they did centuries ago—conducting business and socializing. People from surrounding towns come in to spend the day. Local buses bring in housewives carrying shopping bags that will be full on the return trip. Stalls with bakery goods, clothing, cookware, flowers, cheeses, and most other things you can think of fill the square. Originally the right to have a market in a town was granted by the king, often with the charter going to the Lord of the Manor. Some towns have had the same market day since the charter was first awarded. Market Drayton in Shropshire has had a market every Wednesday for 700 years.

While you're in the tourist office find out about anything relating to special interests you have. Maybe there are museums you didn't know about that you'd like to visit. There may be nearby gardens you could see, or you might learn that a pub was the setting in a novel you've read or would like to read. I have often been told of interesting places I hadn't known existed that I later added to a day-trip. On this first walk, stop in a news agent and buy a local newspaper. You can get the feel of the entire region from the paper. For example, many areas in England are "horse country," and the paper will have news of events for riders. A West Sussex paper I bought had a page called "Sussex Horse World." It had items on dressage events and horse shows, and ads for everything from riding instructions to horse dentists. A Cotswold newspaper listed all the dates and starting places for February fox hunts. You'll read about local problems and controversial issues and gain an insight into the people and the area. And in the details of coming events you might find something unusual that interests you.

If the TIC isn't open during midwinter months there are other places where you can get information. In many towns the library has brochures and bus schedules and the librarians can be helpful in answering questions. Your hotel front desk will probably have much of this material, and the employees will always help. More than once I have stopped in a police station to ask about something. And always, anyone you meet on the street will answer your questions.

On your first day in Britain you might be affected by jet lag and will not want to do much but walk off the effects of hours of sitting. Every time I go to Britain I have one big adjustment to make; it takes me two days to slow down and fit in with the small-town rhythm. Unless I begin my trip in a big city where everyone hurries, I have to consciously make an effort to relax and slacken my usual pace.

Begin talking with people in shops, pubs, and restaurants as soon as you're out. The easy way to strike up a conversation is to ask a question. The fact that you picked this town to visit means you already know something about it, but as you begin to explore you will discover things you'd like to know more about. We leave home to find differences, to learn what makes a faraway place unique and maybe to learn what makes our hometown special. People appreciate travelers who are enthusiastic about seeing Britain, who show a genuine interest in their town. A few years ago I was surprised to learn just how much it really means to them.

One January I spent five days in a small town in Wales. I was the only guest in the B&B where I stayed, and because it was a quiet time it was easy for me to talk with the young lady who managed the B&B. Every morning at breakfast we talked about the town and about Wales. She showed me old brochures with information that was no longer available. A ten-year-old newspaper clipping that recounted an unusual event was of such interest that I asked if I could borrow it to make a copy. She hesitated because the article belonged to the owner, but then told me where I could have a copy made. I hurried out, made the copy, and returned the clipping immediately. I always remembered the lovely Welsh lilt in her voice.

Four years later I went back to the same town and this time I stayed in a lovely old hotel I had read about. As I went to my room one day I met a young lady in the hallway. We greeted each other and as I started to go on she asked me, "Weren't you here a few years ago? You stayed in the B&B." When I said I had, she told me she was the one who had managed the B&B when I was there. She looked quite different with her long curly hair cropped short, but then I recognized her voice. She asked if my name wasn't Dorothy and then said, "Do you know why I remember you? Because we talked so much." I was truly dumbfounded, not because she remembered me, but because of the reason she had. So few guests had cared enough about the town and area to ask about it that one person, four years earlier, was memorable for being curious and showing an interest in what was there. It is a sad commentary on the way many people travel. Of course, they are tourists, not travelers.

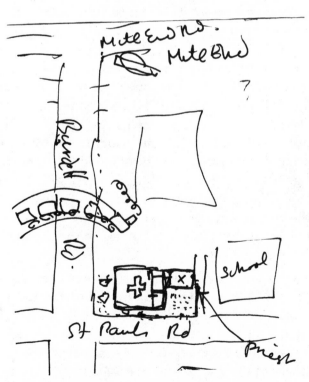

When I asked a shop owner how to find a museum, he drew this little map for me, train bridge and all.

Take the time to talk with those you meet and to learn more about them and their country. It is one of the joys of traveling. If you ask someone for directions the answer might be, "I'm going that way, come with me." Then you'll probably be asked, "You're on holiday, then?" Or, "What part of the States are you from?"

And if you're out and seem unsure of where to go, you might be approached by someone offering to help. Once when I was in a larger town I wanted to walk over a hill to a village on the outskirts. There were two ways I could go. I could walk the entire way on town sidewalks or I could go through a woods where the sea-views were described as spectacular. I stood looking at a map wondering which walk to choose when an older woman stopped and asked if she could help. I explained why I was studying the map and she said it wasn't really safe to walk through the woods. We talked for a few minutes and then she said, "Come home with me, we'll have tea and then I'll walk over with you." We spent an enjoyable hour together. Later, when we reached the village, she showed me another way to walk back to town. It was along a road that followed the sea with the same beautiful views I had read about.

When you take a day-trip it will often be by local bus. In rural areas the drivers and regular riders are all friends and care about each other. Once on a bus in the Cotswolds the driver turned off the main street route to take an elderly woman who was laden with packages right to her door. Then he went down a side street, stopped, ran into a house, and, a few minutes later, hurried out and back on the bus. All the riders asked "How is she?" and smiled when he said, "She's better." The woman across the aisle told me that his daughter had been very ill, so each time he went through this town he stopped to see how she was. I found this congeniality extended to visitors on all the rural bus routes. On an uncrowded bus, sit in front near the driver and you can learn things about the area that won't be in books. Sometimes I have asked a driver a question and other riders have joined in the conversation and I have gotten a mini-education.

Although each place you visit will have its own character, there will be similarities between towns. Two buildings you will find everywhere are the church and the pub; even the smallest villages have these two essentials. Churchyards will often have at least one yew tree. For centuries the yew has symbolized everlasting life. In Painswick the 14th-century churchyard has ninety-nine yew trees. A legend says that when a 100th yew is planted it never survives—the devil will "see it off."

Many towns have an open area in the center called the Bull Ring. This is the site where cattle markets were once held. And most towns have a High Street, usually the main business street. You'll see the work of rural artisans everywhere—in thatched roofs with patterned roof lines, in hedges of layered tree branches, and in drystone walls—all the work of skilled craftsmen.

In many small towns the front door of a house opens onto a narrow sidewalk almost out in the street. You might even find a house whose door is right on the street. Old narrow lanes had to be widened, taking away any private area the houses might have originally had. In some places there is a sidewalk on only one side of the street, and if traffic is heavy, you walk with care. The pattern of village life is said to be changing. Commuters are buying cottages or having houses built on the edge of villages. Others buy cottages just for weekend retreats. Many of these newcomers never get involved in village affairs and don't really become "neighbors." A number of years ago a villager from a northern county said, "Just lately, I have had a horrible feeling, which as a child I never thought could happen. I feel as though I'm becoming a stranger in my own village."

On day-trips you'll want to see the highlights of the town—a museum, an old church, castle ruins, a village green you've read about, or a special pub. But save time to see the town itself. Walk the back lanes edging the town. I still remember an elderly man I met as I walked down a deserted side street in a village one morning. He wore a flap-eared cap and Wellington boots, and he carried a bouquet of long-stemmed garden flowers. We greeted each other and, as often happens, on hearing my American "accent," he stopped to talk. He was born in the village and had never been to the "States," but he had relatives in New Jersey.

As we talked, he suddenly thought of the bouquet and his face crinkled with smile lines as he said, "These are for my wife. It's not that I've been in trouble, it's just that I had the chance." I could imagine his white-haired wife puttering in the kitchen at home, and her face lighting up when she saw him and the flowers. I'm not sure what the famous little church in the village looked like, but I remember him and his smile and his bouquet.

And you'll find serendipity off the busy tracks. You'll uncover surprises not mentioned in any book you've read—the perfect ivy-clad English cottage set back in a garden, a narrow old humped packhorse bridge arching over a ribbon of water, or, perhaps, you'll come upon a sign directing you to some ancient ruin you can walk to. And it is in the back lanes where cottages have names instead of addresses—Thyme Cottage, Wee Cott, Woodbine Cottage, or something just as lovely.

I discovered this old windmill on a lane between two villages.

When you planned your trip you might have made a wish-list of places to see that will outstrip possibility. Karl Baedeker, of guidebook fame, once said, "The traveller's ambition often exceeds his powers of endurance, and if his strength be once overtaxed he will sometimes be incapacitated altogether for several days. . . . 'When fatigue begins, enjoyment ceases.'" Trying to do more than you can enjoy will only bring stress to what should be a carefree meander through Britain. You can't see it all.

Tourists often scurry lemminglike through a town to see a famous sight and then rush on to the next place so they will not miss anything. Travelers, on the other hand, slow down, savor everything, and take home their own special memories. Years later they might recall not the magnificent castle they were in, but the view through an arrow slit high on the castle wall—of the slate-roofed town with fishing boats idling in the harbor and the sea glistening beyond. Or they will remember a tale a pub bartender told them about the town, a story they would never have heard if they hadn't paused to relax in the pub.

Wandering through an old village on a foggy morning adds a tranquil touch to your day.

Following a rigid schedule will take away your freedom. If you had a day-trip planned for a particular day, you can change your mind and stay where you are instead of going. Saunter through the town. Start down the road to the next village; you might go all the way and discover someplace really special. Have a leisurely snack in a pub or stop in a tea-room for the traditional afternoon tea. Just see the town and have an easy, casual day. As poets have suggested, take the time "to stand and stare." You might not pass this way again so relish what there is in the town you've chosen. Relax and spend some time with people you meet.

The British are enthusiastic weekend travelers and even in winter, towns can be bustling and shops and restaurants can be filled from Friday to Sunday. One January Sunday I had planned to have lunch in a highly recommended Cornish pub. As I started up the steps an older couple came out, and the disgruntled husband scowled as he said, "If you want to eat today, don't go in there. You'll never get waited on." I went in anyway. Every table was crowded and people stood three deep around the bar, hiding the bartender from sight. I left and crossed the street to another pub. The couple I had just met was seated at the end of the bar. I said that I agreed that trying to eat in the other pub was futile and sat on a stool near them. We exchanged trip news and they told me about their home in Derbyshire, a county known for "well-dressing." This tradition has religious links and some say it began when villagers gave thanks for the plentiful spring water during a drought. Another version is that thanks were given for the purity of the water when a town escaped the Black Death that killed so many in 1348. Whichever one is true, each year people in a number of towns spend weeks decorating their wells.

Strong board frameworks, described as heavy screens, are soaked, covered with clay and salt, and, after much preparation, an elaborate picture is "painted" using thousands of flower petals and other natural materials. They are usually made in sections because of their size and weight. The screen said to be the largest in the district is nine feet wide and almost six feet high. One village's records showed that 80 people worked 400 hours, puddled a quarter of a ton of clay, and used 10,000 flower petals and thousands of seeds, leaves, and other bits from nature for their picture.

As we talked, another gentleman with a heavy white curled walrus-mustache joined us. The bartender took a picture of all of us with the couple's camera. Before we parted they said they'd send me a photo and we exchanged addresses. When I got home, not only was the photo there, but they had also sent a lovely booklet picturing the paintings of flowers for well-dressing in Derbyshire.

Is every day going to be a perfect and exciting day while you're in Britain? Maybe not. Is every day at home perfect and exciting? Much of your enjoyment will depend on you. If you're friendly at home, you'll be friendly to those you meet in Britain. If you're shy at home, you'll have to make an effort to be interested in the people you meet on your trip.

Americans are sometimes thought of as loud and brash and demanding. If true, that would certainly be enough to turn off anyone they meet anywhere. A man I met in a class one year told me about an American couple who visited his town. He had met the woman previously and had enjoyed knowing her, but he hadn't met her husband. When she wrote that they would stop to see him he made plans to help them enjoy Britain. He would take them to the museums in London, show them historic sites, take them to his renowned local theater, cook gourmet meals, and show them old-fashioned British hospitality.

Each day he picked them up at their hotel and spent the day carrying out the plans he had made for them. The husband made no attempt to hide the fact that he was not impressed by anything he saw. He appreciated nothing and enjoyed nothing. He should not have left home. My friend said that he gave up trying to please the couple when he took them to some famous historic ruins and the husband looked at them and said disdainfully, "At home we'd tear that down."

Fortunately for the rest of us, not many American travelers are that rude and boorish. We know we're guests in someone else's country and travel to enjoy it. And I find that most British people I meet know that most Americans who visit their country want to learn about it and appreciate it.

You might wonder if you'll be lonely traveling alone. Over the years I have spent almost a year touring Britain, a month or two at a time, and I can recall only a few times when I was homesick. It was usually when I was traveling for a couple of months and it was most often when I awoke in the morning.

Momentary homesickness is normal and need not spoil your day. I remember one morning when I awoke feeling unaccountably sad. I was in one of my favorite towns and in a lovely hotel, so my surroundings weren't the cause. It was too early for breakfast to be served, so I dressed and went outside to a still, foggy day. The streets were quiet except for a few people walking their dogs. I passed the poulterer's shop and waved to the butcher who was filling the window counter. With a big smile he waved back. The owner of the fruit shop was setting pots of flowering plants on a sidewalk rack. I saw one I didn't recognize and asked her about it. A bready smell wafted down the street as I neared the bakery. An elderly man rode past on a bicycle. Across the street another older man walked slowly past the shops, his cane tapping the walk with each step. Each time I said "Good Morning" to one of these other early-risers my spirits lifted, and by the time I got back to the hotel I'd forgotten aloneness.

When I awoke with this gentle melancholy on a couple of other occasions it wasn't so easily dispelled. I decided it wasn't a good day to catch trains or buses and strike out to a new place. So I stayed in town and had an easy unhurried day. On one such day I browsed in shops and talked with owners, walked through the outskirts of town and to a village a short distance away. I got back in time to have lunch in a pub I often went to. Then I bought a book about the area and spent a couple of hours having coffee and reading by fireside in the hotel lounge. By the time I settled in here and relaxed I was back to normal.

Even in midwinter greengrocers set flowers and produce outside their shops.

This is almost a formula day for me when I feel like gearing down and having some quiet time for whatever reason. I know I will miss seeing the place that was to be my day-trip, but I remind myself that I can't see everything. This is the kind of day I might have at home if I feel at loose ends and want to pamper myself. You might enjoy spending a rainy day like this, but omit the walk. I never consider days like this wasted. It is a satisfying change in routine and spending a casual day in town gives you an opportunity to learn more about the people.

When you travel, not everything will go according to plan, but if you are flexible and can take unexpected, maybe even unpleasant, surprises in stride, nothing can ruin your dream trip. Generally, little will happen that you can't cope with, and there is always someone to help if you need it.

British mystery writer P. D. James might have been sketching the ideal solo traveler when she wrote,

> My genes are optimistic. There are some of us who are fortunate that way. They are at home with the world and find it a friendly place, and believe people are going to like them and help them along. On the whole, they know they can always get by.

It is the perfect attitude for one traveling alone.

BRITAIN'S TREASURES

I haven't seen Britain's Crown Jewels; perhaps I will someday. To me the jewels of Britain are in the countryside, in the centuries-old towns and villages, and in those who live in them. Those are the treasures I go to see. Those are the ones I remember. The places pictured in the following chapters are some of my favorites, and you will find your own special treasures to remember.

DUNSTER

Amid the green rolling hills that range along the coast of Somerset is the centuries-old village of Dunster. Here in one of England's best preserved medieval villages the unobtrusive new quietly mingles with the old.

Dunster begun as a Saxon settlement more than 1,000 years ago, and grew into the Dunster of today when it became a "castle" town. After the Norman Conquest, William I granted sixty-nine West Country manors and estates to one of his chief supporters, William de Mohun, who built his castle on a hill overlooking Dunster.

The village is on the northern edge of Exmoor National Park and has been called, variously, "one of the most fascinating villages in England," "the most picturesque village of Exmoor," and "an incomparable village." And Dunster is all of those.

The cobbled walks and narrow twisting streets are lined with old buildings—some of red sandstone, some whitewashed or pastel—colored, some timbered and some thatched. They're all hidden from sight when the bus sets you down at the bottom of the hill Dunster stands on. You have what seems a long uphill walk along a tree-shaded street called Dunster Steep. This is one of the places where you'll be grateful for lightweight luggage and for being a walker if you are one.

Near the top of the hill, on the left, is the Tourist Information Centre, a good place to stop, catch your breath, and pick up a few brochures on Dunster and on the local bus service.

Back on Dunster Steep and just beyond the tourist office you turn left into the wide main High Street and immediately face three of Dunster's riches. Ahead, at the far end of the street, is the castle, rising dramatically above the village on a thickly wooded hill. On your right is the 17th-century Yarn Market, and on the left is the vine-clad Luttrell Arms, built in the 15th century and today a Forte Hotel.

The romantic castle that towers over Dunster is the result of major remodeling done in the mid-1800s. All that survives of de Mohun's castle is the 13th-century gateway. In the 900 years since the Norman castle was built, only two families have owned it—the de Mohuns and the Luttrells, who bought it in 1376 and lived in it for 600 years.

As with most castle towns, Dunster was beset by enemies a number of times, but suffered most during the Civil War between King Charles and Parliament. The Luttrells joined the Royalist cause and the castle was besieged by Cromwell's troops and forced to surrender after 160 days. A hole in the roof of the Yarn Market is said to be from a cannon ball fired from the castle during the siege. In 1976 the castle was given to the National Trust. It and the extensive grounds are open to visitors on certain days of the week between April and November.

For several centuries Dunster was a center of the woolen industry. There were specialists in the village, each of whom excelled in a different phase of production, from the spinning of the yarn to the weaving, dyeing, and finishing of cloth. Fast-running streams were needed for finishing the cloth, and Dunster had the River Avill. The Yarn Market was built as a market house for the sale of cloth as well as yarn made by independent spinners. It is octagonal in shape with open sides supported by huge timbers and a heavy stone base. Eight dormers, set in the slate roof, each have three windows with diamond-shaped panes. The Yarn Market was built in 1609, when Dunster was still a prosperous wool town, but by the mid-1700s the woolen industry had declined to the point where workers were leaving the village. One writer reported that at the beginning of the 17th century Dunster had 400 houses, but by the end of the century there were only 190, many of them in ruinous condition.

Today Dunster has a population of about 800 and is again a thriving place busy with tourists. But it is in the same position many British towns are in—trying to protect themselves from unwanted growth and development by outside interests. One retired businessman told me that trying to retain Dunster's unspoiled quality is a continuing struggle. Up until now the village has been able to fend off intruders and preserve its old-world feeling.

Church Street, curving off High Street, has several buildings dating from the 14th century and even earlier. The first one you come to is a beautiful three-story stone building with a slate facade and casement windows. Although it is called the Nunnery, it was the guesthouse of Dunster Priory and was never used by nuns. Standing between two crisp ivory-washed shops, it is as dark and wrinkled-looking as a shriveled walnut.

St. George's Church farther down the street was originally built as the priory church of the Benedictines in the 11th century, but little of this church remains today. At the entrance to the churchyard is the priest's house, a half-timbered structure said to have been built using ships' timbers. For a touch of tranquility, visit the adjoining Village Gardens. The land, given to the monks by the de Mohanses, is now a Garden of Remembrance to those who died in the World Wars and is cared for by the Dunster Village Trust. After a busy day, pause here and spend some quiet time relaxing on one of the benches in the garden.

On a street behind the church is a medieval dovecote that belonged to the priory. This fat, round, squat stone tower held 500 nesting boxes, providing the priory with fresh pigeon meat throughout the year.

On Park Street, leading down to the River Avill, you pass a cluster of pretty pink, ivory, and white thatched cottages. With their flower gardens and climbing vines they are reminiscent of the pictures of Old England that we used to see. At one edge of the road a tiny rivulet flows past the cottages and down to the river. Lilliputian stone bridges cross the streamlet in front of each cottage and become the path into the yard. Just past the last house the runnel suddenly ends. The day that I walked down to the river I wondered where the stream had disappeared to and asked a young workman who was by his van changing into work boots. He said that when the road had been raised to prevent flooding from the river, the watercourse was diverted to run under the road and then down to the river.

He asked if I had been to the water mill yet and I said that that was my next stop. He told me his name was Sully and that when the abandoned mill was repaired in 1979 his father, Gerald Sully, had worked on the restoration. Exactly 200 years earlier, in 1779, an ancestor of his named John Sully had been the head carpenter on a similar reconstruction of the mill. Later I bought a short history of the mill and the story of the two Sullys doing the same work 200 years apart was related just as he had said.

The Domesday Survey listed two mills in Dunster and it is thought that this mill is probably on the site of one of those 11th-century mills. In those days the mill belonged to the lord of the manor and both he and the miller took a percent of the grain delivered to the mill as payment for its use. Most old mills have a nostalgic charm, and this one was a favorite of artists. As recently as the 1930s there was a charge of half a crown to sketch the Mill Walk. Today the mill is a National Trust property and for the last fifteen years it has been producing stone-ground whole-wheat flour.

On the river next to the mill is a tearoom where I sometimes stopped for a light lunch or coffee and dessert. On a mild day you can have your lunch at one of the outside tables and watch the ducks on the riverbank while you listen to the music of the river.

Down by the river near the thatched cottages is an old stone packhorse bridge called the Gallox Bridge. Packhorse bridges were built with low sidewalls so the panniers (wicker packs slung on either side of the horses) could swing freely. V-shaped refuges were built on some bridges so pedestrians who might be caught on the bridge could wait there while the trains of packhorses passed. The Gallox Bridge is unlike most of these bridges for two reasons. First, it has a deep curve in it that makes it almost a rounded right angle. Then, perhaps because of its shape, it has two rounded refuges bulging out into the river.

Dunster's unusual packhorse bridge is called Gallox Bridge.

In Dunster you can study, firsthand, buildings that date back several hundred years, and I enjoyed that. But when I think of Dunster it isn't this wealth of history that comes to mind. When I think of Dunster I think friendly; it's like an invitation to sit on someone's front porch and stay awhile. One afternoon I stopped in a pub on West Street for a snack. Two young men, the bartender and a friend, were talking together at the bar. I ordered a cider and they immediately began asking me questions—where was I from, what was I doing in Dunster, where was I staying, etc. I sat at a table by a window and they came over and sat at the table next to me and continued talking. When I picked up the pub menu I saw that the soup of the day was marrow soup. Thinking of the only marrow I was familiar with—bone marrow—I asked what marrow soup was. Both young men began demonstrating with their hands what a marrow looked like, but with bone marrow on my mind, I had no idea what they were describing. Finally, when we were overcome with laughter the bartender went out to the kitchen and carried back a huge squash—a marrow.

On the deep windowsill next to my table was a row of old books and as I ate I began to study them. The bartender, still at the next table, said, "Those are all old cookbooks; pick out one you'd like and you can have it." As tempting as the offer of an old book was, I didn't think I should take a possibly rare book. I spent a fun hour in the pub and was sorry it was my last day in Dunster; I surely would have gone back for lunch another day. You never know when you'll have an enjoyable hour like this—it is always unexpected and spontaneous.

If you go to Dunster in the off-season you will probably be remembered by the shopowner the second time you go into a shop. In fact, just showing an interest in the village can trigger a long pleasant conversation. These friendly touches add pleasure to your trip.

There are several excursion walks you can take through the village and on paths in the outskirts, and there are day-trips you can take by bus. Minehead is only two miles away. You can take a bus to get there or on a mild day you can walk; there is a sidewalk the entire way. Minehead is the market center of the district, and you will want to see the interesting parts of the town. And since there are no banks in Dunster, this is where you can change money if you need to.

Minehead, once a fishing village, later became a busy port with a brisk trading business, especially with Ireland. Then as early as the 18th century it became a resort town and it remains one today. Small hotels and B&Bs line the streets near the bay and there is the usual resort town kitsch—an amusement park with rides and unsightly "caravan" parks, which are grounds for parking small vacation trailers or where tiny holiday cottages have been built. But that is not the Minehead you go to see.

The areas of greatest interest are the two original old towns. Following the bay will take you to the harbor and one of them—Quay Town. The collection of houses here is more than 300 years old. Near the harbor is the Church of St. Peter on the Quay. It was once a coal and timber store that was given to the town by a mariner who was saved during a storm at sea. Next to the church is an old ship called the *Old Ship Aground* and behind it is Minehead's lifeboat station.

The hill that rises behind Quay Town is North Hill, where the old Higher Town is. You can take a footpath up the hill but it could be muddy and hard climbing and there is an easier way to get there. Walk back toward the town center and then take one of the streets leading up the hill.

From the hill there are spectacular views of Minehead and Exmoor National Park and the sea. Higher Town has narrow, steep, cobbled walks that pass by little gardens and courtyards. Leading up to St. Michael's Church the steep walk becomes a flight of steps called Church Steps. It is crowded with old cottages of cob and thatch.

Cob, a mixture of clay, straw, gravel, and sometimes dung, was used where better building materials were not available. Cob walls, which can be two to four feet thick, were protected by plaster or whitewash. There is an old saying that "cob needs a good hat and a good pair of boots." Thatch was the good hat and the boots were sturdy stone foundations, often painted black. Built well, a good cob house can last for centuries, and many do.

A walk up to Higher Town through the narrow lanes is an uphill climb, but it is well worth the effort to see this old section. One afternoon as I walked through Higher Town I stopped to take a picture of a charming thatched cottage. A man biked up behind me and stopped at the cottage I had just photographed. He set his bike against the house and began talking with me. I commented on his lovely house and he invited me in to see it. The whitewashed living room had mammoth dark beams and a huge stone fireplace. Much of the 300-year-old house was original, with the softly rounded corners typical of cob houses. The owner had moved here with his family from London to live a more relaxing life and did not regret leaving the city. Their home had a snug inviting ambience and an air of serenity.

The fortunes of Minehead rose with both shipping and the woolen industry, but as fishing ports expanded in other areas and factories with new machines sprang up in northern England, there was a sharp decline in Minehead's prosperity. Then in 1791 a fire spread from a barrel of tar to the thatched buildings and raged through what had been Lower Town. By the time night came seventy-one buildings in central Minehead were gone.

It was then that the first notion of being a resort town, of entertaining tourists, surfaced. Today, because Minehead is a major shopping town for the outlying districts, most shops do not just cater to tourists, but serve the area's residents as well. The Parade is the main shopping street and is where the bus stops are. An excellent day-trip, if you enjoy walking, would start here; you can get a bus to Porlock and begin a truly memorable walk. There is a string of quiet villages you can stroll through, starting with Porlock, then Bossington by the sea, then along a country lane to Allerford, and on to Selworthy, perched high on a hillside with magnificent views of the valley below and Exmoor beyond. The experience begins with the ride on the local bus through the incredibly beautiful Somerset countryside. When I made this trip one morning I was the only passenger on the bus from Minehead and the driver told me about the villages and what to look for—tall round chimneys, little roofed bread ovens bulging out from the foot of fireplace chimneys, and the path to take over a hill to Selworthy. As we neared Porlock we turned down a one-lane road so narrow that hedges, higher than the bus, brushed the windows on both sides. Robert Southey wrote a poem about Porlock while sitting by the fire in the village's Ship Inn. He told of the verdant vale, the lofty hills, the musical waters, and woody glens—all still there in this peaceful stretch of Somerset.

My walk began in Porlock, where I spent some time walking through the old town and on through the newer areas that spread out over the hills. The villages I would go through were all part of the vast Holnicote Estate, which was given to the National Trust in 1944. The character of these villages has not changed for more than a hundred years.

Once I left Porlock there were no cars and few people were on the country road. Bossington, with a beach and a channel to Porlock Marsh, is in a picture postcard setting with Bossington hill towering above in the background. I stopped and talked with an artist who sat at an easel painting the cottages in this serene area. As I walked along the road to Allerford I passed red sandstone farmhouses and creamy cottages with round chimneys sending gauzy patterns of smoke against hills dark with evergreens and leafless trees. The patchwork fields were framed with hedgerows.

Hedgerows are as much a part of Britain as rock walls are. There are said to be 600,000 miles of hedges where countless species of plants, birds, and small animals live. One writer called the hedgerows "the world's longest wildlife refuge." Today they are protected and cannot be destroyed without permission.

At Allerford an old stone cottage with a round chimney stands on the bank of the River Aller next to an ancient humpbacked packhorse bridge. The bus driver had told me that to get to Selworthy I should take the path that went over the high wooded hill beyond the bridge instead of the longer route back to the highway and then up to the village. I stopped in the little shop in Allerford, bought some postcards, and asked the shopkeeper about the old track over the hill to Selworthy. He highly recommended taking that route, just as the bus driver had.

It started at the packhorse bridge; a sign said "Selworthy, 1½ miles." After what seemed like at least two miles, I came to a fork at the top of the hill; I took the wrong path and found myself in a thick woods, so I backtracked and followed the other path. On this winter weekday there was no one else in sight. There were no houses anywhere, and the only sound was of the cars I could see on the highway about a mile below the hill. At home I am cautious about where I walk and on this isolated hilltop I felt somewhat uneasy, but I had gone too far to turn back so I hurried on. I was relieved when I heard the sound of a hammer striking metal and I knew I was near Selworthy.

The bread oven at the foot of the chimney stands out in this lovely thatched cottage.

This is truly a special place. From the wooded hillside the views over the valley far below and then beyond to Exmoor National Park are exceptional. Sir Thomas Acland, who built Selworthy to house the pensioners from his estate, wanted his "happy valley" to be old-fashioned and a picturesque part of the landscape. The cream-washed cottages have thatched roofs with deep eaves and dormers and are scattered around a long village green. All Saints Church at the top of the village is coated with a mixture of lime and tallow to protect it. It shimmers in the sun and can be picked out as a sparkle from miles away. Built in the 15th century, the interior has rich stone carvings and tracery and exquisite features. Nothing in the village was open and I spoke only to other travelers who had come just to see the lovely church, but it was well worth the long walk to spend time in this idyllic place. There is no bus service into Selworthy, so from here you walk back down to the highway to get the bus back to Minehead.

When you return to Dunster by bus you walk through a subway (pedestrian walkway) that crosses under the highway to Dunster Steep.

The Exmoor National Park Authority publishes an annual newspaper that gives information on the local area, activities, shopping, museums, and what to do. You might find things of interest to you in it. For example, there is a schedule of group walks and a list of riding stables for riders.

Although Dunster is not a popular destination for Americans as yet, it is for the British. This means there are several hotels, mostly small, for you to choose from. The most famous and most deluxe is the creeper-clad Luttrell Arms, originally built for the monks of Cleeve Abbey. In 1651 it became an inn called "The Ship" and was later changed to the Luttrell Arms in honor of the lords of the manor of Dunster.

From the moment you go through the stone entry you will find touches of the original house. The timbered bar with a massive fireplace, blazing on a winter day, is part of a 15th-century Gothic hall. The hotel bedrooms are attractively furnished with a TV and tea- and coffee-making equipment. For a touch of luxury you might choose one of the guest rooms with a four-poster bed.

Another Dunster hotel I enjoyed staying in is the Exmoor House Hotel on West Street. It is a small hotel—only seven guest rooms—and that might be one reason the owners give such personal and individual attention to their guests. My double room (there are no singles) was decorated in pale green and dusty rose. The hotel lounge is large, with groupings of sofas and upholstered chairs. Everything in the hotel is immaculate.

One morning while at the Exmoor House I was awakened at about 4 A.M. by the clinking of glass. I looked out the window and saw a milkman setting out milk in the old-fashioned bottles I knew when I was young. I remember bottles of milk being left on each doorstoop at home long ago, and this before—dawn delivery seemed to fit this old village.

With several different local bus companies, transportation is good in the Dunster area. You can get schedules from the tourist center or from your hotel. Getting to Dunster from other parts of Britain is easy. Take a train to Taunton and then the local bus to Dunster. Just outside the Brit-Rail station's main entrance a schedule of Southern National's bus service is posted on the wall. There is usually only a short wait for the Dunster bus, which stops across the street and down a short way on the left. If you have questions about trains, buses, or the area, stop in the travel shop just inside the station door. Compared with many areas of Britain, much of this Somerset coastal area is still not touristy, especially in the off-season. Although the British visit the area, it is largely undiscovered by Americans and other tourists, and except for Minehead, you can be in places almost untouched by the progress that has beset and spoiled so many villages and towns. This lovely area is certainly one to consider.

GRASMERE

Crowning the northern verge of England and curving out into the Irish Sea is the great crescent of Cumbria, cradling the most romantic place in Great Britain—the Lake District. It has long, narrow lakes and small looking-glass tarns; soft emerald fells and rugged rock-climbing crags; waterfalls that plunge from as high as seventy feet and crystal streams that thread lace in the valleys. Little of this splendor has changed over the centuries.

When the Romans came they built forts and roads, the Normans added castles and abbeys, and the Vikings left their prints in the names of towns and villages like Braithwaite and Borrowdale, Ambleside and Hawkshead. Now the Lake District is England's largest national park, and the National Trust is the single biggest landowner. And a watch is kept to ensure that it remains as it is.

As a visitor to Lakeland you can stay in old stone villages on the lakes and walk the fells with grazing sheep. You can cross streams on little arched stone bridges and follow miles of footpaths and drovers' tracks.

Several books had been written about the Lake District in the mid-1700s, and Turner, Constable, and Gainsborough were among those who painted it, but credit for making the area famous is usually given to the "Lake Poets"—William Wordsworth, Robert Southey, and Samuel Taylor Coleridge, who all lived here.

Although many others were associated with the district over the years, today this is "Wordsworth country." He was born here and lived most of his life walking and dreaming and writing his poems here. The village he is most linked with is Grasmere in one of the most romantic settings you can imagine; surrounded by mountains, it nestles along one shore of a small lake that holds a tiny wooded island.

The English poet Thomas Gray, who toured the lakes in 1769, described Grasmere in his journal as "one of the sweetest landscapes that art ever attempted to imitate. . . . Not a single red tile, no gentleman's flaring house, or garden walls, break in upon this little unsuspected paradise."

This chocolate-box view of Grasmere is one that Wordsworth particularly loved.

As with most of the lakeland buildings, those in Grasmere are made of dark rough-hewn stone with slate roofs, though some have been plastered over and whitewashed. The colors that brighten the town are from nature—the blue of the lake, the bright emerald of the lower slopes, and the rusts that are woven in the gray of the upper fells. On the main street where the local bus stops is the little village green.

Grasmere is small, but it is spread along the lake and back through the valley to the foot of the hills. Footpaths for leisurely walks wind through the village, follow the meanders of the Rothay River, and wander out into the countryside. A stroll is a good way to spend some time becoming acquainted with Grasmere. Near a bend in the river and on its bank is St. Oswald's church. Wordsworth once observed that the church was "large and massy, built for the duration." The oldest part of the church dates from the 14th century. Wordsworth, his sister Dorothy, his wife, Mary, and three of their children are buried here. Eight yew trees that Wordsworth planted in the churchyard still stand. More than 100,000 tourists visit his grave each year. You can imagine the press of people in the summer.

At the churchyard lych-gate is a tiny building that for almost 200 years was the village school. Since 1854 it has been the Gingerbread

Shop, famous even outside Britain for its delectable specialty. Gingerbread is still being baked from Sarah Nelson's original secret recipe handed down to only three families over the years. The aroma will entice you through the picket gate and into the tiny shop. Unlike the cakelike variety you might know, this is a thin, crispy, but chewy treat.

From the churchyard, Grasmere's main street winds past shops, inns, small hotels, and galleries and leads to the village green in the center. Across from the green is the studio and gallery of a famous artist, W. Heaton Cooper. You don't have to be an art lover to appreciate his watercolors or the work of his father, A. Heaton Cooper. Just off the green is a secondhand bookstore where I bought an out-of-print book that I probably couldn't have found elsewhere.

Visitors flock to Grasmere to see the area Wordsworth lived in and loved. Beyond the church and back down the road, in a hamlet called Town End, is Dove Cottage, where Wordsworth spent some of his happiest years and where he was probably most inspired in his writing. In the 17th century the cottage was a pub known as the Dove and Olive Bough. Now called Dove Cottage, it is where Wordsworth and his devoted sister Dorothy lived and where he brought his bride Mary Hutchison; three of his children were born here. It has been open to the public since 1891 and is furnished with Wordsworth's possessions. Nearby is the Wordsworth Museum, which has exhibits that illustrate his life and poetry.

Those with a special interest in Wordsworth might want to consider joining the classes at the Wordsworth Winter School. In February the school offers a five-day course in Wordsworth with lectures, seminars, poetry readings, walks, and excursions. A number of distinguished experts on the subject lead the classes. Details are available from the school.

Between Grasmere and Ambleside is Rydal Mount, Wordsworth's home for the last thirty-seven years of his life. It was the perfect home for the poet. There was room for his garden, which he designed and loved, and the spacious rooms in the house fit his family—Wordsworth, his wife, their three children, his sister Dorothy, and Mary's sister Sara. Rydal Mount is open to the public. You can wander through the grounds and gardens that are changed little since Wordsworth planted them. Wherever Wordsworth lived he always had many literary visitors; Southey, Coleridge, Sir Walter Scott, Matthew Arnold, and Thomas de Quincey were among them.

It is said that Wordsworth was one of the first people to turn walking through the hills and dales of the Lake District into a pastime. He walked as many as thirty or forty miles in a day. A friend told how Wordsworth would absent-mindedly walk through a flock of sheep without realizing they were there. A servant at Rydal Mount once showed a visitor around and told him, "This is my master's library where he keeps his books: his study is out of doors."

Wordsworth took notes as he walked and from these notes he wrote the well-known *Guide to the Lakes*. If you plan to visit the Lake District you might want to read it before you go; even though it was written more than 150 years ago, it is still an excellent guide to use. There are other guides to the Lake District, written by people who visited or toured the area, but Wordsworth's guide is so good because it was based on his intimate and lifelong knowledge of the area.

If you decide to walk some distance from the village—really from any town or village—there are important commonsense rules to follow. Tell someone at your hotel where you're going and how long you plan to be gone; don't plan a walk that is too far to cover easily in the time you have allotted; never walk in isolated areas alone; stay on the well-used paths. The weather can change suddenly in the Lake District. The sky can turn slaty and fog can develop quickly, blanketing everything, and you can easily lose all sense of direction.

Even people who have lived in the area their whole lives have become dangerously disoriented. The story of a tragedy that occurred near Grasmere points out the peril of being caught in a sudden storm, even in familiar surroundings. One Saturday afternoon in March 1808, George and Sarah Green left their farm in Easedale and walked over the fell to a farm sale at Langdale, leaving their eleven-year-old daughter to care for her five younger brothers and sisters until evening. The children sat up until eleven o'clock that night and then, thinking that their parents had stayed overnight in Langdale because of the bad weather, they went to bed. They waited all day Sunday and finally on Monday one of the boys walked to a neighbor's house to borrow a cloak so his sister could walk to Langdale to find their parents. Immediately all the men from Grasmere and Langdale began a search for them. Their bodies were found on Tuesday. They had become lost in a snowstorm and had fallen on crags. The Greens were buried in the Grasmere churchyard.

There are many walks you can take from Grasmere without going far afield. Wherever you go in the area you will find serene landscapes and breathtaking views. One lovely Sunday afternoon in late February I took a walk that became a favorite of mine. Today I can recall the sights and sounds as if only a month had passed instead of the eight years it has been. The walk began in Grasmere along the road to Ambleside. When the sidewalk along the road ended, steps led down to a wooded path beside the lake. Farther along I could hear the Rothay River tumbling over its rocky bed long before I reached it. The path followed the river for a way and then wound through a wooded glen before it eventually ended at the main road near Rydal Mount. Sunday is a "walking" day in Britain, and many others were on the path going in both directions. One couple had a youngster and an infant in a baby carriage with them as they went.

I had planned to take the bus from Rydal to Ambleside, but a young man waiting for the bus changed my mind. He had just walked from Ambleside and described the walk as being so beautiful that I decided to walk on myself. Opposite Rydal Mount was the dirt road I was to take. It led past a clear valley brook, and then gradually climbed among hills dotted with sheep, leaving the highway far below. The path had once been a car track and maybe it was still occasionally driven on, but that day there were only walkers out, ending their weekend with these gentle pastoral views. Taking this idyllic walk is a perfect way to spend part of a day, especially on a Sunday, when many other walkers are out.

Ambleside is always bustling with foot and car traffic, even in winter. It is a major bus stop with connections to a number of villages you might want to see. The best-known building in town is a curious little 17th-century two-story rough stone building that spans Stock Ghyll. It was built by a prominent town family as a summerhouse, but it also served as a covered bridge across the stream. Known to many as the Bridge House, local residents refer to it as Apple House because it was once surrounded by an orchard. It is now one of many National Trust properties in the Lake District and is a Trust Information Centre.

A mile south of Ambleside is Waterhead, a tiny place with little more than hotels and a boat landing at the head of Lake Windermere. The lake is ten miles long and is England's largest lake. In an 1842 edition of *County Maps of Old England* the lake is called Winander-water. Wordsworth remarked that because of its size and the beautiful cluster of islands on the lake, more fresh beauty unfolds on "Winandermere" than on any of the other lakes. The towns of Windermere and Bowness-on-Windermere, once two towns, have almost grown together now. Windermere, where the railway to the Lake District ends, is not actually on the lake. And Bowness is the district's closest thing to a lake resort. The bus from Grasmere goes to Bowness, but a more enjoyable way to get there is by lake steamer or launch from Waterhead to Bowness pier. On the thirty-minute cruise you get a sense of the peaceful grandeur of the romantic Lake District. Bowness is where most travelers go if they want to be on Lake Windermere. If you are there in the off-season the throngs of tourists that flock to the waterfront and swarm in the streets have left, and the scores of tour buses no longer clutter the parking lots on the bay. As a side-trip from Grasmere you can easily spend most of a day here.

A family of eight was said to have lived in Ambleside's quaint Bridge House in the last century.

You can stroll along the waterfront or delve into some of Bowness's interesting spots. There is an excellent exhibition, the "World of Beatrix Potter," that brings the tales of her beloved animal friends to life. There are enchanting three-dimensional scenes depicting Jemima Puddleduck and the bushy long-tailed foxy gentleman; Jeremy Fisher and his little round green boat; Peter Rabbit and Mr. McGregor's garden; and Mrs. Tiggy-winkle in her tiny kitchen in the hill. While you study these charming displays, country sounds of birdsong and running water fill the air. And there is a biography on film of Potter that includes her work as the pioneering conservationist she became in her later years.

Not far from this museum is the Old Town of Bowness. I wanted to see a particular old inn, the Hole Int' Wall. Charles Dickens stayed here on one of his visits to the area. The afternoon I stopped for a cider, the pub was almost empty. I sat at a small table along the wall and studied the building. The ceiling had old beams and panels that seemed to be decorated with elaborate carvings. I asked the bartender about the old town and about the inn. He said the inn was built in about 1612 and got its name from a small window through which ale was passed into the smithy next door in ages past. A young man came in and sat at the table next to me and joined in the conversation.

All this time an elderly gentleman had been sitting at a fireside table absorbed in a newspaper. Suddenly he laid the paper down and began talking. He was born in Bowness and told us about long ago days in Old Town. He said that some of the old stone buildings around the inn were fishermen's cottages and no buildings could be more than two stories high. It was a poor area where no one could afford good cement, so the mortar used was made from local lime and sand, which could not support higher buildings. When I left the pub and walked back through the old town I stopped and lightly ran a fingernail along the mortar of one building. The old man was right; it crumbled into sand at my fingertip. I wondered how it had held up even two stories for so many years.

If you're interested in steam trains you can ride an old one on the Lakeside and Haverthwaite Railway. A launch takes you to the Lakeside Station, where you board the train. The route follows the southern tip of Lake Windermere; it goes through woods and meadows and past little settlements scattered along a river. The old whistle blows and the steam billows and rushes past the windows. As the train nears Haverthwaite Station it passes through a tunnel of rock and glides past a high rock face left from the cut made when the tracks were laid. There is a small gift and coffee shop at the station where you can spend a few minutes. The engineer told me that when the train leaves the station for the first run each morning it is "fired up" with all the restaurant trash, an inexpensive way to build up energy for the engine. You can get information on the train schedule at the pier ticket office at either Waterhead or Bowness.

If you plan to stay in Bowness instead of making it just a day-trip destination, you might consider booking a room at the Burn How, an excellent small hotel just a short walk from the Bowness pier. A Best Western Hotel, it has a variety of accommodations including motel-type units called family chalets. When I stayed there one February there were few guests and I had one of the huge chalet rooms. The Burn How has a lovely lounge where you can have a drink or just relax before dinner. The dining room overlooks secluded gardens and is small and intimate. It is a perfect setting in which to enjoy the excellent cuisine of this award-winning restaurant.

The bus between Grasmere and Windermere passes the entrance to Brockhole, a National Park Visitor Center that is in a large country house on Lake Windermere. It was the estate of a wealthy textile merchant. The extensive gardens, which were designed almost a hundred years ago, include several terraces on different levels and steps lead to a number of gardens planted with exotic shrubs and trees from foreign lands. A woodland path leads down from the gardens to the shore of Windermere. The house is now the park center and has exhibits and a variety of programs. Brockhole is well worth a stop, especially on a nice day, if you have time.

On my last trip to the Lake District I took the train from Edinburgh to Penrith and then the local bus to Keswick, where I had a snack at an outdoor café while waiting for the bus to Grasmere. When I boarded the bus the only other passenger was a young-looking woman with a backpack who was dressed for hiking.

She was from Australia and had just retired from teaching. She planned to spend a year backpacking through Britain. The Lake District was her first stop. We talked until the bus reached Grasmere and I got off.

One of the places I had planned to visit as a day-trip was Hawkshead, the favorite lake village of many travelers. In Hawkshead a maze of narrow cobbled lanes with whitewashed buildings set around old squares give the village a special charm and individual character. Most of the buildings date from the 17th century and several are of particular interest. The little grammar school is where Wordsworth had been a pupil at the age of eight after his mother's death. Five years later he was orphaned when his father died a tragic death similar to that of George and Sarah Green. Returning from a business trip, his father became lost in the mountains and spent the winter night on the fells. He found his way home the next day but became ill from the ordeal and died shortly afterward.

The school is open to visitors and has reminders of Wordsworth's days there. His desk where he carved his initials is preserved. If you visit during a quiet time, chat with the knowledgeable guide about the school and Hawkshead. The Parish Church, which has fascinating wall paintings I hoped to see, was closed for a funeral service. Beatrix Potter is the other famous writer with ties to Hawkshead. Her stifling life with her parents was brightened with visits to the Lake District, where they vacationed when she was young. Her love of the area finally brought her here at the age of thirty-nine. She bought Hill Top Farm in the hamlet of Near Sawrey, not far from Hawkshead. She called her farm as nearly perfect a little place as she had ever lived. Many of her tiny books for children are set on the farm and in the nearby lanes.

At the age of forty-seven Potter married William Heelis, her longtime solicitor. His former office in Hawkshead is now the Beatrix Potter Gallery, which has changing exhibits of her watercolors and sketches and photos depicting her life there. On her death Potter left fourteen farms and many cottages—a total of 4,000 acres—to the National Trust so her property would be preserved. Her journals of more than half a million words were written in a secret code that wasn't deciphered until twenty-two years after her death.

After I left the school I still had a couple of hours before my bus left to wander through the crooked alleys and peek into the many hidden nooks and crannies of Hawkshead. As I walked toward Main Street to begin my prowling I saw the Australian teacher I'd met on the bus. She saw me at the same time and for each of us it was fun to see a familiar face. It was almost noon so we decided to have lunch together in the 16th-century Queen's Head, known for having some of the best pub food in the Lake District. She was staying at a youth hostel near Hawkshead and had begun her hiking that morning by walking around Esthwaite Water, the small lake near the village. We had a leisurely lunch and lingered until it was time for me to get my bus back to Grasmere.

I didn't get to wander through Hawkshead, but I can do that another time—it will still be there when I return. My schedule is always flexible enough to allow for these pleasant encounters, and I am always glad to spend a couple of hours enjoying a fellow traveler.

Many of Wordsworth's poems are reflections of his years at Hawks-head. One excursion he never forgot was a walk to the Red Bank Road overlooking Grasmere and its lake. Years later he wrote a poem about that roving schoolboy who looked down on Grasmere and said, "What happy fortune were it here to live!" and "here to die!" And, of course, that happy fortune became his.

Wordsworth so loved the Lake District that he detested anything that marred its beauty. He complained about a white house on a mountain-side; it impaired the majesty of the mountain. He disliked the narrow road that was built along the shore of Grasmere Lake, calling it a "broad highway." And he decried the destruction of a fringe of woods that had long stood beside the lake. When plans were being made to extend the railway from Oxenholme to Windermere he sent lengthy letters of oppo-sition to newspaper editors. He wrote a sonnet of protest, asking, "Is then no nook of English ground secure from rash assault?" He was supported in his views by poet, artist, and critic John Ruskin, whose home, Brant-wood on Coniston Water, is said to be on the most beautiful site in all of Lakeland. They would both have been pleased to know that planning controls do limit the number of major eyesores today.

But the Lake District does have ugly caravan parks and controversial time-share developments. And I have seen a picture of tents lining Gras-mere Lake in the high season. Tourism is the main industry in many lake towns, and scenes like these are unavoidable, but if you're there in the off-season you won't see much of this "progress."

Mountain Goat Tours and Holidays is a company that runs tours from Keswick and Windermere. It offers interesting all-day and half-day excursions. Your hotel will have a schedule of the tours and also have information on what is available if you'd like to be taken to places that might not be easy to reach by local bus.

If Grasmere interests you and you avoid the high-season, you should have no problem finding accommodations. There are many small hotels and B&Bs in all price ranges. I have stayed in two hotels that I especially like. One is the Gold Rill Country House on the edge of Grasmere near the tourist center. The Gold Rill was built as a country gentleman's home at the turn of the 18th century, and it has been a hotel for almost fifty years. There is an air of spaciousness throughout the property; it begins in the two acres of grounds and gardens and flows inside into a comfortable lounge with a window wall that looks out onto nearby fells. The dining room, which is known for good service and food, faces the gardens. The Poet's Bar serves light lunches and snacks. My bedroom was attractively furnished and had a color TV and tea- and coffee-making facilities.

My other favorite, the Red Lion Hotel, is in the town center near the village green. Built in the 1700s as a coaching inn, it has been receiving guests for 200 years. It has been modernized a number of times over the years, and today it has lovely bedrooms, a pleasant bar and dining room, and an attractive lounge. The hotel publishes the *Red Lion Gazette,* a mininewsletter with details of current special events. When I was there, the hotel was taking reservations for a Murder Mystery Evening and offering arrangements for hot-air balloon rides.

Transportation to and within the Lake District is good. Depending on where you travel from, you can take a train to Penrith or to Windermere (via Oxenholme) and then get a bus to Grasmere. The area's main tourist information center is next to the Windermere train station, so if you arrive there by train do stop in before getting the bus. Also, pick up a bus schedule there. The tourist center in Grasmere is closed during the midwinter months, but all hotels will have brochures on the area. Wherever you decide to go in the Lake District you will be in the midst of splendid beauty and you might agree with Dorothy Wordsworth, who pictured it this way: "Grasmere was very solemn in the last glimpse of twilight; it calls home the heart to quietness."

STOW-ON-THE-WOLD

The Cotswolds! If you have ever been there, images will rise and flicker across your mind like the flames of a fire when you hear those words. Images of golden-stone hamlets sheltered by rolling hills; clear purling streams winding beside village greens; country lanes passing cottages from fairy tales; life, slowed down.

The Cotswolds have been called the true old English countryside. Even the village names fit the area—Snowshill, Windrush, Didbrook, Dovedale, and Milton-under-Wychwood. Lying mostly in Gloucestershire, the Cotswolds begin at Chipping Campden in the north and reach almost to Bath about sixty miles south. At the widest point it is about thirty miles from Painswick to Burford, just inside Oxfordshire.

Melville Bell Grosvenor, of the National Geographic Society, once suggested that if you ask any British naval officer what he would like most when he retires, he would probably say, "Give me a cottage in the Cotswolds, with a garden, a dog, and a pipe."

The area has been described as "buffered, padded England—England in an armchair." And that is what it is. There is a softness here and an air of unhurried, easy living. It's as if the hills and valleys were tuned to "easy-listening" music.

The name Cotswold is from the old Anglo-Saxon word *cote* for "sheepfolds" and *wold* for "high open ground." It was sheep that made the area comfortable—sheep that because of their fine fleece were called "Cotswold Lions." In medieval times it was said that "in Europe the best wool is English. In England the best wool is the Cotswold's." This wool was highly valued in Europe; long trains of packhorses carried it to the coast, where it was shipped to the Continent. It is said that the fine woolen cloth used for the Pope's cape was of Cotswold wool.

The richness of the Cotswolds came from sheep, and in almost every town or village there is one of the famous "wool churches," and there are beautiful manor houses built by merchants who became wealthy on wool. Almost every building in the area was constructed of a rich, warm stone called oolite limestone, which was quarried from nearby hills. Think of honey in the shade—that's the color of Cotswold cottages.

Grayer in the rain and often darkened with lichen, the villages tucked in the hills still glow, even on a gloomy day. Writer J. B. Priestley wrote of it, "Even when the sun is obscured and the light is cold . . . these walls are still faintly warm and luminous, as if they knew the trick of keeping the lost sunshine of centuries glimmering about them."

Today tourists are attracted to the area by these stone villages. Some of the buildings, centuries old, lean a little now or have a roofline that sags a little, but stone-mullioned windows, flagstone floors, high gables, and steep roofs of split stone tiles lend charm to Cotswold cottages.

One of the most popular Cotswold towns is Stow-on-the-Wold. At an altitude of 800 feet, it is the highest town in the area. An ancient saying goes, "Stow-on-the-Wold where the wind blows cold and the cooks can't roast their dinners."

Stow's large market square is the center of activity in town, and streets and lanes curve and fan out from it in all directions. You can tell from the number of hotels and inns (eight by recent count) that this is a tourist town that would be thronged in the summer.

There was a day when the square would have been crowded, not with tourists, but with sheep. Generations of drovers brought them up Sheep Street or Shepherd's Way to the great Stow fair. Daniel Defoe wrote of 20,000 sheep being traded here in one day. Leading from the square are several narrow alleyways called "tures" just wide enough for sheep to be driven through and counted.

A small village green has the old stocks once used to punish those guilty of minor offenses. As we might expect, the green is smaller than it once was; the space was needed for parking cars. At the opposite end of the square is St. Edward's Hall, now the library. Behind it is the market cross. In the Middle Ages all market towns had a market cross. The simplest ones had a stone shaft rising from a base of steps and crowned with a cross. It seems that none survives from that time, but Stow's steps and shaft are the original. Surmounting it today is a gabled headstone with carved figures that was added in the 19th century.

Many of the buildings around the square are from the 16th and 17th centuries, but most have been altered or "improved," so only parts of the original structure remain. Down Digbeth Street, just past the market cross, is the Royalist Hotel, believed to be the oldest building in Stow and advertised as the oldest inn in England. Radiocarbon dating tests showed timbers more than 1,000 years old. The hotel has other remarkable features, such as leper holes and marks to ward off witches. There is an

Islamic "houris" frieze thought to be from the time of the Crusades. It is one of only two such friezes in the country. I haven't stayed in the Royalist, but I had a delicious lunch there and a long talk with the owner. Just off the square, behind a row of shops, is St. Edward's Church. The eighty-eight-foot church tower was built in the 1400s and can be seen rising above the hill and marking Stow from as far as twenty miles away. The church was mentioned in the Domesday Book, but little of it survives from Norman days. There is a wall monument to the Chamberlayne family, manorial lords of Stow and Maugersbury, who were great benefactors of the church. One of the church's most prized possessions is a large 17th-century painting of the Crucifixion by Flemish artist Gaspar de Craeyer, a gift from the Chamberlaynes.

In 1646 the church played an unexpected part in history. During the Civil War and for some years after, the troops and officers of both sides passed through Stow and sometimes stayed for several days, at Stow's expense. King Charles himself, who came with 1,000 horse and foot soldiers, stayed one night at the King's Arms, which he declared "the best inn between London and Worcester."

Then came the battle of Stow. The Royalist troops, on their way to Oxford, were almost surrounded by Cromwell's men just outside of town. They retreated into Stow, where the fighting continued into the center of town. According to local legend, Digbeth Street and the tures leading out of the square flowed with blood. The Royalists finally surrendered after 200 of their men were killed and 1,500 prisoners were crowded into the little church. There is an incised stone slab that covers the grave of Captain Hastings Keyt, a Royalist soldier killed in the battle.

The first time I visited the church I found several small iron crosses on a table. Some were on chains and others were set in wooden bases. A sign said the crosses were made by a local blacksmith who donated them to the church. I bought one on a chain and on my next visit to Stow I bought one set in wood. I was intrigued by the crosses and on a recent trip I stopped at the Stow tourist center to ask who made them. It was Austin Nicholls from the Old Smithy in Lower Swell.

When I contacted him he told me the crosses were each made of three horseshoe nails and brazed together using a form of brass rod, which adds a hue of gold where the nails cross. At that time he had made almost 1,400 crosses for the church. He sent me a news clipping showing a special figurine he had made when he finished cross number 1,000. He had made only three of the figurines and offered to make one for me set

This is the lovely figurine made for me by Austin Nicholls of the Old Smithy in Lower Swell.

in either wood or stone from the old church tower. Now I have a treasured figurine set in 15th-century stone standing on a bookshelf.

Nicholls is the last blacksmith in the northern Cotswolds; he has seen the other nineteen smithies close in the last twenty-five years. Knowing that adds even more value to my lovely figurine.

Behind the church on the back edge of Stow and away from the Square is one of the most famous Roman roads in Britain—the Fosse Way. The road, built in A.D. 47, started in Seaton on Lyme Bay in Devon, headquarters of the Roman second legion, and ran in a straight line through Bath, Stow-on-the-Wold, Leicester, and on to Lincoln, where the fortress of the ninth legion was. The Fosse Way was two hundred miles long and never deviated more than six miles from straight. The sound of the Roman legions marching along the Fosse Way must have echoed across this countryside.

Stow has become known as an antique lover's town. When I was last there Stow had thirteen antique shops, all on the square or on the narrow side streets. They ranged from small places with only a few items to elegant shops with two floors of fine old English furniture and decorative pieces, including metalware, tapestries, and paintings.

The shops that are members of the Cotswolds Antique Dealers' Association display a sign with the logo—a sheep on a woolsack—taken from a brass rubbing in the Northleach Church. You can get a directory listing the association's fifty members from any of these shops when you stop to browse.

Stow-on-the-Wold is a delightful place to stay and spend some time. It is an easy town to find your way around in, with only a few streets branching off from the square. The first thing to do after you're settled in your hotel is to get a town map from the tourist center. For a small charge you can buy the "Town Guide," which includes a directory of all local businesses and services, a large painted map showing Stow's main streets, and a wealth of interesting little blurbs about Stow. With a map you can wander along the streets and maybe stop in a tearoom or hotel for tea or coffee while you study the map and get your bearings.

Just as Stow has more hotels than most towns its size, it also has more shops than you'd expect. Besides the antique shops and several art galleries there are news agents, stationers, and booksellers. There are shops with quality crafts where you can stop and talk with the shopkeepers about their work. I have found lovely one-of-a-kind gifts, small enough to carry in my suitcase, in the gift shops there. And the town has everything a traveler might need—tea shops, restaurants in hotels, banks, a pharmacy, and, if you'd like to have a picnic, you'll find a fruit seller, a bakery, and two butchers.

When you have a few extra hours one day, stroll through the back streets and see how Stow grew. On a walk down to Shepherd's Way, one of the old streets, I came to what seemed to me a steep hill. An elderly man was biking up it more easily than most young people could. When he reached the top where I was, I remarked what a steep hill that was to bike up. He smiled, not at all out of breath, and said, "When you've done it for ninety years you don't notice it," and biked on.

A short walk for a pleasant day is one to the nearby hamlet of Maugersbury. The Domesday Book lists Edwardstow (now Stow-on-the-Wold) as part of the estate of the Manor of Maugersbury. You can walk along a road that had little traffic when I was there, or take a footpath, both leading out from Park Street. The walk takes you through the quiet partly wooded countryside, leading to pastures where horses graze and where views across low rolling hills lead to Icomb Hill.

One of the first places you'll see in Maugersbury is a two-story crescent-shaped building. In 1800 Edmund Chamberlayne, then Lord of the Manor, built this house for some of his poorer tenants. In the building were four cottages with a central area used as a Sunday school; underneath this was a public oven. This was at a time when caring lords watched over their tenants. Maugersbury has no special places to visit, but beautiful views and interesting 17th-century farmhouses along the country roads will give you a tranquil hour if you've had a busy morning.

Stow-on-the-Wold has eight roads radiating from it like the spokes of a wheel, so there is a choice of longer walks you can take. A favorite walk of mine is a circle trip to Upper Swell, then on a country road to Lower Swell, and finally back to Stow. There is some traffic on the roads to and from Stow, and if it has rained, the roadsides can be muddy. But on a mild, sunny day, if you're used to walking several miles at a time, this is a side-trip you might enjoy. Drystone walls hem in fields and in places the road is overhung with trees. There is an old saying, "The squirrel can hop from Swell to Stow, without resting his foot or wetting his toe." The first sight you have of Upper Swell is an old stone bridge over the rippling River Dikler. A 19th-century mill with a great mill wheel stands beside it; beyond a moss-covered weir is the millpond. The small church and the manor house are the center of the small village.

The walk from here to Lower Swell is on a quiet country road through farmlands. Lower Swell is larger and busier than Upper Swell partly because it is on a busy road to Cheltenham. There are old stone cottages, a hotel, and a church with Norman parts. I have taken this walk twice while in Stow and both times I stopped at the Golden Ball in Lower Swell for a pub lunch of homemade soup and good British bread with a glass of cider. There was also a good lunch menu with other choices. The pub is on the main road back to Stow. If this is farther than you'd like to walk, check the bus schedule for service. At one time a bus went to Lower Swell on certain days of the week, and you might ride there and walk the rest of the way back. Either way it is a good walk through Cotswold country.

If you have time for only one walk while you're in Stow, perhaps the one to choose is to Upper and Lower Slaughter. The villages are not as bloody as their chilling names sound. I have heard two explanations for Slaughter. One version is that it stems from *slohtre*, the Anglo-Saxon word for a marshy place; the other says that a Norman landowner, de Sclotre, left his name here. These are not only two of England's most beautiful villages, they are "perfect Cotswolds."

To avoid a very long walk, the easiest way to visit these villages is to take the bus that goes to Bourton-on-the-Water and ask the driver to let you off at the Lower Slaughter road. If you plan to take the bus back to Stow, ask where to wait for it and verify the return schedule. Lower Slaughter is one of the most photographed villages in England. You'll see it pictured in calendars, books, and magazines.

The little River Eye, sometimes called Slaughter Brook, winds through both villages. When you reach the river at Lower Slaughter you are at one of the best-known spots in the Cotswolds. White ducks ripple the brook, and tiny stone bridges, some with simple white railings, straddle it. Cottages follow the wide greens beside the brook, leading to a 19th-century corn mill. With its tall brick chimney rising above the cottages, it is one of the few red brick buildings you will see in the Cotswolds. Behind the mill is Collett's Shop—the local store and post office. Saunter down the few lanes and imagine living in one of these cottages with old stone walls two feet thick. You will not find many places as placid as this.

It is an easy walk from here to Upper Slaughter. One footpath begins beyond Collett's Mill; if you don't see it, ask someone. The path, fenced on both sides, goes through the middle of a horse pasture. You pass through several kissing-gates along the way. If you keep left when you near Upper Slaughter you will come to the Manor Hotel. Once the village manor house, it is now a luxury hotel. A pause here, in this lovely 17th-century building, to have a light lunch or a snack by a log fire, will add a storybook quality to your day.

A walk through the village takes you past St. Peter's Church. The cottages grouped around the church were remodeled in 1906 and little building has been done since then. On a lane dropping down from the church you come to a ford where cars drive through the shallow brook and walkers cross on a small bridge. A massive old tree watches over the crossing. A number of those who live in the Slaughters have retired here to enjoy an easy, unhurried life.

If you'd like a longer walk you can take a rural road back to Stow from here. The road wanders through farmland and eventually joins the main road into town. Otherwise, you can go back through Lower Slaughter to the bus stop. This way is probably not more than a couple of miles roundtrip.

Because of Stow's location there is a wide choice of day-trips you can take. You can get an early morning bus to Moreton-in-Marsh and then take the train to Oxford for a few hours, or to some other town on the train line that you'd like to see. Or you can just spend some time in Moreton-in-Marsh.

The town is built along the straight, wide High Street, once a part of the Fosse Way. Standing in the middle of the broad street is the Town Hall. It was built in 1887 to mark Queen Victoria's Golden Jubilee. It was originally open on the ground floor, but unfortunately, the arches have been closed in, detracting from its original beauty. Most of the town's hotels were once inns and taverns that served stagecoach passengers. You can window-shop along High Street, which has a number of gift and antique shops, or stroll down the lanes that shoot off from the main street.

If you want a day of shopping while you're here, take a bus to Cheltenham. It is a beautiful spa town with gracious Regency architecture, wide tree-lined avenues, and the Promenade, once described by the *London Times* as "perhaps the most beautiful thoroughfare in Britain." Made famous as a spa town by a chance discovery of a healing spring, Cheltenham became a social center, and the result was its gardens and elegant buildings, many decorated with delicate ironwork balconies.

The Promenade is a boulevard of some of Britain's finest shops. It continues on to Montpellier Walk, with many individual boutiques and antique shops. Adding a touch of grace to the walk are white female statues, modeled after those in a temple in Athens, that stand on pedestals spaced along the store fronts. Branching down side streets from the Promenade are streets with department stores and shopping arcades.

Just behind the Promenade is the Tourist Information Centre, where you can get directions to the Gustav Holst Museum or to any other point that interests you. The main bus station, called Royal Well, is on the street behind the tourist center. This is where the Stow buses arrive and depart.

Horseracing fans will be interested in steeplechasing at Cheltenham Racecourse. The racecourse is open from September to May. Its most popular event, the National Hunt Festival, takes place in mid-March every year. Hotels in the entire are filled for this three-day festival. You will also find that most hotel brochures note that seasonal reduced rates exclude Cheltenham Gold Cup Week. The bus ride between Cheltenham and Stow takes almost an hour, so this trip will fill most of a day.

Another day-trip that is a short bus ride from Stow is one to a village that everyone wants to see—Bourton-on-the-Water, sometimes known as the tourist mecca of the Cotswolds. A well-known travel writer who made the mistake of trying to see Bourton during the busy tourist season wrote that, with the miserable crowds, Bourton was "worth a drive through but no more." He was not alone in his opinion. Another writer dubbed Bourton the "most remorsefully touristy of all the Cotswold towns." Weekends can always be busy, but if you go on an off-season weekday you'll be one of only a few visitors. Then you can sit on a bench in the shade beside the Windrush River and have a picnic lunch. Because of the sparkling river flowing through the center of Bourton and the low stone bridges arching over it, Bourton is called the "Little Venice of the Cotswolds." A broad sweep of tree-studded lawn borders the quiet river.

Bourton-on-the-Water is famous for its low stone bridges that arch over the Windrush River.

Bourton has a number of interesting attractions and most of them are open year-round. Many travelers start their sightseeing with the Old New Inn on High Street. Sixty years ago the landlord's father began laying out a garden in the yard behind the inn when he got an idea for a model village of Bourton. With the help of six local craftsmen, an exact replica of Bourton was built of local stone to 1/9 scale. The Windrush flows under miniature bridges, and trees and gardens grow next to tiny stone walls. It took four years to finish the tiny Bourton.

Bourton-on-the-Water has a perfumery exhibition with a perfume garden where all plants are chosen for their fragrance. There is also an audio-visual show in a "Smelly Vision" theater. A 400-square-foot Bourton Model Railway on High Street is one of the finest layouts of its kind in the country. A visitor can operate models of more than forty British and Continental trains that run on three main displays.

Down a side street is a pottery studio with a good selection of handmade pots a craftsman would like to see. Farther out is Birdland, which has a varied collection of birds and flowers. There is a penguin rookery with underwater viewing and a house where tropical birds and plants thrive. Watching flamingos, cockatoos, cranes, Chinese quail, and dozens of other kinds of birds in the gardens and by the fishponds and waterfalls is a peaceful way to pass some time.

An 18th-century water mill houses both the Motor Museum and the Village Life Exhibition. Vintage cars and motorcycles are set in an atmosphere of the past with more than 7,000 items from the early days of motoring. Upstairs is a reconstruction of an Edwardian village shop and a blacksmith's forge.

Bourton-on-the-Water is only a ten-minute bus ride from Stow, so if your stay here is short you can combine sightseeing in Stow with a trip to Bourton in one day.

Many travelers from foreign countries, including Americans, make the Cotswolds a stop on their first trip to Britain. Henry Ford loved the Cotswolds so much that when he built Greenfield Village in Dearborn, Michigan, he bought a cottage in Chedworth and moved it, stone by stone, to Michigan. He also bought a blacksmith's forge from Snowshill a few miles from Stow. It seems that when the cottage, the forge, and a barn and fence were being assembled in Greenfield Village, no one could get the roof tiles back together even though each stone in the buildings had been carefully numbered. A stone tiler had to be brought over from Snowshill to hang the roofs.

When I was in the area one time I bought a copy of the magazine *Cotswold Life*. In it was an article about an Englishwoman who spent years of her life restoring neglected Cotswold cottages. One of those was Rose Cottage in Chedworth. When it was completely restored an agent offered to buy it for a very large sum. He considered it a perfect example of a traditional Cotswold cottage and hinted that it might be removed to another site. The woman discovered that the other site was America only after seeing workmen numbering every stone and timber and taking photographs of the cottage. Rose Cottage is now in Greenfield Village. She was always saddened by the Cotswolds' loss.

Stow-on-the-Wold has more attractive hotels than most towns of its size. The Old Stocks Hotel where I stayed several times occupies three 16th- and 17th-century buildings on the square facing the village green. It has 300-year-old stone walls and some of its old oak beams are ships' timbers. The hotel has one closet-size single room that is too small to be comfortable for a stay of several days and you will not want that room.

The atmosphere of the Old Stocks Hotel is casual and friendly, and the small bar has a log fire in cool weather. On my second stay at the hotel the female bartender remembered me from my first visit a couple of years earlier. On one visit as I sat in the bar before dinner, an Australian gentleman sat down at the table next to mine. He and his wife and their two teenaged children were traveling through Europe. His family joined him at the bar, and when my table was ready he invited me to join them for dinner. We traded travel stories and their enthusiasm about their trip made the hour at dinner seem like fifteen minutes. It was a nice close to the day.

Another hotel I've enjoyed is the Unicorn, a Forte Heritage Hotel. Located just behind the church on the corner of Sheep Street and the Fosse Way, the Unicorn is a traditional British hotel that has changed little since it was built in the 17th century. Antiques are tucked everywhere and in the pub bar elaborately carved furnishings add a touch of old. The decor throughout, including the bedrooms, is warm and lovely and designed for relaxing.

On my next trip to Stow I plan to stay at the Stow Lodge Hotel. This attractive hotel, in a peaceful corner of the square, is reached by a tree-shaded pathway that leads through gardens to the hotel entrance. As soon as you open the front door you are met by old-world charm. The entry has a high stone archway through which you first see the interior of rich wood and old fixtures. Fires glow in the bar and lounge in season, and you can see where a secret priest-hole once was. It was used in the days when it was a crime to harbor a Roman Catholic priest. Bedrooms are located in the hotel and in a Coach House on the hotel grounds. The only single bedroom is upstairs in the main building and would be a charming place to snug in for the night.

Another lovely hotel that I have not stayed in, but where I had tea one afternoon, is the Grapevine Hotel just off the square. It is a Best Western Hotel and maintains very high standards of comfort, decor, and service. With so many inviting places to stay in Stow, your only problem might be choosing one.

The Stow Tourist Information Centre is excellent. In addition to providing maps and brochures of Stow, the nearby towns, and the Cotswolds, it offers detailed help to those planning to spend time in Stow. If you're interested in joining a group walk, check to see if one is available while you're there.

A brochure called *Guided Walks in the Cotswolds* lists local walks planned by the Cotswold Warden Office for the Cotswolds Area of Outstanding Natural Beauty. The walks, which start at various locations, range from about four to ten miles and are scheduled to take from three to seven hours. At the tourist center you can also get information on local bus service and train schedules and buy tickets on National Express, the long-distance bus service.

There are two easy ways to get to Stow, depending on where you come from. One is through Cheltenham by bus. If you take a bus to Cheltenham it will probably stop at the Royal Well station, where you can get the bus to Stow-on-the-Wold. If you go to Cheltenham by train you will have to take a taxi to Royal Well bus station, which is several miles from the railway station. If you're traveling by train it is much easier to go to Moreton-in-Marsh. The train station there is only a couple of blocks from the Town Hall, where both National Express buses and local buses to Stow stop. Ask someone where to wait for the bus as there are two waiting areas.

If you decide to visit the Cotswolds, do go in the off-season. Another travel writer wrote that these appealing towns are "heavily overcrowded and their undoubted charms hidden by a tragic burden of traffic." That, unfortunately, is true of most areas of Britain during the tourist months.

A stay in the Cotswolds can be a delightful, relaxing experience, and at some time in your travels you will want to see these picture-postcard villages that nestle in the lush Cotswold hills.

BRADFORD-ON-AVON

"Bradford-on-Avon wears its many-splendoured coat with a modesty which befits an old town with such an embarrassment of riches. If true charm be unconscious, then Bradford has it in abundance." So wrote a local man for a Bradford brochure. This beautiful old town is a luscious hors d'oeuvre, a town of character that has grown comfortable with age.

Bradford has two ancient churches and a medieval chapel that stands high on a hill above the town. Old stone cottages, like limestone outcrops, clutch hillsides that rise from the town center. One has to climb flights of stone steps in narrow walled passages to reach the top of the steep hills.

Bradford is another gem that is not on the tourist trail. One reason could be that, although it is on the main London–Bath train line, not all trains stop there, and most major highways skirt the town. Bradford, on the southern edge of the Cotswolds, was recorded in the Domesday Book as Bradeford, after the ancient broad ford that crossed the river where the Town Bridge now stands. There are several rivers in southwestern England named Avon, which is a Celtic word meaning water. Bradford's Avon is not the famous Stratford-upon-Avon river.

Travelers who wrote about the town in olden days described it as looking Dutch, or like Spain, or like the hills of Italy, where houses hug the slopes. In fact, many Dutch weavers were brought here to modernize the cloth industry, and there are houses still called Dutch Barton where these early weavers lived.

On arrival in Bradford one of the first unusual sights you'll see is the little stone chapel built out over the water on a pier of the old Town Bridge. In medieval days pilgrims on their way to Glastonbury stopped there to pray. Later the chapel became a tool house, an ammunition store, and a lockup known as the Blind House because drunks were often locked up there. The bridge is the center of town. When it was widened in the 17th century two of its 13th-century arches were kept.

You'll find the Tourist Information Centre in the library near the bridge. When you stop there ask if a brochure called *Bradford-on-Avon Discovery Trail* is still available. If it is, be sure to get one. It has a marked

*This little stone chapel has stood on a pier on Bradford's old Town
Bridge since medieval days.*

walk through town and describes the ancient historic sites. The walk
leads up to terraces built into the steep hills and then down to the Avon
and the canal where you can walk for miles along the towpath. Although
the brochure has a small town map, you'll want to get a more detailed
one with a street index.

The first thing you'll notice about the streets that fan out from the
bridge is the traffic. The roads from surrounding towns converge at the
bridge and, except where the street is marked for a pedestrian crossing
and at a stoplight at the end of the bridge, it is not easy to cross these
main streets. When I first went to Bradford I stopped at a news agent for
a paper and the owner made a point of telling me just where to cross the
street safely. A guide I bought at the tourist office also warns you to cross
the street with "extreme caution." Perhaps by now there will be another
pedestrian crossing at these corners.

To really appreciate Bradford-on-Avon you have to walk along the
cobbled streets and up steps with names like Barton Steps and Rosemary
Steps to the top of the hill, where you can look out over not only Bradford but the hills and valleys and plains for miles around. The paths you

walk, the buildings you pass, and the walls you brush against are all built of pale yellow Bath stone quarried right here.

There are three terraces that climb the hill from the center of town. The first is named Newtown. Here you can wander past old houses that glow with the warm richness of the stone. Newtown is linked to the two higher terraces by a steep hill called Conigre Hill, from an old word meaning "rabbit warren." Up a series of steps is the next terrace, Middle Rank, with rows of 17th-century cottages where weavers lived during the peak of the cloth industry.

One day as I wandered along the path here I saw an interesting little narrow dead-end lane between rows of cottages. There were brilliant red and yellow flowers blooming in tiny gardens and vines cascading over stone walls. The dirt path that led into the quiet corner was overhung with flowering shrubs. Hoping I wasn't trespassing, I went in to take a few photos. I came to a small alcove formed by the walls of a cottage. Water trickled down from under the house and splashed into the foam of a minute pool. A sign said "Lady Well Spring."

It began as a stream in the highest terrace and had once flowed into a stone trough used to water horses and then it continued down the hill. Today the spring still runs down under the road, then under Ladywell Cottage, where I stood. From there it flows on down to Newtown.

As I took a picture of the well a lady came out of one of the cottages. When I said I hoped I wasn't intruding, she said I wasn't and agreed it was a lovely corner for a photo. Then she asked if I'd like to see her cottage. She explained that from where we stood at the back of the cottage it looked only two stories high, but these two stories were the third and fourth floors of her home. From the front side of the cottage you see a four-story house, with an entrance on the first floor. We walked past the end cottage in this row and around to her front door. These four floors were once homes for two weavers' families, with two floors in each cottage.

We went in to one of the most precious living rooms I have ever seen—and one of the smallest. On one wall was a fireplace carved from one huge piece of Bath stone, and though it was not oversized it filled much of that wall. Another wall was lined with shelves of books that went up to the low beamed ceiling.

A circular staircase that was too narrow to hold an overweight person stood in one corner. It continued up to each of the upper three floors. Each floor had just one smallish room. The second floor was a study; the third, a bedroom and bath; and on the top floor was the kitchen. Each room was filled with a lifetime of memorabilia—paintings on easels, antique mirrors, collections of lovely pieces of china, and on wall shelves in the tiny room that held only the toilet were a small puppet stage with characters, dolls, and ceramic figures.

In this small four-story cottage each room was as dear as the next. It was hard to imagine a large family living in just two of these rooms as the weavers' families had.

In Middle Rank and on up to Tory, the highest terrace, there were miniature gardens and creeping vines on stone walls. The views of the countryside were spectacular. Bradford is spread out over the hills that rise from the town center. Some of the steps leading up to Tory, once called Top Rank Tory, are very steep, but if stairs don't bother you it is worth the climb to see this old part of town and the views. Many-gabled buildings with tall chimneys that pierce the sky line streets that curve and wind and come to sudden dead ends. At the end of Tory is St. Mary Tory, well marked on every map. This 15th-century chapel, later reconstructed, had rooms for pilgrims on their way to Glastonbury Abbey.

From here you can go back down the hill to another of Bradford's famous buildings—the Saxon Church of St. Laurence. You don't have to be a history buff to appreciate this. Thought to have been built about A.D. 700, it was "lost" for eleven centuries until the vicar of Holy Trinity Church across the street discovered it in 1856. Other buildings that crowded around it had hidden the church all those years. It had once been used as a charnel house, where bodies of the dead were left. Later it became a school, and then cottages. The vicar, Canon William Jones, had noticed the cruciform shape of the cottages, and when some repair work was being done on them workmen uncovered two carved angels built into one wall.

The vicar realized it must be an ancient church, but he had to wait fifteen more years to find out. Then the owners agreed to sell the cottages, and the surrounding buildings were cleared away and the Saxon church was uncovered. It is one of the oldest surviving churches in England. Leaving the church, you can cross the river on a graceful arched footbridge and take a tranquil walk on a riverside path leading to Barton Farm. Trees edging the river hide the town from this countryside park. You come to the old stone packhorse Barton Bridge and from here you can walk to Avoncliff downriver. You can take the path along the river or follow the towpath beside the Kennet and Avon Canal. You might decide to walk here on a fine sunny day and have a picnic lunch beside the river.

If you'd like more exercise you can rent a bicycle for a ride on the tow-path.

This country park was part of the original Barton Farm, the grange that supplied food to Shaftesbury Abbey. Just beyond the bridge is a magnificent 14th-century tithe barn. In the 10th century parishioners were ordered to give one-tenth of their income in cash or in grain or animals to support the church. This barn was built to hold the abbey's tenth, or tithe, of the produce given. It is one of the largest and finest tithe barns in the country. Its massive timbers support a roof of 100 tons of stone tiles.

The other farm buildings—a granary, barns, and sheds—are now used as crafts shops and galleries. The granary, near the tithe barn, has become an emporium packed with things massed on tables and hanging from rafters. If you enjoy browsing or have small gifts to buy, allow time for a stop here.

The main shopping streets in Bradford fan out from the town bridge. The Shambles, on a narrow flagged walk between two main streets, was the medieval marketplace. The slaughterhouses this street was named for disappeared long ago and today produce stores, a bakery, and an excellent china and cookware shop have taken over. The post office is at the end of the Shambles. In nearby Market and Silver Streets you'll find tearooms, art galleries, and antique shops.

In this central area are a number of places that make good stops for lunch or a snack. One of them, the Bridge Tea Rooms, is a "must" stop for chocolate lovers. The mouth-watering chocolate cakes and other desserts will tempt you to stop here once a day. Lunches and homemade soups are also served all day. The building, c. 1675, looks so old and crooked that you might wonder if it will stand long enough for you to have coffee. Inside it is a Victorian tearoom with old beams and a blazing fire. The waitresses wear floor-length dresses with long white aprons and white ruffled bonnets. A sign inside the door warns you to watch your head as you leave, and you do have to duck to avoid a head injury in this old doorway. The Bridge Tea Rooms are across from the library.

Another lunch stop in the center is the Scribbling Horse. The name is taken from a wooden frame used for preparing wool for spinning, a remnant of the days when Bradford was famous for its wool and cloth. When I ordered a toasted sandwich here it came with two pieces of toast crimped together on all edges, forming a pocket for the filling, which was hot. I thought of buying one of those toasters on another trip, but when I checked with an electrical expert at home about a converter for it I was told that depending on the wattage used, a converter could cost more than $100. The toaster made a delicious sandwich and I am still checking on buying one.

The Swan Hotel at the foot of the bridge serves meals and also pub snacks. The tourist office has a brochure listing places to eat and drink in town.

As you walk around Bradford you'll see many handsome houses built by professional men and cloth merchants made wealthy on the wool trade. Some are rambling Georgian houses; others have tall stone—mullioned by windows and striking pillars. Even the halls and schools in Bradford are rich buildings.

Because Bradford is not on the tourist trails, it doesn't have the number of hotels in the center that many towns have. The 16th-century Swan Hotel is the only one. When I stayed there my room was a small single room, clean, very nicely decorated, and with a private bath. And it had something I always appreciate—good reading lights. The hotel staff is always pleasant and very helpful and the atmosphere is warm and friendly. The Swan is especially remembered for one period that was made wretched by one notorious man. It seems that the infamous Judge Jeffreys held court in the Swan for a while. Known for cruelty and corruption, he executed between 150 and 200 people and sold many hundreds more into slavery in the colonies.

I have also stayed in two guest houses that are a short walk from the bridge. One of them, Priory Steps on Newtown, was converted from six 17th-century weavers' cottages. There are only five rooms, so you should make reservations early if you'd like to stay here. The beautiful building is built of Bath stone and has shiny white painted windows and doors. The rooms, all with private baths, are decorated with great care, each one different from the others. My room was done in blue and white and had a ceramic-trimmed brass bed covered with a blue-and-white quilt. And there were dried flowers and a lovely antique drop-leaf table in the room. The lodge has a well-stocked library where you can find a book to curl up with some evening. In the rear of the house is a large garden area overlooking town.

I also enjoyed the other guest house I stayed in—Bradford Old Windmill. Once a functioning windmill, today the sails are gone and the round tower is given over to round rooms. My room, round and beamed, had a huge round bed. It was well furnished with a ceiling-hung wicker basket chair and a small table with a mirror that could double as a writing desk. From the tall, narrow windows with pointed Gothic arches you looked down on Bradford spread out below. Cases of books for guests to use were in the halls and stair landing. Interesting pieces that the owners had collected on trips around the world were displayed throughout the house.

Like many B&Bs, the house is closed from ten in the morning until five in the afternoon. I found that to be a disadvantage one day when I returned to Bradford early after a busy day; I spent a couple of hours walking while I waited to get in the house. If you plan to return early, you can arrange in advance to get in before five. The owners are eager to help guests in any way they can. They gladly set up an iron and ironing board for me when I needed it. If you call for reservations while the owners are out, expect to hear a lengthy recording before you're able to leave a message.

Both Priory Steps and Bradford Old Windmill are a short uphill walk from the Town Bridge, where the buses stop. If you come by train you might want to take a taxi to either of these, as the walk from the station is long if you're carrying a suitcase. Bradford has several other small inns and B&Bs as well as two deluxe hotels that are each about a mile from town.

Aside from Bradford being a lovely and interesting town, another reason to stay here is that its location makes day-trips to many places easy. Bus and train service is good; however, you do need a train schedule to know which trains stop in Bradford. You also might have to change trains or buses in Bath to get to some places, but that is a short ride. From Bradford the train to Bath follows the Avon River; on a nice day fishermen, picnickers, and walkers will be on the green riverbanks, making it a pleasant train ride. Trowbridge, a larger town south of Bradford, is also a connecting point for some buses you might take.

Bath is a city that everyone wants to see, and many visitors travel more than a hundred miles from London to spend a day there. Beautiful, blond Bath! It has been called the "Timeless City of Gold" and is often called the most elegant city in England. So splendid is Bath that it has been selected as one of UNESCO'S World Heritage sites.

The Romans were here soon after they arrived in Britain. When they discovered a hot spring in this land of chilly mists they named the place Aquae Sulis, the "Waters of Sul," after a Celtic deity and linked it to their Goddess of Health and Healing, Minerva. And they built a temple in their joint honor.

Today Bath is a showplace of fine architecture, a city of parks and gardens spreading over hills. Graceful ironwork adorns houses and squares and hundreds of small shops line narrow passages branching out from the Abbey Churchyard. And there are more museums and galleries than you'll ever have time to see.

Over the centuries Bath has been written about by more writers than probably any one place in Britain except London. Chaucer, Shakespeare, Jane Austen, Celia Fiennes, Henry Fielding, and Robert Southey are just a few. Charles Dickens found Pickwick here, and in 1857 William Thackeray wrote, "As for Bath, all history went and bathed and drank there."

When you arrive in Bath by either bus or train (the bus and train stations are across the street from each other), one of the first famous landmarks you'll see is the Pulteney Bridge, which gracefully spans the Avon River. The buildings that crowd the bridge have stood on these arches for more than 200 years. And you'll see the great tower of Bath Abbey rising above the city center. The abbey was called the Benedictine "lantern of the West." When the present abbey was begun in 1499, Oliver King, bishop of Bath and Wells, had a dream that was later preserved on the West Front of the abbey. Carved angels climb up and down ladders to heaven on the turrets, and at the sides stand the Twelve Apostles. The building of this last great abbey was interrupted by Henry VIII's Dissolution of the Monasteries. It was plundered, as were most abbeys, but was finally restored and finished during the reign of Henry's daughter, Elizabeth I.

The Abbey Churchyard is the large square on the west side; much of your sightseeing will begin there. The Tourist Information Centre and the Roman Baths and museum are here. The great bath is one of the finest Roman remains in Britain. It has an open-air lead-lined swimming pool. In the museum are mosaics, sculptures, and other finds from old Aquae Sulis. Underneath the Pump Room you can see the recently excavated precinct of the Roman Temple of Sulis-Minerva. The gilded bronze head of the Goddess Minerva, unearthed in 1727, is said to be the finest exhibit here.

Bath is a city to be walked through, and the TIC can give you directions to the architectural showcases you'll read about. The shops in the little passages and corridors where only foot traffic is allowed might tempt you to not take the longer walk to the Circus and the Royal Crescent. But if it's a nice day, do go on to see these buildings, which are among Bath's treasures. In these rows of townhouses the famous people of Bath lived in luxury—David Livingstone, Thomas Gainsborough, and Lord Robert Clive, to name a few.

On your walk from the churchyard you will come to the Circus first. (In Britain, an open area where streets converge is often called a circus.) In Bath's Circus three arc-shaped buildings are separated by three streets leading into a great circle. When you approach the Circus by any of these streets you will see a magnificent clump of huge plane trees spreading over a circular green in the very center. The arcs of houses have three tiers of columns and above the ground-floor windows is a frieze of 528 symbols of the arts and sciences that curves along the three buildings.

Nearby on Bennett Street, one of the three streets leading out from the circle, are the Assembly Rooms that figure in novels set in Bath. The rooms house one of the finest museums of costume in Britain, with displays of dress from the 16th century to the present day, all in period settings.

Brock Street, branching out from the Circus in the opposite direction, leads to the Royal Crescent. In one sweeping 600-foot-long curve are thirty houses graced by 114 columns in a palace facade. Composer Franz Joseph Haydn described the crescent as "a building shaped like a half-moon and more magnificent than any I had seen in London." It faces Royal Victoria Park, a fitting view for a building of such elegance. In the park are gardens, a lake, one of the finest collections of trees in Britain, and avenues of cherry trees with blossoms of beauty in the spring.

The Royal Crescent and the Circus are only two of Bath's architectural gems. Wherever you go you will find more. Along the flagged walks are ornamental wrought-iron lamp holders, ornately carved doorways, and plaques on buildings telling of famous people who lived there. On a building next to the beautifully restored Theatre Royal hangs a large plaque that tells the story of the uncrowned King of Bath, Richard "Beau" Nash. He and his mistress, Juliana Popjoy, lived here in what is now Popjoy's Restaurant.

Beau Nash came to Bath in 1705, attracted by gambling and women. He set the standards for Bath society and even made rules dictating the "right" dress and manners. He became the official Master of Ceremonies and made Bath one of the most fashionable cities in Europe.

Of the many writers who used Bath as a setting for their books, Jane Austen is probably the one associated most with Bath. She was not alone in describing the social activities, from the morning baths to the afternoon walks to the theater and the evening balls; Daniel Defoe called a day in Bath a "round of the utmost diversion."

As you might expect in a city with all these attractions, there are restaurants and tearooms everywhere. For an early cup of coffee, Sally Lunn's Refreshment House and Museum, just off the Abbey Churchyard on North Parade Passage, is an interesting stop. It is said to be the oldest house in Bath and is the home of the renowned Sally Lunn bun. Young Sally came to Bath in 1680 and was hired by a baker to sell his goods in the street. But the brioche buns she baked were such a success that customers began requesting them and they still do today.

Sally Lunn's Refreshment House and Museum has been famous for its buns since the 17th century.

Excavations in the cellar of the small museum have revealed medieval foundations and stone walls. Roman artifacts unearthed show that buildings stood on the site as far back as A.D. 200. Most interesting is a faggot oven of a design that originated in Rome in about 100 B.C. In the ground floor restaurant is a secret cupboard in chimney paneling where Sally's recipe was discovered. When I was there, the cellar museum was open only in the morning.

The Pump Room, where a trio of musicians plays during the morning, is also a delightful place for a coffee stop. Brochures from the TIC refer you to these and other restaurants in Bath's center.

In the fall of 1993 a shopping center with discount factory prices had just opened in Street, a town some thirty miles south of Bath. An article in the Bath evening newspaper described it as "based on an exciting American idea, the first of its kind in Britain." It went on to say that "like a shark in the water," this center, with twenty-two stores, threatened to devour trade as far away as Bath. This Clark Village (from the famous Clarks shoe company) opened to mixed reviews. Some residents in the Bath area said they would continue to shop in Bristol or Cheltenham and others said they'd wait a few months to see if the crowds thinned out at the shopping center. There have been attempts to establish supermarkets in Bath, and, in fact, some chains are still looking at sites where they would like to build their superstores. So far, the residents have been successful in keeping them out, but it will probably be an ongoing struggle. A recent count showed that Bath has about two million tourists a year, so the time to go there is in the off-season. If you stay in Bradford-on-Avon, or in any town near Bath, you will want to spend a day here in one of Britain's loveliest cities. It is only a short ride from Bradford by either bus or train.

Because Bradford has good transportation, the list of possible day-trips is long. You can take a train into Wales or ride south to a town on the English Channel. Local bus service covers a wide area, offering a choice of many towns you might like to spend a few hours in.

If you are interested in great cathedrals, you might want to visit Wells, which has one of the finest in the world. In a letter to his brother, novelist George Gissing wrote of Wells and its cathedral, "That glorious Cathedral, set amid surely the most beautiful Close that exists. . . . A marvellous spot, civilized with the culture of centuries, yet quite unlike the trimness of other cathedral towns."

Time spent at Wells's 12th-century cathedral will be spent studying art. Begin with the west front. Decorated with more than 300 statues of saints, angels, and prophets, as well as of scenes from the Old and New Testaments, the front has been called the "Bible in stone" and "a magnificent song of praise," and is said to be the most important gallery of 13th-century sculpture in England." Above this mass of sculpture, in the cen-

*This magnificent cathedral in Wells is one of the most
beautiful cathedrals in Britain.*

ter gable, is a great Christ in majesty over a row of statues of the Twelve
Apostles. The carvings had so deteriorated that recent restoration work
took more than a decade. Painstaking cleaning with toothbrushes, spatu-
las, and mist sprays prevented further decay, but several statues, including the Christ, had to be replaced entirely.

The most outstanding feature of the inside of the cathedral is the set of
great "scissor-arches." These were added to support the central tower
after it began to lean and crack, and today the arches are one of the cathedral's greatest attractions. Other highlights of the interior are the sixty
misericords decorated with scenes carved by artisans (said to be among
the finest in existence) and the ornate stone carvings above the columns
and roof supports and between arches. One scene carved around a capi-

tal topping a column is particularly well known. It is of a man and boy stealing fruit. The boy is holding a basket of the fruit, probably grapes. A farm hand points them out to the farmer, who chases them and hits the thief over the head. This is only one of the unique carvings you'll see.

Everyone who visits the cathedral seems to know in advance about the 14th-century clock. I got there just before noon and sat on a bench with others who were waiting to see the clock strike. The clock is six feet across and is intricately painted. An outer circle marks the twenty-four hours and a star moves around an inner circle as the minutes pass. A center circle shows the days of the month. At noon a quaint figure kicks a bell with his heel and above the clock knights on horseback appear and gallop in a circle, and at each turn one of them is unseated.

From here a walk through the cathedral will bring you to a graceful stone staircase that curves and appears to flow down from some hidden place above. The old stone steps are worn down from the footsteps of centuries. You often find stairs worn like this, but each time I see them I am filled with awe. I think of how many people had to step there to wear down stone, from the humblest peasants and farmers, to the knights, bishops, and kings. These stairs turn into the Chapter House and a narrower flight continues up to the Chain Bridge, which passes over a busy street and joins the Vicars' Close to the cathedral. Vicars' Close has a series of stone houses lining each side of a cobbled street with a vicars' chapel at the far end. Behind a low stone wall on both sides of the street, each house has a small garden. This is where the men of the Vicars Choral, who made up the Cathedral Choir, lived. It is the oldest continuously inhabited medieval street in Europe.

On the opposite side of the cathedral is the Bishop's Palace, which is like a medieval castle—walled and surrounded by a moat with a drawbridge. Swans that grace the moat have learned to pull a string that rings a bell outside a gatehouse window when they are hungry; someone then throws food out the window to them. I walked beside the moat for a while, hoping to see a hungry swan ring the bell, but my timing was wrong and it didn't happen.

There is an attractive cafeteria-style restaurant in the cathedral cloisters overlooking a courtyard. The atmosphere suits the cathedral, and the setting is so perfect it is worth a stop. The British lunch I had was excellent.

Wells is Britain's smallest city. It would not take much time to explore the whole city. Otherwise, combine Wells Cathedral with a few hours in another town. It is truly time well spent to wander these old stones and this beautiful cathedral.

Another easy side-trip from Bradford is the village of Lacock, most of which is owned by the National Trust. Because this was the home of William Henry Fox Talbot, a pioneer in photography, Lacock is of special interest to photographers.

The Domesday Book records that the manor, mills, vineyards, and woods belonged to the son of one of William the Conqueror's knights. King William visited Lacock with his court in 1086.

There is a marvelous mix of buildings here. Many of the timber-framed cottages have jettied (overhanging) upper stories, to accommodate weaver's looms. Seventeenth-century stone cottages stand next to elegant brick mansions, and buildings with mullioned windows and steep gables crowd together on narrow lots. Lacock has the atmosphere and character of medieval England; there are no telephone poles, electric lines, or TV antennas to remind one of this century. In fact, it was said on a recent British TV program that the only blemish in this idyllic village is the throngs of tourists that fill the old streets and byways. Lacock was a planned estate village built for the employees of the abbey. The abbey was a 13th-century Augustinian nunnery and was one of the final 800 monasteries and nunneries that were broken up by Henry VIII. It was then bought by Sir William Sharington, who demolished the church and converted the rest of the abbey buildings into a mansion for himself.

The story is told that Sir William's niece, Olive, leapt from the manor's tower into her lover's arms rather than renounce their love. Her billowing skirts saved her, and she and her lover, a Talbot, were permitted to marry. The property, including the abbey mansion and village, then passed to the Talbots.

The growth of Lacock stopped in the mid-eighteenth century when the Talbot family made sure a planned railway line and station were not built there. Their foresight in not wanting to spoil the village is probably the reason for Lacock's beauty today. In 1944 Matilda Talbot gave the abbey and most of Lacock village to the National Trust.

Near the gate to the abbey is a 16th-century barn, which is now the Fox Talbot Museum of Photography. An audio-visual presentation and changing exhibits complement the collection of cameras and equipment used by Fox Talbot. His pictures (calotypes) and his many international awards are displayed. In the past, the museum has been open from

March to November, but if this is a must for you, check the dates before making plans to see it.

Lacock is a village to just unhurriedly wander through. Built as a square with four main streets, there are lanes extending into the country-side. You can stroll out to a packhorse bridge over the Bide Brook or take a footpath to a medieval bridge that crosses the River Avon. It is an opportunity to get away from traffic and spend some time in the rural quiet. If this is to be a lunch stop, you have three inns to choose from— the Sign of the Angel, the Red Lion, and the George, all of them centuries old.

Another exceptional day-trip you can take is to lovely Salisbury. There are several daily trains between Bradford-on-Avon and Salisbury, and good bus service is also available. The trip can take anywhere between half an hour and two hours, depending on how you travel.

Salisbury did not begin where it now stands—on the banks of four rivers. It began on an ancient windy hill two miles north. The hill-fort built there was occupied in turn by the Celts, the Romans, and the Sax-ons. Then the Normans came. They built a castle and a bishop's palace on the mound that was called Sarum. Today you can take a bus from Salis-bury to Old Sarum and walk up to the old settlement. A bridge crosses the deep ditches that encircle the steep, broad mound. The ruins of Sarum, mostly low walls and foundations, are well preserved. From this high point you can look over red-roofed Salisbury, its cathedral spire soaring to heaven above New Sarum.

It was Bishop Richard Poore who decided to move his city down to the plain below. The story is told that the bishop had an archer shoot an arrow from Old Sarum's mound, and where it fell the new cathedral would be built. If the story is true, the arrow fell on a water meadow beside the River Avon where the cathedral now stands. Work began in 1220 and with great ceremony the consecration of the cathedral took place just thirty-eight years later. The graceful arcaded cloisters, the earli-est surviving in England, were completed in 1270 and enclose a great square of tranquillity. Today the spreading branches of two cedars of Lebanon, planted in 1847, fill this lovely square. Lingering awhile in the hush of these cloisters will add a quiet glow to your day.

Adjoining the cloisters is the octagonal Chapter House, where the cathedral's greatest treasure is preserved—one of four surviving copies of the Magna Carta. A frieze of sculptured scenes from the Bible runs completely around the walls of the Chapter House. Another of the cathedral's prized possessions is an ancient clock. Dating from 1386, it is the oldest working clock mechanism in England. It has struck every hour for more than five centuries, except for one seventy-two-year period when a new clock was used and no further interest was shown in the old one.

Salisbury Cathedral was one of only a few cathedrals that developed an extraordinary custom—having a Boy Bishop. On December 6, the Feast of St. Nicholas, the choirboys elected one of their own to be the Boy Bishop. From that day until December 28, Childermass Day, he occupied the Bishop's Throne, attended by the rest of the choirboys, who were his canons. The Boy Bishop preached a sermon and recited the offices except for that of the Mass. Crowds of people came to see the unusual ceremony on Childermass Day when the choirboys, dressed in robes, took part in a procession through and around the cathedral.

The crowning glory of Salisbury Cathedral is its spire, the highest in Britain. It was added almost a century after the cathedral was completed. The original foundation had not been intended to support the spire's 6,400 tons, and over the years measures have been taken to strengthen the supports of the spire. Although the spire leans 29½ inches to one side, it has survived for more than six centuries to lead travelers to this great city.

On a gray, frosty, winter morning in Salisbury, the cold of centuries seems to seep out of these ancient stones. Although the chill somehow befits the tombs, effigies, and monuments to those who lived as long as seven hundred years ago, it can still bring a shudder, just as would have some of the tragic events these old stones witnessed over the centuries. The cathedral was flooded, plundered by soldiers during the Civil War, and abused by the prisoners it held. Weather and pollution deteriorated its exterior stonework and lightning struck its spire. When I was last there, scaffolding mounted the tower and spire where craftsmen worked to repair damage. Some of the statues from the west front niches had been removed and were being restored by artisans in a workshop on the cathedral grounds.

Outside the cathedral is the finest close in England. Enclosed on three sides by walls built of stones from Old Sarum, it is a separate world from the bustle on the other side of the walls. The fourth side of this lovely picture is framed by the River Avon flowing peacefully behind the houses across from the cathedral's west front.

When the cathedral was being built, the church authorities needed housing. That's when the present layout of the close, with houses arranged along the edges of the great square, was established. A Bishop's Palace and several mansions for the clergy were also built. Over the centuries, some of the houses have been reconstructed, but many original features remain. The Deanery, for example, is said to have its original 13th-century roof. A few of the buildings are open to the public for part of the year.

One of the grandest buildings in the close is now an excellent museum. Originally the Salisbury residence of the Abbots of Sherborne, it was named the Kings House after James I visited here. Now the Salisbury and South Wiltshire Museum, it offers history buffs an excellent look at the area. There is a Stonehenge Gallery that illustrates the building of this World Heritage site. The Early Man Gallery has an important collection of archaeological finds spanning the Stone Age to the Saxon period. Other displays contain items of medieval life in Salisbury, and you'll see a model of Old Sarum. There are also fine galleries of ceramics, including an extensive collection of Wedgwood pieces.

The High Street Gate, or North Gate, leads into Salisbury Close from the center of town.

An impressive array of famous people have lived in and visited the houses in the close over the years. Former Prime Minister Edward Heath lives in the close today. W. S. Gilbert (of Gilbert and Sullivan) and Canon Izaak Walton, son of the author of *The Compleat Angler,* lived here. Henry Fielding wrote part of Tom Jones in a close house, and the composer Handel stayed here when he gave his first English recital in a chapel over St. Ann's Gate.

There are three gates leading into the close. St. Ann's Gate, with the room above that was the chapel of the Vicars Choral, is entered from St. John's and Exeter Streets. The High Street Gate, or North Gate, is considered the main gate and has the colorful Royal Arms over the archway. The third gate is Harnham Gate, which leads across the Avon to the small town of Harnham. In olden days these three gates were locked at night, and today they still are. They are closed at 11 P.M., and high security is kept by a constable.

When Bishop Poore chose the site for Salisbury Cathedral he also laid out the city. His plan was a rectangle with five streets running north and south and six from east to west. The squares formed by the wide streets were called Chequers and you will still find references to them today. For example, the Red Lion Hotel is listed in the Antelope Chequer. Because most medieval towns grew haphazardly out from some central point with alleys and passageways added anywhere, this urban planning made Salisbury unusual for the times.

Just outside the High Street Gate, on the corner where High Street meets New Street, is Mitre House, named after the bishop's headdress and said to be the first house built in Salisbury. This is where Bishop Poore lived while the cathedral and Bishop's Palace were being built. It still has the rooms where every new Bishop of Salisbury robes for his enthronement, just as each has for seven centuries.

Bishop Poore laid out the marketplace as the center of activity. Originally the square was much larger than it is today. There were designated areas for each activity. The corn market, the wool and yarn market, and the cheese market, where fruits and vegetables were also sold, were on the north and east sides of the square, with wheelwrights, butchers, and the poultry markets on the south and west sides.

The square had four crosses, but only the Poultry Cross survives. This cross was first mentioned in records in 1335, but today's cross dates from the 15th century. It was modernized at one time, but has now been restored to its medieval style, with open arched sides and pinnacles above. It still offers shelter to traders as it has for more than 600 years. Starting in the 14th century, the portable temporary stalls used were made more permanent and eventually became a row of houses. Market places all over England were reduced in size in this way. Market Square is still the center of importance in the city. The Tourist Information Centre is on Fish Row adjacent to the square.

Walking the streets of Salisbury is truly a delight. Some of today's shops are in old black-and-white half-timbered houses with gables and leaded windows. A number of restaurants and inns are worth a stop just to see the buildings that house them. On Milford Street, a short walk from Market Square, is the Red Lion Hotel. One wing of this rambling inn dates back to the 13th century. In a section of the dining room the original "wattle and daub" wall is exposed to view. The wattles were a web of interlocking twigs that were plastered over with clay called daub. Although many buildings still have some walls with this old style construction, few have areas that are uncovered for you to see. The Red Lion is one of the finest examples of a staging post for coaches in the country. It has a 150-year-old hanging Virginia creeper in the courtyard that turns brilliant red in the fall—truly a sight to see.

Another building of interest is the Bay Tree Restaurant, formerly the George Inn, on High Street. Much of the original building dating back to 1314 is preserved. On old beams in one room are carved the heads of Edward II, king from 1307 to 1327, and Queen Isabella. Charles Dickens mentioned the inn in *Martin Chuzzlewit* and Oliver Cromwell slept here, as did the diarist Samuel Pepys. In 1668, Pepys described his "silke bed" and very good diet. However, he found the bill so "exorbitant" that he had a row with the landlady and moved to a cheaper inn where the beds were "good but lousy."

There are more interesting spots here than you can possibly see. Brochures from the TIC describe the highlights. On New Street just outside the close's High Gate are two more historic inns, the 500-year-old New Inn and the 700-year-old Old House, both of which are good places to stop for coffee or lunch.

If you have time for a longer stroll you can walk along the meadows across the Avon from the cathedral. This is where Constable and other artists sat to paint their famous pictures of Salisbury Cathedral. The walk begins at the Harnham Gate in the close. Just outside the gate the walk leads to the bridge crossing the Avon. From there you look down on the riverside gardens of another historic building—the Rose and Crown

Hotel. The north end of the inn was built in about 1380 and still has the heavy oak timbers from that age. In the Oak Bar there is an original square wooden window facing the road. You are now in the village of Harnham, meaning "enclosure of the hares." Harnham was settled before New Sarum was built. If you turn right at the corner and walk along Harnham Road you pass lovely old thatched cob cottages. When you turn right into Lower Street farther on, you will be going toward the old village which has more beautiful houses. A path leads to the River Nadder and Harnham Old Mill. Ducks laze on the river, and from this peaceful spot the cathedral can be seen rising high above the trees. As you walk along the town path you have the finest views of the cathedral. If you don't have time for this longer walk through Harnham you can walk to these famous meadows from the town center. Most maps from the TIC will have this famous walk marked. Whether you come to Salisbury by bus or train, it is a short walk to the TIC, where you will want to stop before setting out to see Salisbury. The center is compact and, thanks to the 13th-century Bishop of Salisbury, is so well laid out that getting around is easy.

Salisbury is also a good place to stay for several days. It takes more than one day to stroll through the historic streets and spend time in the cathedral and close. And you could visit Old Sarum if aged ruins interest you. There is an excellent repertory theater here. It is a major entertainment center in Wessex. If you decide to choose Salisbury as a stopping-place for a few days, you can gain an insight into the city before leaving home by reading Edward Rutherfurd's epic novel *Sarum*. His meticulously researched book is a chronicle of Old and New Sarum, covering almost 10,000 years.

Visiting Salisbury will be an exceptional experience. When the 19th-century English architect Augustus Pugin stood in the northeast corner of Salisbury Cathedral's close he remarked, "Well, I have travelled all over Europe in search of architecture, and I have seen nothing like this." The cathedral and close are truly masterpieces.

From Bradford-on-Avon you can visit so many lovely places—all within day-trip distance—that it is a town to consider when you choose a home base for your trip. If your plans don't allow a stay in Bradford, do make it a day-trip destination if you are in the area.

SHREWSBURY

The border country of England and Wales—called the Welsh Marches—is a gallery of history. Battles raged here for centuries; in wars fought among the English for the throne of England; in those fought against foreign invaders; and in many fought by the English against attacks by Welsh raiders.

In this now peaceful corridor of wooded valleys and rivers, of mountain foothills and rich farmlands, is a string of outstanding towns that are off the typical tourist track. Among these towns is one of my favorites—Shrewsbury, an old market town in Shropshire. Shrewsbury will not only lure you in, but also hold you long after you had planned to leave. It is set in an almost encircling meander of the River Severn, and is often called England's finest Tudor town with its black-and-white timber-framed buildings.

Beyond this passage is a beautiful area of old buildings where scenes from the movie A Christmas Carol, *with George C. Scott, were filmed.*

Winding streets from medieval days skew up and down the steep town hills. Passages, called "shuts," slip under arches of buildings and lead to little back alleys. The origin of the word *shut* is uncertain, but one source says that shuts were short-cuts between streets. A Shrewsbury guide told me that shuts originally had gates at each end that were closed at night, protecting the cottages in the lane. These little alleys are centuries old and many still have their original name—Gullet Passage, Seventy Steps, Peacock Passage, Sheep's Head Shut, and Grope Lane. The names of many streets can be traced back just as far; Dogpole, Mardol, and Wyle Cop are some of the oldest streets. Milk Street and Fish Street were named for the tradesmen who had shops there. In the 13th century, Butcher Row was called Ffleshomeles ("flesh shambles,") a name for butchers and fishmongers. Meat hooks still hang under the eaves of shops there.

One of Shrewsbury's charms is its treasure of stunning buildings, especially those still half-timbered. Some buildings have intricately shaped timbers with skillfully carved designs and upper stories that overhang the ground-floor shops. There are windows that project and have many-paned, leaded glass. And many buildings have two- and three-story bays. When Charles Dickens stayed at the Lion in 1858 he wrote to his family, "We have the strangest little rooms, the ceilings of which I can touch with my hand. The windows bulge out over the street. . . and a door opens out of the sitting room onto a little open gallery . . . where one leans over a queer old rail and looks all down hill and slantwise at the crookedest old black and yellow houses." Some of the crooked old houses have been restored and modernized but they are still there down the hill and slantwise from the Lion.

One building that was of particular interest to me is the King's Head, a 15th-century pub on Mardol. On my first visit to Shrewsbury in 1987, I walked down Mardol and came to a spot where the sidewalk was curtained off and an entire building was covered, closing it off from the street. I asked a workman about it and he told me it was the King's Head being renovated. He said the overhanging third story had gradually listed until it leaned out eighteen inches more than when built and had to be repaired.

A year later I was in another part of Shropshire and found an article about the King's Head in a local newspaper. The pub had reopened that November, and during the restoration a 15th-century wall painting had been discovered. Hidden behind a chimney that had been built against a wall, and covered with tar and soot, was a faint picture of a lion. After studying it, experts from the University of Cardiff carefully cleaned it figure by figure until the entire painting appeared; it portrayed religious scenes, including the Last Supper.

It was another year before I got to see the painting. While making a train connection in Shrewsbury, I had an hour wait for the next train. I checked my bag at the station and walked to the King's Head. The painting is incomplete and somewhat obscured, so it is difficult to make out clear details. A description on the wall points out figures that are probably Christ and some of the Twelves Apostles. Another part of the painting is said to most likely be a picture of the Annunciation. The beautiful exterior of the King's Head is still timbered and has the old diamond-paned mullioned windows, but even after restoration the upper stories still seem to lean precariously.

Many of Shrewsbury's black-and-white half-timbered buildings date from the 16th and 17th centuries, but in later years other beautiful buildings were built. Elegant red brick Georgian and Queen Anne houses changed the look of Shrewsbury. The Market Hall in the square and the public library were built of white sandstone. Anyone with even a slight interest in architecture will find Shrewsbury one of the most fascinating towns in Britain.

As early as the 11th century there were four churches within the loop of the Severn. St. Mary's Church goes back to the 10th century. It has a 200-foot spire and some of the finest stained glass to be found anywhere. St. Chads, considered one of Shrewsbury's most beautiful buildings, was built at the edge of the Quarry, one of the loveliest parks in England. The second spire in Shrewsbury's skyline is St. Alkmund's. You can see an unusual painted glass window there. The fourth church, St. Julian's, was old when Shrewsbury was granted its charter; it is now a Shropshire craft center. All four churches are worth a visit.

Much of the town's history is tied to its castle. After the Norman Conquest, William I granted lands in the Welsh Marches to his loyal followers so that a long line of strongholds could be built to defend against Welsh attacks. Roger de Montgomery, who was given control of Shrewsbury, built a motte and bailey castle in the narrow neck of land formed by the River Severn. Over the years the castle was destroyed, rebuilt, and altered, but the old red sandstone castle still guards the only land approach to town.

Roger de Montgomery also founded what is probably today's best-known Shrewsbury landmark—the Benedictine Abbey of St. Peter and St. Paul. The medieval life of the abbey has been brought to life by the *Brother Cadfael Chronicles*, written by the late Edith Pargeter under the pen name of Ellis Peters. Her Brother Cadfael, a Welshman, had fought in the Crusades and been an adventurer on the seas before entering the Rule of Saint Benedict when he was almost sixty. In the chronicles the monk-herbalist became a solver of mysteries who roamed through the border countryside seeking clues. The stories, based on historical events and real locations, have been translated into more than twenty languages and read by millions. Today they have been televised and shown throughout the world. If you know Pargeter's books, you will recognize the settings in Shrewsbury.

In 1994 an excellent exhibition, the "Shrewsbury Quest," opened in Abbey Foregate, where the Benedictine monastery stood for 500 years. Nothing of the monastery exists today except a small part of the original church, but a view of Brother Cadfael's life and times has been re-created at the Quest.

There is an excellent booklet, *In the Footsteps of Brother Cadfael*, that guides one on walks around Shrewsbury. One walk weaves over the crooked little cobbled streets and alleys where the houses and shops in the Cadfael books stood. You pass the site of the High Cross, where the body of Sir Henry Percy, known as Hotspur, was beheaded and quartered. Shakespeare dramatized Hotspur's death in the play *Henry IV*, when Falstaff told of killing him after fighting "a long hour by Shrewsbury clock." This is a walk through the town's medieval history with descriptions of the historic sites along the way. Following this booklet is the best way to see Shrewsbury on your own.

"The Shrewsbury Quest" has a re-creation of Brother Cadfael's herb garden and workshop, and the abbey church and cloisters. It is an educational center where you can solve a mystery, play a game, or try your hand at medieval calligraphy. With the Brother Cadfael mysteries so widely known today, this new center will probably draw crowds of tourists, and on weekends, even in the off-season months, British tourists could fill the center. If you want to spend a day here you might plan to do it on a weekday.

Long before the idea for "The Shrewsbury Quest" was born, the town had enough attractions to warrant a week's stay. The Shropshire Regimental Museum in the castle is filled with relics of past battles and mementos of famous regiments. Rowley's House Museum occupies both a 1590 black-and-white timbered building and a later brick mansion. It has Roman treasures and displays of natural history from old Shropshire to the present day.

If after a day walking Shrewsbury's hilly streets and alleys you feel a need for some quiet time, find the Quarry on your map and spend a leisurely hour there. This riverside park, with its manicured lawns, lovely gardens, and a pond in the "Dingle," is one reason Shrewsbury is known as the "Town of Flowers."

If you'd like a guided walking tour through this historic old town, you can arrange it at the Tourist Information Centre. The center is just off the square, and it should be your first stop on arrival. You'll need a good map to find your way in these tangled streets and to get your bearings in this loop in the river. You can also get a schedule of what's going on in town. There are theater and musical programs as well as sports events.

If you are interested in taking classes, walk down to Chester Street, past the railway station to the Gateway. There are many crafts classes offered there, from one-day sessions on musical instruments or working with salt dough, to four- and five-day courses on machine-embroidered pictures or woodcarving. You can write to the Gateway for its schedule of classes. The center has no living accommodations so you find a hotel in town on your own.

There are several centrally located hotels in town. Of the four I have stayed in, the Lion is my favorite. The Lion is a Forte Hotel and has all the amenities you would expect. Rooms are well furnished with lovely decor and have private baths. Single rooms are small but have a television, telephone, and tea and coffee-making facilities. Massive fireplaces dominate both the bar and the cozy two-story lounge, where comfortable upholstered chairs invite a long stay.

The Lion was made famous during coaching days, when it was the base for stagecoaches that ran between Shrewsbury and London. In the mid-1700s the journey took five days; just half a century later, cheering crowds met the legendary stagecoach the *Shrewsbury Wonder* when it arrived in a record fifteen hours and forty-five minutes. Samuel Hayward, the *Wonder*'s most famous driver, claimed he was never more than ten minutes late in his sixteen years of driving. But he was better known for his speed in racing up Wyle Cop and into the Lion yard. He would drive the horses at full gallop up the hill, swing the team around in a circle, and without slowing down, they would racket through the narrow stableyard entrance with only inches to spare. No other driver ever attempted to imitate this performance.

In 1770 the Lion added a grand ballroom with a decorated plaster ceiling and oval mirrors lit by glittering chandeliers. It became the social center of town. Jenny Lind was a guest at the Lion; violinist Paganini played here, and Prince William, later to become King William IV, danced in the splendid ballroom.

As early as 1695 the town had excellent shops. There were watchmakers, vintners, dancing masters, booksellers, milliners, a furrier, and amazingly, fifty-two tailors. When Daniel Defoe toured Britain in the 1720s he wrote of Shrewsbury, "This is indeed a beautiful, large, pleasant, populous, and rich town; full of gentry and yet full of trade too . . . they speak all English in the town, but on market-day you would think you were in Wales."

In the early 1700s a visitor wrote of the busy Market Hall that it had "the most Coffee Houses around it that ever I saw in any town." Today the narrow winding streets and little shuts are lined with old buildings with ground-floor shops. Some streets have been "pedestrianized," that is, made open only to walkers.

Although Shrewsbury has more than 1,000 buildings listed for protection, "progress" has also hit here. Some of the old buildings have been modernized beyond recognition, and fast food places and "dime stores" are now in business.

As with any town whose history goes back many centuries, medieval Shrewsbury could be in danger of being overwhelmed by busloads of tourists who want to scurry through town just to have "been there." Now might be the time to see this beautiful old town. There is good bus and train service to Shrewsbury and there are other towns of special interest nearby that make good day-trips. Two in particular that are easy to reach are Chester and Ludlow.

It is said that the first guidebook to Chester was written in 1781, but travelers had been describing Chester in books long before that. Today this city in Cheshire is an overnight stop, or at least a one-day stop, on most tours that circle Britain and hit the high spots—and for good reason. Chester has things of interest that you won't find anywhere else in Britain.

Like Shrewsbury, Chester is not a small town. And just as Shrewsbury's center is almost completely encircled by a river, the central part of

Chester is also enclosed—by medieval walls, the most complete town walls in England. You can walk the broad path atop the walls for all of the two-mile circuit.

Built by the Romans as their fortress Deva, the enclosed part of Chester is laid out following the original Roman plan. Two main streets intersect each other near the town center where the town cross stands. At the far ends of each of these streets is a gate in the wall—Northgate, Eastgate, Bridgegate, and Watergate. There are steps leading to the wall walk at each gate and at several other points, so you can walk for just short sections if the entire walk seems too long.

From the walls you can almost see the history of Chester. Just outside the wall are the ruins of a 7,000-seat Roman amphitheater, said to be the largest one that has ever been uncovered in England. In one corner of the wall is King Charles's Tower, with an inscription telling of a lost battle during the Civil War: "King Charles stood on this tower, September 24th, 1645 and saw his army defeated on Rowton Moor."

Near Eastgate you pass the red sandstone cathedral that was founded by the Normans as a Benedictine abbey in 1092. It is now famous for its richly carved choir stalls, considered to be among the finest examples of 14th-century wood-carving in Europe. The misericords and canopies are magnificent. At the foot of Eastgate, the Old Dee Bridge crosses the River Dee, which rises in the Snowdonia National Park and winds its way to Chester. The armies of England's kings crossed here on their way to fight the Welsh in the hills that rise to the west. At another point you can look down on the Shropshire Canal, which was built over a Roman defense ditch and is now used by canal boats that cruise to Llangollen in Wales.

There is also a series of steps on the wall called the "Wishing Steps." The legend is that one who makes a wish, runs up the steps, then down, and up again without taking a breath will have his wish granted. If you're in Chester on a mild sunny day take this exciting walk on the walls. You will have the view that soldiers of Rome had as they patrolled the wall.

The Chester TIC has an excellent booklet, *Chester Walls Walk*, that describes everything you see on the walk. It is divided into four sections, each of which covers the area between two gates. It details every step of the walk—what you'll see within the walls, on the walls, and outside the walls. It is history come alive.

Just as famous as the walls are Chester's two-tiered walks known as the Rows. The Rows, which are unique to Chester and are thought to date back to the 13th century, were best described by J. S. Howson, Dean of Chester in 1875:

> The Chester "Rows" . . . are covered galleries, raised several feet above the street, so that there are shops under the feet of those who walk to and fro, while the front rooms of overhanging houses are above their heads. Thus there is this singular fact in Chester, which it shares with no other city, that, partly along the pathway supplied by the Walls, partly by the aid of these Rows, the foot-passengers can move about on a higher level than the carriages and the horses. Flights of steps at short intervals connect the Rows with the Streets.

Steps lead from the street to Chester's famous galleried Rows which are lined with shops.

There are superb shops in the Rows and on the street level below. A good place to stop for coffee is Browns, a famous store in the Eastgate Row. It has a little coffee shop in a 13th-century crypt where small table lamps bring a soft glow to the old red sandstone walls that arch to the low ceiling.

The way to experience the old and new of Chester is to walk along the streets where beautiful black-and-white timbered buildings stand. The Town Hall is near the center where the four "Gate" streets meet. This is where you'll find the Tourist Information Centre. It has the usual maps and brochures as well as information about town walks you might want to join. The walks are led by a local guide who knows Chester—its history, its nooks and crannies, and the tales from olden days that you won't find in books.

There are two excellent museums within easy reach. The Grosvenor Museum is famous for its displays of both Roman and local history. The Chester Heritage Centre, Britain's first Heritage Centre, has an audio-visual presentation and exhibits illustrating Chester's heritage and its famous buildings.

Much of old Chester was lost in disasters. A fire in 1278 raged through the inner city, and during the Civil War many buildings burned to the ground or were largely destroyed. But there are many restored buildings dating from the 13th to the 15th centuries.

When I stay in Chester I like the Blossoms Hotel. It's in a prime location, just outside the wall at the Eastgate. The hotel was named after St. Lawrence the Deacon, who was depicted in pictures after his death surrounded by blossoms. Once a coaching inn, the Blossoms has been rebuilt and restored several times and is now a Forte Hotel.

If you're in the Chester area, make this city one of your "must-see" stops. For a day-trip from Shrewsbury you can take one of several trains a day; the ride takes about an hour. The railway station in Chester is quite a walk from the walls but you can get a bus to the city center.

James Boswell, who traveled with and wrote about Samuel Johnson, said of his visit to Chester in 1779, "Chester pleases my fancy, more than any town I ever saw." You might feel the same way after seeing Chester.

Another easy day-trip from Shrewsbury is to Ludlow. Sometimes called "the perfect historic town," it is set in a curve of the River Teme with its castle perched on high ground above the river gorge. Ludlow Castle is one of the fortresses built by the Marcher Barons to keep out the Welsh. The town was laid out by the Normans in the shadow of the great castle.

A market town from the beginning, Ludlow still offers fine shopping, with antique shops, bookstores, and art galleries among the many businesses that line the bustling medieval streets. The Tourist Information Centre has a brochure with walks through town that are mapped out for easy following. Many old buildings dating as far back as the 15th century are described in the walks, and wood-carved figures and brackets that were added in the 16th and 17th centuries are pointed out. Of particular interest is a walk that leaves the town activity and circles behind the castle along a tree-shaded path above the river gorge. As is true of many castles, tales of treachery and intrigue are still told about Ludlow Castle. Perhaps the most famous story is the one called the "The Princes in the Tower." The two little princes spent much of their lives in Ludlow Castle. There are no accurate portraits of the young boys, but they are usually pictured with fair, wavy, shoulder-length hair, both dressed in black velvet and wearing a heavy gold chain around their necks; and always, with bewildered, apprehensive looks as they clasp hands and the younger Richard clings to the twelve-year-old Edward.

When their father, Edward IV, died in April 1483, young Edward was in the castle, and two days after his father's death he was proclaimed King of England. Their Uncle Richard, appointed protector of the children but intent on being king himself, took immediate charge of them. They were taken to the royal apartments in the Tower of London. The two boys were sometimes seen at the windows or playing in the tower garden. A few weeks later all the king's attendants were denied access to him, and gradually the boys were seen less and less often, until finally they ceased to appear at all. Less than three months after Edward IV had died, their uncle became Richard III and the princes were never seen again. No proof has ever been found of their murder, but almost two hundred years later, when a stairway was being demolished, a wooden chest was discovered hidden under a heap of stones. The chest contained what was later concluded to be the bones of the two little princes.

It is said that Ludlow Castle is haunted by a White Lady who died there and whose ghost wandered for years among the ruins on dark nights. A 12th-century minstrel's song tells how the lady, Marion de la Bruyere, had a Welsh lover during the border clashes. One night, as was her habit, she lowered a rope to him and realized too late that he had left the rope hanging and a hundred Welshmen had overrun the castle—Ludlow was in the hands of the enemy. Marion killed her lover with his own sword and threw herself from the tower, plunging to her death on the rocks below. Some say that curious gasping sounds can be heard coming from the tower; they are thought to be the last gasps of Marion's lover. When you see the castle on a lovely day it is hard to believe any tragedies took place there.

Another walk you can take follows Broad Street, known as one of England's most beautiful streets. It has long been admired by writers and painted by artists. A painting by Samuel Scott, who lived on Broad Street in the 1760s, pictures the beautiful Georgian houses. Many of them are still there today. In a 14th-century building I found De Grey's Cafe, a good lunch stop. There is little left of the original building except possibly the huge rough timbers in one room.

In the Bull Ring near Broad Street is one of Britain's most famous inns—the Feathers. With one of the most magnificent half-timbered fronts in England and with an interior to match, it is certainly worth stopping in. The Feathers was named after the three ostrich feathers that make up the Prince of Wales's badge. Originally the building was the home of Rees Jones, a Welshman who became a Ludlow attorney. The initials, RI and II, for Rees and his wife, Isabel, appear on the lock-plate of the massive iron-studded entrance door. The Feathers first became an inn in about 1670.

The inn was once advertised as a posting inn, where horses could be hired for riders or carriages and then dropped off at the next "post," possibly Bewdley or Leominster in this case. In 1749 the inn had "stabling for above 100 horses." Later, for a brief time, the hotel became the terminus for a coach service known as the *Red Rover*. Today, with transportation by train and car, the Feathers is a deluxe hotel for travelers. There are several bars and a lounge, the James I Lounge, which has an elaborately decorated ceiling and a richly carved mantlepiece. Beautiful antiques and tapestries throughout the public areas make the hotel almost a mini-museum.

Study the facade, with the ornamental metalwork in the windowpanes and the carvings that decorate almost every piece of timber. I stayed here on one trip just so I could browse in the Feathers. Although it has been altered and restored over the years (as have most of the buildings of Ludlow), it is still a work of art.

The ashes of the poet A. E. Housman, whose poetry was centered in Shropshire, are buried in the parish churchyard.

Ludlow was a planned medieval castle town that became a social center. It is an excellent place for a day-trip from Shrewsbury. Train service is frequent, and the ride through the border country is a pleasant forty-minute trip. The train station is behind Ludlow's main business center, which cannot be seen from the station; ask someone the easiest way to get to the town center. Ludlow is another fine example of a Marcher border town with its history open to view.

Another worthwhile trip, somewhat farther afield but still easily reached, is one to Llangollen in Clwyd County, Wales. Llangollen, cradled in the valley of the Dee Valley and bordered by the soft green Berwyn Mountains, is not a medieval town like many of those in nearby Shropshire and Cheshire.

Llangollen has been painted by artists and written about by poets for hundreds of years. In 1792, the young artist J. M. W. Turner wrote that the church and bridge, the river and the descending road, surrounded by mountains, "all Combine to give a complete romantic landscape." The 14th-century stone bridge, considered one of the wonders of Wales, crosses the Dee in the center of town and as you approach it you can hear the capers and splashes as the river rushes over its rocky bed. On my first visit to the town I stood on the bridge and just listened to the music of the river and watched the patterns of the water gushing over the rocks.

To leisurely see Llangollen you need at least two or three days, so this is not just a one-day trip from Shrewsbury. In addition to the natural beauty of the area, two major points of interest are Castell Dinas Bran and Plas Newydd. High above the town on a conical hill sit the ruins of the Welsh castle Dinas Bran. A path up the hill leads to a splendid view of the hills and valley. The day that I planned to walk to the top opened to heavy gray clouds; sudden rays of sun would break through and splash a bright spot on the dark hills, holding a promise of possible clearing. Then, without warning, black clouds came scudding down the valley and by the time they reached Llangollen, sheets of rain were swept along the valley floor by a lashing wind. The storm passed on down the valley as quickly as it had come, but it left a soft all-day rain behind. I didn't climb to Dinas Bran but spent the day wandering and browsing in the shops.

Up Butler Hill at the opposite end of town is Plas Newydd. Once the home of the "The Ladies of Llangollen," it is an exceptional house in a peaceful setting in spacious grounds. In 1780 Lady Eleanor Butler and Miss Sarah Ponsonby left their homes in Ireland and settled in Llangollen, where they lived for more than fifty years. Over the years they enlarged the small cottage they had bought and added features such as the beautiful carved panels that embellish the outside of the entry. Plas Newydd eventually became an intellectual retreat where literary greats of the day were welcomed.

Llangollen was on the old coaching road that ran between London and Holyhead, the terminus of the ferries between Wales and Ireland. Llangollen also had train service for about a hundred years, but it was discontinued in 1968. Now a steam train runs between town and

Plas Newyyd, where the "Ladies of Llangollen" entertained literary greats in the 18th century.

Glyndyfrdwy, about five miles away. And there is still the Shropshire Union Canal.

Today Llangollen is probably best known for the International Musical Eisteddfod. The Eisteddfod is a festival of group and solo singing, orchestral music, and folk dancing that has been held each summer for almost fifty years. The festival draws participants from all over the world; in 1995, for example, there were 105 choirs from forty-seven nations. World-famous artists like Placido Domingo, the Royal Ballet, and the Vienna Choirboys entertain with evening concerts.

The Eisteddfod's motto *Byd gwyn fydd byd a gano, gwaraidd fydd ei gerddi fo* (Blessed is a world that sings, gentle are its songs) fits this land of song.

In 1955 the male choir from Modena, Italy, was to compete in the Eisteddfod. One young man, who was supposed to be studying for his teaching exams, decided to go to Wales with the male choir instead. He and his father sang together in the choir. That year, with twenty-two male choirs participating, the Modena choir won the competition. The young man was Luciano Pavarotti. Maureen Jones, one of today's Eisteddfod directors, remembers this wonderful event and recalls the concert as being "fantastic." In 1995, forty years later, Pavarotti, his father, Fernando, and ten of the original choir members returned with the Modena choir to sing in the festival.

ETARC is a European cultural center in Llangollen. It has an exhibition hall with books, crafts, and music-related items. And it has a year-round program of top quality traditional concerts.

Llangollen has its own male choir, Cor Meibion-Llangollen. If you decide to stop in Llangollen, make it a night when you can sit in on one of their rehearsals at the Hand Hotel. You'll hear rousing war songs; stirring songs of faith; songs of the sea; songs of love; and songs of Wales. Eifion Jones, one of the choir managers, said that the choir's members include bakers, ministers, mechanics, salesmen, court officials, and a clay worker. He said that most members live near Llangollen, but one man drives 8,000 miles each year to rehearse and sing in the concerts. The choir tours foreign countries and joins other groups for concerts in which as many as 1,000 male voices sing together. To support the choir they have "Coffee Mornings, Christmas Fayres, and Lotteries" and receive various donations. I saw them practice in the lovely lounge of the Hand Hotel. Cushiony red velvet chairs, soft gold decor, and a blazing fire all set a mellow mood for listening to the choir's songs.

I stayed in the historic old Hand Hotel on the bank of the Dee with gardens leading down to the river. Built in 1700, the hotel was once a coaching inn and has had many distinguished guests—Wordsworth, Sir Walter Scott, Tennyson, and George Borrow, among others. In 1886 Robert Browning and Elizabeth Barrett Browning (who wasn't able to leave England at the time), spent autumn at the Hand. Robert later told about enjoying the peaceful beauty of the Welsh valley. The suite the Brownings had is named after him.

If you are interested in visiting Llangollen and would like to hear the choir rehearse, check to be sure of their practice times. For a current list of the many Welsh male choirs who welcome guests, write to the Overseas Marketing Department of the Wales Tourist Board in Cardiff. The brochure will give the days and places where the choirs practice.

Bus service to Llangollen is good and frequent, but you will have to make a connection to get the bus to the town. You can get train schedules at tourist offices or railway stations for the towns that have bus service to Llangollen. For example, if you begin your trip in Shrewsbury, take the train to Ruabon, Wales, and change there for a bus to Llangollen. Buses leave hourly from a point about 200 yards from the railway station.

Settled below the great shoulder of Offa's Dyke, the historic counties of the Marches offer a view of Britain unlike any other. There are more "magpie" towns, and the hills shelter little stone villages among quiet lanes.

Shrewsbury is not a small town; it has a population of about 100,000, but the Old Town within the loop of the Severn is where you'll stay and spend your time. This center has fewer than 5,000 residents and has the feeling of a small town. It is an area to consider visiting.

ST. IVES

From the moment you think about going to Cornwall you know it's going to be different—different from other English counties. With the sea on three sides, the Duchy of Cornwall is almost an island. Except for a short stretch of land in the west that joins Cornwall to Devon, the Tamar River severs Cornwall from the rest of England, and for centuries, the river separated the Cornish people from the English.

In the mid-1400s, a traveler wrote of the Cornish, "They were not English and had their own customs and their own language." And almost 500 years later a newcomer said, "One forgets that these people are not Englishmen."

A few years ago I met an old gentleman in a Cornish church. He told me in a hushed voice that Cornwall was like a separate country. He hesitated and said, "When we cross the Saltash," meaning the bridge across the Tamar, "we are in England."

Cornwall has always been a land of legends and superstitions, of saints and smugglers, and of tales of disasters underground and on the sea that were a part of Cornish life. For more than 3,000 years it was famous throughout the known world for tin mining and for mining technology. "Submarine" mines, worked under the sea, extended as far out as a mile beyond the coastal cliffs and as deep as 2,100 feet below the seabed.

Scattered in the southwest are the ruins of Cornish engine houses that held the giant pumps that drained the mines. Their tall chimneys still pierce the sky. The largest of these pumps could lift 450 gallons of water per minute from a depth of 1,700 feet—one of the great achievements of Cornish mining technology.

The great days of mining are in the past, as are the times when fishing in Cornwall made history. But as mining and fishing declined, a new wave began—tourists discovered Cornwall. Drawn by quaint seaside villages and by a mild climate where subtropical plants thrive, tourists swarm south like a colony of ants leaving their nest. At the far southern edge of England, poised like the toe of a ballerina's slipper, is the western tip of the district called Penwith. The Cornish coast is one of the most treacherous coastlines in the world, and the granite crags with jagged rocks hidden under water make this toe one of the most dangerous.

The coastland beginning just south of Penzance and Mousehole on Mount's Bay, rounding the headland at Land's End, and all the way north to St. Ives is designated a Heritage Coast and an Area of Outstanding Natural Beauty. At the top of the toe is the town of St. Ives. Jutting out into the sea is a misshapen thumb—St. Ives Head—called the Island. The town stretches out like wings from the Island, with the harbor and Porthminster Beach sweeping south and Porthmeor Beach turning back into the Atlantic on the north. These sand beaches are one of the attractions to tourists.

Courtesy of British Tourist Authority

Cottages climb the hills that rise from the horseshoe-shaped harbor in St. Ives.

St. Ives was built straggling up the hills from the sea. Old gray stone cottages are jumbled together beside narrow crooked lanes cobbled with more gray stones. The old slate roofs are orange with lichen. Along some of these higgledy-piggledy walks are handrails to help you up the stony ways. When climbing these hills, if you're not in shape, just as you're gasping for breath you'll probably come to a bench placed just where it is needed. In his book *St. Ives*, Michael Williams wrote of this little warren,

"They dropped houses anywhere that room could be found. The streets ran zigzag as if planned by an inebriated surveyor."

Little alleys curve and run into dead-end courts, but they all wind back down to the harbor, always the center of life here. The harbor curls in an arc with piers at either end. For many years fishing was the leading industry here and as many as 300 boats once crowded the little harbor. The mainstay was the pilchard, a herringlike fish that traveled to Cornish waters in late July.

When it was time for the fish to come in, lookouts, called huers, were posted in huts on the cliff tops and the entire town waited for the fish to arrive. When the huers saw the dark streak moving in under the water, their shouts of "Hevva! Hevva!" (an old Cornish word for a shoal of fish) brought everyone rushing to the beach. Then the huers signaled the fishermen, guiding them toward the shoal. At the right moment a huer shouted "Shoot the seine," and in a few minutes the nets, churning with silvery fish, would be drawn in. As many as thirty million pilchards could be caught this way in a season.

But fishing was year-round work and the boats also had to go far out to sea for catches. With Cornwall's rockbound coast and a sea that could suddenly become a raging terror, there was a fine line between safety and disaster at sea. There are stories of heroic rescues, of fishermen who, at great risk, saved men clinging to debris from a boat that had foundered in a storm. And stories are told of men plucked from the sea when their boat capsized—sometimes in sight of those on shore. In 1803 Cornwall got its first lifeboat—at Penzance. Gradually more lifeboat stations opened around the coast, but even though motorized lifeboats were built and helicopters aided in rescues, the sea was often the victor.

Lifeboats are always launched whenever a boat or ship is in distress, no matter what country it is from. Just before Christmas in 1981, on the worst night anyone could remember, the lifeboat *Solomon Browne* slid into a raging sea near Mousehole, to the rescue of the *Union Star*, an Irish coaster whose engine had failed several miles offshore. The coaster was being tossed like a matchstick toward the jagged granite cliffs. When the *Solomon Browne* finally reached her, she was near the rocks. Three times the lifeboat tried to close in, but each time it was slammed into the 1,400-ton ship. When last seen, the lifeboat was turning for another try when a tremendous swell broke over both the coaster and the lifeboat and they went down together. The captain of the *Union Star*, his wife, and two stepdaughters, and four crewmen died in the wild sea with the eight men from the lifeboat *Solomon Browne*.

The widow of one of the Mousehole men told the Bishop of Truro that her husband had warned her a few weeks earlier that this might happen and that if it did she was not to make a fuss. Another lifeboat was sent to nearby Newlyn to cover Mount's Bay and a new group of volunteers began training in Mousehole for lifeboat duty.

The lifeboat station in St. Ives was opened in 1840. A list published in 1989 of those rescued in Cornish waters shows that St. Ives boats saved 950 lives, more than any other station in Cornwall. One of their rescues occurred in St. Ives. In a severe storm one January evening in 1938, the 3,700-ton steamer *Alba* ran aground on the rocks on the northwest side of the Island. St. Ives's first motor lifeboat, the *Caroline Parsons*, was launched and battled through heavy seas to the steamer. When the *Alba*'s crew of twenty-three was on board the lifeboat, it was hit broadside by a massive wave that capsized her. All but three crewmen were thrown into the sea. Those three pulled most of the others back into the boat, but the boat's engines failed to restart. A line was thrown from shore and made fast on board, and with this, the men struggled to shore. Hundreds of townspeople risked their lives to help the exhausted men over the rocks to safety. Five of the *Alba*'s men died, but all of the lifeboat crew made it in. Almost a year after this rescue, five of that crew went out on another wild night and didn't come back. In 1824 the Royal National Lifeboat Institution (RNLI) was founded to unite the lifeboat groups along the coasts of Britain and Ireland. Since then the RNLI has rescued more than 120,000 people.

When you walk along the beaches of St. Ives on a calm, sunny day, with waves gently washing on the sand, it's hard to imagine the sea thundering in a storm and a crew manning its lifeboat to go out in the frenzy to rescue those in peril.

When I was in St. Ives two years ago a huge new red lifeboat stood high on the harbor wall waiting for its new boathouse to be finished. It is named *Princess Royal*. There is still fishing here but it's not like the old days when the great shoals of pilchards came in. Ann Kelley, a St. Ives photographer and writer, published a lovely little book, *Born and Bred*, with portraits and thoughts of people whose families go back genera-tions in St. Ives. I like the way Robert Care summed up his life of fishing: "I was born in 1907. I've lived in St Ives all my life, born and bred. Come from a fishing family. . . . At one time there was seven hundred fishermen in St Ives. Not like it is now. I went fishing at the age of fourteen. . . . If I had my time to go over again I should still do it because it's a carefree life and more or less no bosses. You only got tide times. It's a marvellous life if you like the water."

Even those who aren't fishermen share the love of the sea. Gascoigne Paynter, who does all the sign writing for the lifeboats, told of the five youngest boys in his family, who, instead of going fishing like their father, learned a trade. One became a mason, one a painter and decorator, and the other three a carpenter, a plumber, and an electrician. But after work they all go down to the boats, either fishing or sailing: "You're sea-minded, you know. You combine it with your trade. The saltwater's in your blood."

Wherever you are in St. Ives, you never forget the sea. You see it from almost everyplace on the hills; you feel the moistness; you hear the sea gulls screech, and on a windy day, you hear the Atlantic pounding the granite crags; and always there is the tang of the sea and a whiff of fish in the air.

The Sloop Inn is said to have fronted the harbor in St. Ives for almost seven centuries.

The harbor area is a good place to begin getting acquainted with St. Ives. As with fishing waters everywhere, gulls crowd the harbor and wait. They perch like sentinels on posts with postured heads; they hang in the air and then plummet like dive-bombers; they dip and wheel and glide and gather on the beach, waiting—always with their raucous cry. It is said that Cornish fishermen have an affection for the gulls. There is a strong feeling, not quite superstition, that to intentionally injure a gull is to invite disaster. Even during times of great need fishermen used to carry a few crusts or scraps in their pockets for the gulls.

The Wharf, the street that curves along the harbor, is lined with small businesses. Most of them cater to tourists—souvenir shops and restaurants. Many have take-out food if you'd like to sit on a harbor bench and have lunch. The landmark Sloop Inn sits near the center of the Wharf. With low beamed ceilings and slate floors it is one of Britain's old harbor inns of character. The public bar has long tables and benches and is a favorite of artists and fishermen. The sign outside the inn has a painting of a sloop, an old swift sailing vessel, and reads "Circa 1312," believed to be fairly accurate.

Around the harbor toward Smeaton's Pier, where the lighthouse stands, you'll find little alleyways climbing the hill to the Island. Strolling along these lanes past old granite cottages, you'll see part of old St. Ives. Miniature flowers creep through old stone walls where vines trail and spill over onto the walks. On one of these back streets I found Whistler's Coffee Shop, a tiny place where I would stop for homemade soup and coffee. A couple of streets lead up to the Island, which is not an island but a peninsula. A British author, W. H. Hudson, was up on the island in 1905 and wrote, "From the little green hill, called the 'Island,' which rises above and partly shelters the town, you look out upon the wide Atlantic, the sea that has always a trouble on it and that cannot be quiet; and standing there with the great waves breaking on the black granite rocks at your feet, they will tell you that there is no land between you and America."

On the crown of the Island is St. Nicholas's Chapel, a fishermen's chapel. It is believed that Saint Ia, who is said to have sailed from Ireland to St. Ives on a leaf, built her first chapel on this hill above the sea. Here on this exposed place on the top of the Island, and on the other hills that rim the town, the air can be warm and still. But when the Atlantic is in a fury it flings spray over the Island's granite rocks, shrieks across the flat crown, and whips down the slopes and through the streets to the town center.

A film company found out too late how destructive a gale off the Atlantic can be. Part of a movie, *Raise the Titanic!*, was being filmed in St. Ives a number of years ago. The company wanted to use the lovely old seaside cemetery in one of its scenes but the town council would not agree to that. So, instead, a fake cemetery of fiberglass, or some such material, was built on the Island. But the "sea that has always a trouble on it" brewed a tempest and a gale stormed across the Island and picked up the fake cemetery stones and the film company's heavy trucks and dumped them into the sea. It damaged roofs in town, including that of the council building. The movie company offered to repair that roof if they could film in the old cemetery, and the council finally agreed.

One windy day I walked up Porthmeor Hill to look out over the Atlantic. The wind tore at my hair and grabbed my coat, but it was a bright day that disguised danger. Near the top of the hill I met two women who were coming down. They stopped me and said, "Don't go up there, you could be blown away." Remembering the trucks being tossed into the sea, I believed them and went back down to town.

Just below the neck of the Island, leading back toward Smeaton's Pier, is the St. Ives Museum on Wheal Dream. It has dozens of exhibits that show this seaside town's history. Enlightening displays bring out the lives of a fisherman and a miner and their families. There is a Cornish kitchen with a "slab," a coal-burning range that even had a clothes-drying rack. The St. Ives Museum also has an American flag that has flown over our Capitol in Washington, D.C. It was presented to the museum in memory of those of our 29th Infantry Division who trained near St. Ives in World War II and died in the European campaign.

At this time the museum is run entirely by dedicated volunteers and is closed from November until May. Because the museum is of such a high quality, it is possible that it might open year-round in the future. If you go to St. Ives, be sure to find out if it is open in the off-season months. Its depiction of the hard life of the Cornish people in this area will give you an understanding of St. Ives that you won't gain on the street.

From the Island, you go back to the Wharf and the town center. The parish church, dedicated to Saint Ia, is more than 550 years old. In the church is a Madonna and child by Dame Barbara Hepworth, a well-known 20th-century sculptor. When I first visited St. Ives years ago, the church was open and I talked with the church sexton about St. Ives. On my last trip the church was locked, as are many churches today.

Walking beyond the harbor toward the railway station, you can see a different side of St. Ives. When you get to a little one-lane street called the Warren, you will see a narrow lane that shoots up a hill and almost immediately disappears around a curve. This is Skidden Hill, named after a term used to describe how carts were brought down the steep hill to the shore. Metal skids were set in front of the cartwheels and then edged down the hill by workmen. Skidden Hill was known for another kind of traffic—smuggling. Customs duties were high in the 18th and 19th centuries, and it is said that more "goods," mostly tobacco and brandy, were smuggled in than came in legitimately. Stories are told of nights, heavy with fog and rain, when horse-drawn carts of goods made for Skidden Hill, where fresh horses waited and then racketed up Skidden and disappeared. The smugglers had the help of many townspeople who delayed or misdirected the customs officers who chased them.

Smuggling was so well organized that those on land lit hilltop fires to signal the vessels whether to land or run. There was contraband hidden in cellars, storerooms, and caves, and it is believed that if you knew where to look on the Island, you could still find stores of tobacco buried there.

Revenue men did search houses, and a story is told of one woman who easily outwitted them. When the men came to check her house in the Warren, she feigned embarrassment and asked them to wait while she made her bed. She then threw all the tobacco onto the rocks below her house. After the men left she retrieved the tobacco and concealed it again. In the 1880s, the proprietress of the Sloop Inn once pled guilty to hiding tobacco. Town officials, including the mayors, were often involved in the smuggling, and there is an old saying, not entirely true, that "a Cornish jury will never convict a smuggler."

St. Ives was once a tin mining center, and I was told that at one time there was a working tin mine at the far end of the Warren. When you walk along the Warren you'll be going past old miners' cottages. These cottages, usually built by the miners and a few friends, were often not much more than four walls and a roof. As the families grew, an upper story was added with a ladder leading to the drafty room where the children slept.

Just as the fishermen's families knew tragedies, so here the miners' families lived with disasters. Fires in mines, sometimes started by the careless use of candles, were fed, not by combustible materials, as in coal mines, but by the huge timbers used to support the roofs and walls of the mines. One of the most common mine accidents was caused by the collapse of previously mined ground overhead. You can visualize these huge timbers, breaking like toothpicks when tons of rock broke through the roof.

It happened at a mine called Dolcoath, where miners were working almost half a mile underground strengthening timber supports. A group of seven were at one end near the tunnel opening and another group of eight, including a boy, were farther in under the timbers. The ground overhead suddenly cracked and dust and stones fell. This was called a "God send," or warning. The men near the opening dashed for safety and just got clear when tons of rock crashed down, burying the eight who were under the timbers. Rescue parties dug tunnels from both sides, but only one man was brought out alive.

The worst disaster in Cornwall's mining history was caused by flooding, the result of a severe, long-lasting rainstorm. A mine not far from Newquay, north of St. Ives, was inundated, trapping the men working underground. Many managed to fight their way to the surface, but thirty-nine men and boys were drowned. The average life span of a miner was forty-seven years. Robert Southey wrote of the Cornish mining areas, "Nothing can be more desolate than the appearance of this province, where most part of the inhabitants live in the mines. 'I never see the greater part of my parishioners,' said a clergyman here, 'till they come up to be buried.'"

An exceptionally lovely walk, called Hain Walk, begins at the far end of the Warren just past the railway station. It follows St. Ives Bay high above the water, and trees line the path on the bay side. As you walk, you hear a torrent long before you reach the waterfall; as if to match the roar of the sea, it gushes down the rocky hillside. Farther along, stone walls covered with trailing vines edge the paved path.

The day I walked here I came upon three young boys who had tethered a pet goat to a shrub and laughed as they took turns swinging on a rope tied to a high branch of a tree. They swung out over the brush covering the hill that fell down to the bay. Each one showed me how far out he could swing. After I walked on I could still hear their shouts of laughter.

The path turns up a hill and leads to St. Ives Road. When I reached the road I stood on the corner looking at my map, deciding whether I should walk farther on or go back toward St. Ives. A man and a little boy drove up in a car and stopped beside me. The man asked if he could help me with directions and when I thanked him and said I was just getting my bearings he smiled and drove on and I started back toward St. Ives. On the heights overlooking town is Tregenna Castle, a deluxe hotel that is an especially pleasant place for coffee or lunch. If you take this walk, plan on time to stop here.

Today St. Ives is a major art center. It began when J. M. W. Turner wintered here in 1818, and later the artists Whistler and Sickert followed. They all reveled in the magical Cornish light. Toward the end of the 19th century, artists began streaming into the toe of Cornwall. Some went to Newlyn, outside of Penzance, where they formed a school and painted the everyday life of a fishing village. Others came to St. Ives, where the landscape and the sea and the harbor stirred their imaginations. And they kept coming. By 1910 about eighty artists had studios in St. Ives. Bernard Leach came to St. Ives in 1920 and set up his pottery studio on the steep hill called the Stennack. He was said to be the first Western potter to study in the Orient. New Zealand critic C. L. Bailey declared Leach to be "the greatest teacher and the greatest influence there has ever been in the oldest craft known to man." Since Leach's death in 1964, his wife, Janet, has run the Leach Pottery. When I was there Trevor Corser showed me around. He worked under Bernard Leach and is now a renowned potter in his own right.

An earlier arrival, Alfred Wallis, had moved to St. Ives in 1890. He was a rag and bone merchant who didn't begin painting until he was in his seventies. With no training he began with childlike paintings of houses, lighthouses, ships, and the sea. He became famous as a somewhat eccentric primitive painter, and today, more than fifty years after his death, he is as well known in the St. Ives art world as any area artist. He once said, "What I do mosley is what use To Bee out of my own memery."

Two major 20th-century artists, sculptor Barbara Hepworth and abstract artist Ben Nicholson, moved to the area in the 1930s. Hepworth is probably the best-known artist to settle in St. Ives. Her studio is now a museum that includes both the cottage where she lived and worked and the garden where her huge sculptures stand among palm trees and lush plantings. Hepworth said that finding Trewyn Studio was a sort of magic; she had walked past the twenty-foot walls for ten years not knowing that behind them lay a cottage and garden that would become her

A Barbara Hepworth sculpture stands above St. Ives Bay and faces Godrevy Lighthouse, the setting for Virginia Woolf's novel To the Lighthouse.

studio and her home. She died there in a fire in 1975. Several of her pieces are placed around town.

The Tate Gallery St. Ives opened in late June 1993. The gallery's spectacular setting overlooking Porthmeor Beach was described by Tokyo Art Museum Director Seiji Oshima as "the best site for a gallery anywhere in the world." It was the light and the sea and the landscape that first attracted artists to St. Ives, and the gallery has them all in view.

The St. Ives Tate is an extraordinary building of huge white curves and glass that dominates the hillside it stands on. One of the first things you see on entering is a large Patrick Heron stained-glass window. There is a ceramic gallery and a curved glazed gallery where paintings and sculpture are lit by natural light. St. Ives art, from the Tate's collection of more than 300 works from the early years, will be shown on a rotating plan.

Prince Charles, Duke of Cornwall, opened the gallery. When I was there less than four months after it opened, the gallery had already been incredibly successful. In that short time, there had been more than 100,000 visitors to the gallery. The number originally anticipated was

70,000 annually. St. Ives might now become world-famous as the art center it has quietly been for more than half a century.

For centuries the Cornish in St. Ives had been shaped by the sea and fishing, by tin and mining, and it looks as if that will become just a part of their history. The old town seems to be changing. It brings to mind the thoughts of St. Ives native William Care, who said in Ann Kelley's book, "It's not St. Ives now. We was one big family you know. If there was anyone ill they would say, 'who is going to stay up with Bill or Sarah tonight?' And they'd have a cart-load of sand outside the cottage to deaden the sound of the horses and carts."

If you choose St. Ives as a place to stay for a few days you will find that, unlike most towns with all these attractions, there are few hotels near the town center. Most are on the hills that surround the town. My favorite place to stay is the Garrack Hotel. High above town on Burthallan Lane, the vine-clad hotel has the atmosphere of a country house. It is set in spacious grounds above Porthmeor Bay and has beautiful views of the sea and the Island. The Garrack has been run by the same family for twenty-five years. My room was nicely furnished and comfortable. When I arrived, a tray with a carafe of Cornish Mead was on my dresser as a welcome.

Rooms are in two buildings, and there is a small "leisure center" that has a pool, Jacuzzi, and sauna. There are a couple of cozy sitting rooms for guests to use. The meals I had in the dining room were excellent. You can walk to the Tate from the Garrack, but be prepared for a steep hill with handrails to help you get both down the walk and then back up. From the gallery you can walk to the harbor and the town center to spend a day. Because the Garrack is high on a hill, you might find that the walk from the hotel to the harbor and back is too long and you might have to take taxis. That could add more expense than you'd like to have.

Another hotel recommended by guides is the Porthminster Hotel, a Best Western. I haven't stayed there, but the rooms I was shown were all well furnished and attractively decorated. The Porthminster is a rambling hotel of several stories that overlooks the beach and is not far from the harbor.

You reach St. Ives by train, and because of steep hills, the distance from the railway station, and having to carry even a small suitcase, you do have to take a taxi to most hotels.

Although the Porthminster is not far from the station, the streets wind and are all uphill, so it is best to take a taxi. And a taxi is the only way to get to the Garrack. Wherever you stay in St. Ives you will probably be on a hill overlooking the town or the sea. I would request a room with a view in either of these hotels.

The weather in southern Cornwall is mild, almost tropical. In fact, tropical plants and trees flourish there. In January, on a train ride to Penzance, we passed fields of daffodils being picked by workers in bright yellow slickers. The flowers were for the London markets.

There are many day-trips you can take from St. Ives—to Penzance, Newlyn, Mousehole, or even Plymouth. Oates Travel, a travel agency in the town center, has off-season day tours that might be of interest. They have frequent trips to the Theatre Royal in Plymouth for matinees.

Train service to St. Ives is good. You take the Penzance train and get off at St. Erth, the last stop before Penzance. The train from here to St. Ives follows the bay, and the outstanding scenery is a preview of St. Ives. The writer D. H. Lawrence, who lived here for a time, wrote, "This Cornwall is primeval: great, black, jutting cliffs and rocks, like the original darkness, and a pale sea breaking in, like dawn. It is like the beginning of the world, wonderful: and so free and strong."

St. Ives might become a favorite of yours. With the flavor of the old fishing and mining days, the old gray stone cottages rising on the hills, and now, the new, with the art world closing in, it has a lot to offer.

PORTMEIRION

Portmeirion—a sort of song in Wales!

This remarkable cluster of buildings, towers, and monuments is at the southern edge of the Vale of Festiniog, and just skirts Snowdonia National Park. Fairy-tale cottages washed in ice-cream colors—vanilla, strawberry, banana, pistachio, and chocolate—clamber from Tremadog Bay up a craggy tree-clad hillside.

The village was the dream of a distinguished Welsh architect, Sir Clough Williams-Ellis. He had long wanted to show that one could develop a beautiful place without defiling it and perhaps even enhance what nature had provided. Over many years he had searched for the perfect setting, remote and unspoilable, where his romantic vision could become a reality. He sailed to some two dozen islands around Britain looking for the ideal site, but without success. And then an uncle asked him if he knew of anyone who might want to buy a place that was in a state of wilderness on Tremadog Bay. When Sir Clough saw it he knew instantly that he had found his site. He described it as having

> all and more—much more—than I had ever dreamed of as desirable for my perfect site—beetling cliffs and craggy pinnacles, level plateaux and little valleys, a tumbling cascade, splendid old trees and exotic flowering shrubs; a coastline of rocky headlands, caves and sandy bays, and on top of all, a sheltered harbour for my boat at the nearest possible point of the sea.

The strange old lady who had lived on the property had just died. She had let the peninsula become a tangled jungle in order to have privacy for herself and her many mongrel dogs. After her death, woodmen had to hack their way through the wild growth to get the hearse to her door. At one time a little fishing hamlet called Aber Ia (Ice Estuary) had stood in the cove. When Sir Clough saw the property there was the large house where the old lady had lived and a couple of other buildings. He bought it in 1926 and renamed it Portmeirion, said to be a combination of Portofino, Italy, which he loved, and Meirionnydd, the old Welsh name for the county the land was in.

As an architect, Sir Clough often created elaborately landscaped gardens, and he planted this once-upon-a-time village with a potpourri of eclectic buildings and architectural bits and pieces, much as he would have planted a garden. Portmeirion has been called a bizarre little kingdom, a Welsh Xanadu, a magical otherworldly village, a fantasy, and even a cuckoo-wonderland. It is all of these, and it is exactly what Sir Clough had envisioned.

I first saw Portmeirion with my photography class from nearby Plas Tan-y-Bwlch. We had visited the little gray stone villages nestled at the foot of Snowdonia's mountains for the first two days of our class, and, to me, that was Wales. And then we went to Portmeirion—it was like walking from winter into spring. After passing through the arches of the Gate House and the Bridge House, we were in the village. To come upon it unawares was a stunning experience. It seemed not to belong here, to not fit Wales; but when I stood near the Piazza in the center of the village, with the buildings set on hills between two rocky headlands, and then looked out across the bay, I knew that it was in the perfect setting.

Courtesy of British Tourist Authority

The fantasy village of Portmeirion was the dream of the Welsh architect Sir Clough Williams-Ellis.

There were domes, galleries and columns, statues in niches, arches and balustrades and terraces, and cobbled walks leading to the Piazza, where a pool reflected this embroidery of fanciful fragments. Stone steps led to terraces and cottages that perched on hilltops. Enfolding this on three sides were the woods Sir Clough had originally found and kept. Below the craggy hill was the sweep of Tremadog Bay, beige with sand at low tide and sparkling blue at high tide.

Sir Clough said he planned Portmeirion with a "gay, light-opera sort of approach," in order to entice the casual visitor into taking an interest in architecture, landscape, and design; to show that architecture could be fun, entertaining, and intriguing. He began the work by converting the old mansion into a hotel and the two waterside buildings into cottages. In 1981 a fire destroyed the old hotel and the luxury hotel of today replaced it. Shining white, against a backdrop of green trees, as if it were frosted with confectioner's icing, it is trimmed with the sea-blue of the bay. It faces the water and the green hills of Wales, offering what Sir Clough believed was "one of the noblest views in Europe."

There are dramatic, elegant touches in all the public rooms of the hotel. The bar has carved panels and furniture that came from Rajasthan; it is named the Jaipur Bar after that Indian state's capital. The library has heavy, ornately carved woodwork, and the great fireplace in the main hall is of hand-carved limestone. A wall of windows in the dining room seems to arch out over the bay. A three-part mural on a curved wall is an artist's interpretation of the estuary, and the crewel draperies were worked in Kashmir.

On a stair landing, a small window faces a black rock wall that rises steeply to the upper village. The hotel bedrooms are all individually decorated, and furnishings vary from English antiques to lacquered chests from Canton, to pieces from a desert village in India. My room had a draped Irish half-tester bed. Wallpaper and fabrics had a delicate botanical print and the ceiling lamp was an Italian star lantern that Sir Clough often used.

The village cottages can be rented as apartments. Each one has a sitting room, bath, kitchen, and one or more bedrooms. Each cottage has a name—the Mermaid, the Dolphin, Whitehorses, and the Unicorn are just a few. The Angel was one of the first cottages in use. Its walls curve like the top of a question mark. Another early building is the Watch House, which is perched on the edge of a cliff.

Staying in the village is an experience you won't have anywhere else. Looking out over it in the early morning is like seeing a carousel at rest. The Campanile rises over Battery Rock; the Pantheon, or Dome, with its lavishly decorated facade, looks down on the Colonnade and Piazza. And everything is still, as if waiting for Portmeirion to be turned on and the music to begin.

I rented Telford's Tower, a spacious cottage where the kitchen/dining room and two bedrooms were in a three-story tower, and the living room was in an attached annex. There was a low-walled patio where a peacock settled in the sun early every morning. The tower was on a little rise and overlooked the Piazza and most of the village. Down the rocky hill in front of the tower was the Gloriette, a building that, according to Sir Clough, served no purpose except to look handsome and at home where it stood at the end of the pool. He had bought a colonnade from a hall being demolished when an old friend insisted that it belonged in Portmeirion. He also bought great Ionic columns and tons of other pieces of stonework, not really knowing what to do with them. Thirty years later, when he had the Gloriette idea and looked for these old pieces, none of them could be found. Finally they were discovered buried under a garden, and the Gloriette was built using a part of the colonnade.

Telford's Tower, the cottage that I rented, overlooks Portmeirion's Piazza.

Other buildings came from materials accidentally found in the same way. The elegant Bristol Colonnade had been damaged by bombs and was in a state of decay when Sir Clough bought it. It had to be dismantled stone by stone and reassembled where it now graces the Piazza.

Sir Clough wanted a miniature opera house in the village and was drawing up plans for it when he read about a Welsh mansion being demolished. He remembered seeing the beautifully sculptured ceiling, representing the life of Hercules, in the mansion's ballroom and knew it should be saved. He caught a train and reached the place just as the sale began. Since there was little interest in such an awkward piece, he bought it for thirteen pounds. Then, of course, he had to buy the rest of the room—mullioned windows with leaded glass, oak cornices, and a fire grate. Before the ceiling and other pieces became Portmeirion's Town Hall, it had to be taken apart, crated, and hauled over snow-covered mountains to Porthmadog, where it was all stored. In order to move the ceiling, it had to be reinforced and then cut into more than 100 pieces and packed in straw-filled crates. Today the Town Hall (also called the Hall of Hercules) is used for concerts, dances, private parties, films, or whatever occasion it is needed for. It even became the headquarters for an army staff during World War II.

Eventually Portmeirion earned a reputation as a "home for fallen buildings," and today it is home for more than buildings. A collection of ornamental pieces, some rescued, some gifts, are set in unexpected places in the village. An imposing 17th-century lion rests on a pedestal, a giant Buddha is almost hidden in an alcove, and a great statue of Hercules stands prominently in front of the Town Hall. Everywhere you look are touches of whimsy—lanterns and fragile swinging signs hang from buildings; a copper boat stands on the hotel sea wall; gilded figures dance atop columns from Siam; statues appear in little nooks; and frescoes adorn cottages.

The village has shops of all kinds, though some were closed when I was there in January. Various shops sell books, gifts, ladies' fashions, antiques, and jewelry. There is a delicatessen as well as a self-service restaurant. If you're interested in Portmeirion pottery, the Second Warehouse is the only place in Wales where "seconds" are sold. Sir Clough's daughter, Susan Williams-Ellis, designed the pottery that became so popular that it is now made in the china town, Stoke-on-Trent.

At the back of the village, near the Triumphal Arch, is a small building where an audio-visual presentation is shown every half-hour. *Portmeir-*

ion: The Place and Its Meaning, narrated by Sir Clough, is the story of the village. I saw it several times because the film covers so much you can't absorb all the details in one viewing.

Portmeirion was also built for wandering. Stone steps near the Triumphal Arch lead up a hill to "the Wilds," *Y Gwyllt* in Welsh. This woodland area was neglected for years but is now crisscrossed with paths to stroll. At the top of the hill is a gazebo designed by Susan Williams-Ellis. From it you can view the entire village. In one area, century-old rhododendrons border paths, some blooming as early as Christmas. Because of the mild climate, a great variety of trees and shrubs, both native and exotic, grow here. Palms, eucalypti, cypresses, azaleas, and camellias are just a few. Although never measured, it is said that twenty miles of footpaths wander through these woods. It is easy to become confused and get lost in this vast wooded area, so if you want to walk in these wilds, get advice and a map before starting out.

Near the center of the woods is an unusual plot—the Dogs' Cemetery. The eccentric lady who had lived in the mansion thought more of her many dogs than she did of people. The elegant drawing room of the house had been the dogs' kennel, and this cemetery, complete with headstones, was where her beloved dogs rested.

Portmeirion will be of special interest to fans of the television series *The Prisoner* because the show was filmed here. British actor Patrick McGoohan starred as the prisoner known only as Number 6. The quirky plots in this cult series are too baffling for many to follow, but there are thousands of devotees worldwide. A Prisoner Appreciation Society, founded in 1977 and called "Six of One," holds an annual convention in Portmeirion.

Sir Clough allowed the series to be filmed here only on the condition that the location remain a closely guarded secret. Long after filming was completed, it was finally revealed that "the Village" was Portmeirion. In the cottage where Number 6 lived, there is now a Number Six Shop selling memorabilia of *The Prisoner.* The series was filmed here because McGoohan had worked in Portmeirion previously and had been so impressed with the village.

Resplendent peacocks strut about the village ignoring guests as if tolerating these temporary intruders. Their iridescent trains brush the ground as gracefully as a Victorian lady's elegant skirt.

If you find Portmeirion enchanting, you are in the company of notables who were also captivated by it. Dramatist George Bernard Shaw and philosopher Bertrand Russell, who lived outside nearby Penrhyndeudra-eth, were frequent guests. Among other distinguished visitors were a king, a prime minister, and a Prince of Wales. Writers H. G. Wells and John Steinbeck came, as did Noel Coward, who wrote *Blithe Spirit* while staying in a cottage here.

Architects who came to see Portmeirion later wrote about it. After praising the use Sir Clough had made of the hilly site, Frank Lloyd Wright took him on a tour around the village and pointed out features he particularly liked. And travelers from many foreign countries come to this remote Welsh hillside to see this unusual place.

In order to safeguard Portmeirion's future, Sir Clough established a trust with his daughter Susan and her husband, who are Portmeirion's joint chairpersons. In the early days Sir Clough formed a company to run the village, and his grandchildren, who are the shareholders, are maintaining and preserving the village for future generations. In 1973 the Department of the Environment made Portmeirion a place of "Architectural and Historic Importance," and no alterations or changes can be made without the department's approval.

Although Sir Clough was known for many architectural achievements, he expected to be remembered most for Portmeirion. He said it was so much more him than anything else he had done. In the early days of the village, Sir Clough built somewhat hurriedly, hoping to see Portmeirion finished in his lifetime. As it was, he lived to be ninety-five and enjoyed the completed village for a number of years. On his ninetieth birthday a celebration was held. It began with a morning party for architects, held in the Pantheon. After lunch an afternoon tea party was accompanied by a band that played in the Colonnade. Then followed a tour in a decorated pony-trap, dinner for 200, a ball with two bands, and finally, after midnight, a fireworks display beyond anything the guests had ever seen. Apparently, Sir Clough never lost his enthusiasm or zest for life.

His grandson, Robin Llywelyn, who manages Portmeirion, called the village an expression of Sir Clough's "sense of visual poetry." He had wanted to "rescue the present time from its aridness . . . and recover some of the elegance of the past." And he did it with panache. With a twinkle in his eye he sprinkled this craggy hillside with pixie dust and created this fairy tale.

To really appreciate Sir Clough's masterpiece, I think it helps to be a romantic. Not everyone delights in this fantasy village as I do. It has been described by some as a flimsy film set, or a faded movie set. The "lived-in" look of the village is a result of careful planning. To assure the appearance of an ordinary village, some cottages are allowed to lose their freshness while others are painted and spruced up, all in their turn. As Sir Clough said, "What the whole complex really adds up to must still be judged by every individual for himself. . . .You will approve or detest what it is trying to say according to your own individual bias."

The route of the Cambrian Coast Line train you take to get to Portmeirion is one of Britain's most scenic rides. It leaves from Shrewsbury, crosses Wales, and then follows Cardigan Bay to Minfford, the Portmeirion station. It goes through little seaside villages and along beaches that would be thronged with people in high-season. In places the coast is blighted with hundreds of huts and small trailer-homes, called caravans. Empty in the off-season, they wait for the summer crowds. When the train stops at Harlech you can see the town's imposing 13th-century castle perched on a rocky crag high above the town. Built by King Edward I, Harlech Castle, with its great round towers, is said to have played a far more prominent role in history than any of Edward's other Welsh castles. Here Cardigan Bay becomes Tremadog Bay and as it narrows you can look across to Portmeirion, with its pastel buildings shining white amidst the forest.

In the off-season, November to March, you can either stay in the luxurious hotel or rent one of the cottages for short three or four-day "breaks." If you take a cottage, you can make basic food purchases at the small store in Minfford. The walk into town is probably half a mile and it is mostly through Portmeirion's property. You can have your meals in the cottage or dine at the hotel, and you can have coffee and snacks in the village restaurant or in the hotel lounge.

There are day-trips you can take by bus or train to see more of Wales. Bus service from Minfford goes to different areas—to Caernarfon or into the Snowdonia mountains. The train goes east to Pwllheli on the Lleyn Peninsula or you can go back toward Harlech and to the string of towns across the bay.

Portmeirion is visited as a showpiece in Wales by thousands who come for a few hours or for a day. At the time I was there, the record number of paid visitors for one day was 3,000. In January only a few wandered through the village each day, but you can imagine the hordes that come in the busy season.

Sir Clough had wanted to show that architecture could be fun and entertaining, and with this wonderful pastiche of morsels he certainly did that. There have been some who came and missed what Portmeirion really is, and they were disappointed. Perhaps they didn't hear the music Sir Clough stepped to, or they missed the twinkle in his eye when he shaped this whisper of fancy, this scherzo, to grace this corner of Wales.

HAY-ON-WYE

Southeast of Portmeirion and just outside Snowdonia National Park is the mountain ridge called Plynlimon. On its slopes rises the River Wye, one of the most beautiful rivers in Britain. When George Borrow wrote about his walk through Wales in 1854 he called the Wye the "most lovely river, probably, which the world can boast of." From here the Wye sweeps south, crossing old drove roads that long ago bulged with great herds of cattle and sheep; it winds past ruins of fortresses where battles once raged; it skirts the Black Mountains and then, suddenly, veers northeast toward England. From here it curls and twists and swings in loops as if sightseeing—as if afraid it will miss something. But just before it reaches England, it enters a broad valley at the edge of the Brecon Beacons National Park and makes one more loop before it placidly nudges the old market town of Hay-on-Wye.

Known to the Celts as *Y Gelli Ganddryl*, "the shattered grove," today it is Hay, after the Norman name *Le Haie*, meaning "an enclosed area." Tiny Dulas Brook branches off the Wye and becomes the border between England and Wales, with some of Hay spilling over into England. At one time Hay was a walled town with three gates, but only fragments of the walls remain.

Hay's town center is a roughly shaped triangle with a muddle of streets, lanes, and alleys so tangled that they become a jigsaw puzzle. Buildings seem to have been plunked down in any wide place in a street; where one was put down, another was quickly attached to it, in such a tiny space that there was room for only three sides to the added building—it became a triangle. To find your way in this maze of odd-shaped blocks you must have a town map, which you can get in every shop.

Black-and-white buildings crowd whitewashed shops, and cottages of stone fill lanes so narrow it seems the sun must never reach the deep gaps. Standing above the town are the ruins of Hay's castle. The history of the castle is the history of Hay. Built in 1200, it was burned by the English and burned by the Welsh; it was rebuilt and then captured by the English and sacked by the Welsh. It was a center of battles between the Norman Marcher barons and the Welsh, just as all the border towns were. Hay Castle is said to be haunted by Matilda de Breos, wife of William, who built the castle. In a dispute between King John and William, the king demanded that Matilda turn over her sons to him. When she refused, the king became so angry that he ordered all of them arrested. William escaped, but Matilda and her sons were taken to Windsor Castle, where they were walled up alive and starved to death.

By the early 1500s the castle and the town were declared ruins. In the 17th century a mansion was built into the castle, and over the years a number of different families owned it. Two fires in this century severely damaged the castle and mansion. In the 19th century Hay flourished as an important town. The railway was extended to Hay and new buildings went up—among them the colonnaded Butter Market, the Cheese Market, and the Swan Hotel. But in the mid-1900s Hay fell on hard times. There was unemployment, shops were empty, train service was about to be canceled, and the young were drifting away to find jobs elsewhere.

And then Richard Booth came. He single-handedly put Hay on the world map. An Oxford graduate, Booth had become a fervent lover of books while a student. In 1961 he moved to Hay, bought an old fire station, filled it with secondhand books, and started his book business. He was so successful that he soon had to add more shops to hold his books. And then he bought Hay Castle. Twenty years later the *Guinness Book of World Records* listed Richard Booth Ltd. as the world's largest secondhand bookseller, with "9.9 miles of shelving and a running stock of 90,000 to 1,100,000 in 30,091 sq ft of selling space."

Today Booth buys up to 50,000 books each month. His Lion Street bookshop, the largest in Hay, couldn't hold this great number of volumes and they have spilled over into the outbuildings in the castle grounds. The cobbled courtyard is lined with sheds, piggeries, granaries, a stable, and a coach house—all filled with stacks of book. "Honesty" stalls, opensided and roofed with corrugated metal, are crammed with books. A sign tells you where to drop your fifty pence for any book you buy.

Hay-on-Wye is truly an international town of books. When I first went to Hay there were fourteen bookshops. One shop sold only books of poetry; another carried children's books; and another specialized in information on bees and insects. Several antiquarian shops sold rare books. One had a sign in the window that read, "We have the best stock of rare early printed bibles of any bookshop in Great Britain (16th to 19th centuries)." Lovers of Dickens could find a place that had Dickens first editions and Dickensia, and there was a place that stocked secondhand records, cassettes, sheet music, and books on music, theater, cinema, and dance.

A number of shops sold antique maps and prints. A book search business was not a bookshop, but concerned only with finding out-of-print books on request. It advertised "Perseverance over years if needed." In a hand bindery, leather and cloth bindings were repaired and restored. And there was a jigsaw world, with every type of jigsaw puzzle, including one made up of 8,000 pieces, and the "World's Most Difficult Jigsaw Puzzle, only 529 pieces but double sided with a 90-degree twist in the tail."

Unattended "Honesty" stalls have signs telling how to pay for books you want.

As you might expect, bookshops open and close, and a shop you see today might not be there next year. "Honesty" stalls are everywhere. One of the largest shops has a huge front lawn bordered with metal cases holding low-cost paperbacks with instructions on how to pay. A shop on Castle Street had cartons of books on the sidewalk in front, with signs that said "Free" and "Take what you want."

This is the perfect place for bookworms to browse. Everything about these places packed with books is seductive to a book lover. The smell of old leather mingling with the faint must of aged pages pulls one just as the aroma of fresh coffee at sunrise does. The soft shush of books being pulled from crowded shelves, the creak of old wooden stairs, and the timeworn stone floors and heavy darkened timbers of cellar shops all entice one.

Visitors have books tucked under an arm or in bags; they sit on steps or on the floor between stacks as they examine books; mothers bring babies in carriages. All are drawn to Hay for one reason—books.

Early one morning I met two women—one a poet, the other a writer of short stories—who came to Hay the second Saturday of every month while their husbands went to nearby farm sales. The shop had been open for only an hour and already each carried about six books to buy.

Many of the larger shops occupy two or three connected buildings. One has an arrangement of rooms so complex that you find yourself back where you started from before you've found the room you were looking for. You might go down three steps to one room of books and then up seven steps to another crowded area. There are shelf-lined corridors and tiny alcoves up or down four or five steps in different directions. I tried to draw a map of the rooms so I could find a particular one later, but the layout was too perplexing with these many different levels of floors. Some of these combined buildings have signs warning you to "Mind Your Head" and "Mind the Step." They are to be taken very seriously; ignoring them is to invite injury.

Of course, the grandfather of bookshops is Richard Booth's. Between the Limited, his shop on Lion Street, and Hay Castle he has books on every subject I could think of. You can find books on canaries, capitalism, and caving; books on anarchy, auditing, and Asia; books on magic, Milton, and monsoons; and thousands of books of fiction. The Limited has a directory of more than one hundred categories of books carried. The categories are then subdivided—under Economics there are about fifty subcategories. The foreign language section includes books in Laotian, Urdu, Somali, Tamil, and, of course, Welsh. The script in some of these books was so beautiful that I thought of buying one to have as a work of art, but my bag was getting full. Next time I will pick out a lovely one to own.

In the Hay Castle bookshops are sections that might be of particular interest to Americans. A military shop with books on American forces in Europe is named the Five Star Bookshop after Eisenhower. The American Indian department was listed in a 1988 Booth newsletter as having 4,000 books.

The beginning of this largest secondhand book town in the world was not accidental. Booth chose Hay-on-Wye as his home because his family

Richard Booth began romancing readers with the first secondhand bookshop in Hay.

had long lived in the area and because he loved country living. He found, however, that rural areas were in a state of decline and he railed against those he thought were responsible—"countless government officials," boards and councils made up of "bureaucratic bunglers," and outside meddlers telling locals how to run their towns.

He deplored the loss of the old craft economy when blacksmiths and cobblers and carpenters marketed their skills from their own shops. And he wanted to return to the days when long-time locals ran the inns and hotels without outside interference. So Booth took action on several fronts. His most famous move took place on April 1, 1977. He declared Hay-on-Wye independent of England and Wales. The news was covered by television stations and national newspapers.

Booth declared himself King Richard of Hay, issued passports and currency, and sold knighthoods, dukedoms, and earldoms. When international journalists came for interviews he pointed out that because Hay was really between England and Wales it should be reasonable and easy to establish Home Rule, and he called attention to Andorra, Luxembourg, and Monaco.

He founded a new political party called Rural Revival to give the voice back to the countrymen instead of to the bureaucrats. He advocated bringing back horses and the old craft economy. He even suggested closing the road to Llanthony to all except residents and horses, and said tourists could travel the road by stagecoach. He wrote and published booklets supporting his positions on independence. He wrote one that was an address to Russell Means, of Wounded Knee fame, whom Booth had met at Yellow Thunder Camp on a visit to the Midwest in 1981 and with whom he felt a kinship.

How much of Booth's talk is tongue in cheek and how much is deepfelt is hard to tell. He is known as a master marketer, and the publicity he has gained could be an astute man's shrewd promotion. He also was successful in campaigning against a supermarket chain that wanted to open a store in Hay.

Most will agree affectionately that Booth certainly is eccentric and flamboyant. And a description of him will almost always include mention of his untidy dress and "drooping trousers." When I first met him I was surprised to find him neatly dressed, as any businessman would be. The next time, true to his reputation, he was unshaven and disheveled, his shoelaces dragging on the floor. I had also expected to see signs of his well-known eccentricity, or at least some unconventional traits. Instead he was mild-mannered and soft-spoken, with a quiet superior knowledge of books. While we talked, an employee interrupted to ask about a particular book a telephone caller wanted to find. Without hesitation Booth said it would be hard to find and would be costly—possibly as high as 2,500 pounds. He said, "I've seen a copy in New York and one in Bond Street. If cost isn't important, we'll try to get a copy." On my last trip to Hay I wondered how many books he had in stock then. He thought that between his shops and warehouse, it would probably be about one and a half million. Then he added, "But it's not the number, it's the love of books that counts, isn't it?" He seemed to echo Henry David Thoreau, who said, "Books are the treasured wealth of the world."

All book lovers and collectors of books should plan to spend a few days in the Town of Books. When you consider that printing as we know it began in the 1450s and that you'll find books in Hay that were printed in the same century, you know this is truly a book town.

The first time I went to Hay-on-Wye I arrived by bus on a gloomy sludge-colored day with a misty rain darkening everything.

I got off the bus at the Oxford Road stop; there were no businesses in sight. This was a spur-of-the-moment trip and I had no hotel reservations. I found the police station, and the officer on duty gave me the names of a couple of B&Bs. One of them would not rent a room to a single, but I got a lovely room in the other one. As I walked the rain-slicked gray streets with the gray stone houses I said to myself, "Well, I certainly won't stay in this town more than a couple of nights."

And then the sun came out and I found the town center and the bookshops. I had time to look in the bookshops and to learn about the town. I bought books that I mailed home and I walked in the green countryside. I stayed for six days and have gone back whenever it fits my schedule.

That year there were leftover signs in store windows announcing the previous summer's annual festival—"A Romp in the Hay," a fun-sounding name for a country fete. But there is no "Romp in the Hay" anymore. It has been replaced by the Hay-on-Wye Festival of Literature. Every May the town and area overflow with people from Britain and many other countries for ten days of events. There are interviews, lectures, and workshops as well as readings by renowned writers, poets, and stage and screen dramatists. Bands entertain and Welsh male choirs sing. Maya Angelou sang with the Welsh National Opera Male Choir at a recent festival. You might hear a talk by Dirk Bogarde, Lauren Bacall, or Toni Morrison. One year Salman Rushdie made an unexpected appearance. Celebrities come from all parts of the world, if not to participate in one of the seventy to eighty events, then to just attend.

One festival included a seven-mile "Kilvert Walk," following one of the curate's favorite routes. The Rev. Francis Kilvert was a country clergyman in Clyro, a town a mile or so from Hay. His diaries of the countryside and the people who lived there are a classic picture of life in the 1870s. He watched the seasons change as he walked the hills in all kinds of weather to minister to those who lived on the hill farms. He wrote of Hay fairs and of Hay Castle, where he was a frequent guest of the Bevans family who lived there. And he wrote, "I like wandering about these lonely, waste and ruined places. There dwells among them a spirit of quiet and gentle melancholy more congenial and akin to my own spirit than full life and gaiety and noise." Kilvert died at age thirty-nine, just one month after he was married. This is Kilvert country, and there are many reminders of him in Hay. Most bookshops have *Kilvert's Diary*. One shop has a selection of other publications on Kilvert. In the center of town is the hotel called Kilverts. You can get information on Kilvert here and in most other places you would stay.

In a town devoted to books you would expect to find other forms of art, and Hay has them. There are antiques, paintings, pottery, and a wide selection of quality crafts by professional artisans. I found a lovely piece of artwork in a place called Tabby's Shed down a little alley from Kilverts Hotel. The art is called Bark Art. Beautiful, delicate paintings are done using fine chips of bark. The artist uses no paint or stain or dye to create her portraits, landscapes, and wildlife scenes. If you find the originals too costly, you can buy a print instead. On Oxford Street, across from the bus stop, is a building housing the Tourist Information Centre and a number of craft shops. The interesting thing here is that you can watch each artisan create works from leather, glass, wood, or dried flowers. Other artists design jewelry, pottery, or clothing.

Over the years I have stayed in Hay in January, February, and March, and, for the most part, the weather was mild while I was there. I found Kilvert's notes on the unpredictable weather interesting. One year on January 11, he wrote that early in the morning the air was "as warm as the air of a hot-house and the thrushes singing like mad thinking that spring had come." Then an entry dated Sunday, February 13, reads, "Very few people in Church, the weather fearful, violent deadly E. wind and the hardest frost we have had yet." He went on to tell of his whiskers being stiff with ice and of baptizing a baby in broken ice swimming in the font.

One book I read about Hay before my first trip mentioned that it was almost impossible to get a good photo of the town from the surrounding hills. On a sunny day I decided to walk up a hill that led to Cusop, on the English side of Dulas Brook, to see if I could find a photo spot overlooking Hay. The road following the brook was too wooded to get a view of town, but I saw a clearing ahead and went up to it. It was a farm driveway with a locked gate. Just as I looked for a spot where I might see Hay the lady who lived on the farm drove up. She told me to ride with her up the hill to the farm, where there was a good viewpoint. She stopped at the top of the hill and we got out to a 360-degree view. Hay and the hills beyond were spread out in front of us and behind us rose the Black Mountains. She pointed out one hill and said that it was the one in the late Bruce Chatwin's novel *On the Black Hill.* He stayed in Hay while writing the book, and many local people think the fictional town of Rhulen is Hay-on-Wye.

There is a story told of a man in a cloak and black-brimmed hat who appears to those lost in the mountains. He guides the walker back to the right path and when they reach it he disappears into thin air. He is said to be a farmer of old who long ago knew every inch of the Black Mountains he loved and he stays to help anyone who loses his way on the slopes.

There are a number of B&Bs in Hay and several hotels. The Old Black Lion is an old coaching inn; a part of it dates back to the 13th century. Oliver Cromwell is said to have stayed here during the siege of Hay Castle. The inn's bar is named "The King Richard Bar," and a picture of Booth with his crown and furred robe hangs in a prominant place. Old black timbers are hung with horse brasses. I stayed in this old inn on one trip. My room was a comfortable double room with private bath, TV, and, of course, tea- and coffee-making facilities. I had an excellent Welsh dinner here one night. It isn't always possible, even in Wales, to find real Welsh food, but even if you don't stay here, do at least have a Welsh meal here.

In the very center of Hay is Kilverts, a gray stone hotel on Bull Ring. When I stayed here a few years ago new owners were scurrying to polish and update things. They had previously owned a successful restaurant in town and their excellent menu is now used in the hotel dining room. The bar is a good place to relax over lunch. The hotel has a friendly and fun staff helping guests. My room was small and cozy and was nicely furnished. There is another hotel I haven't stayed in, the Swan Hotel, a Best Western hotel. I stopped for a cider one afternoon. The bartender was very friendly and the hotel seemed to live up to its good reputation.

Bus service to Hay is from Hereford. You can take either a train or National Express bus to Hereford. The bus station is only a ten-minute walk from the train station. There were about five buses a day to Hay-on-Wye when I was last there.

A lovely little book to buy in Hay is *Hey Days in Hay.* Written by an author who lives near Leominster and illustrated by an artist from Clyro, it is a personal and affectionate record and is filled with details of Hay beginning with the days of the Normans and ending with about 1990. Years after you've been to Hay you can look at these drawings and recognize the streets and buildings and remember each one.

If books are important to you, this greatest library in the world is a place to stay for a few days. Some of the bookshops are as neat and orderly as your home library, while others are in a friendly state of disorder, with books piled on floors and heaped in cartons. With the number of books Booth receives monthly, there will probably always be unshelved books everywhere in his shops. W. Somerset Maugham said, "One of the minor, but delectable and innocent, pleasures of life is to wander about a well-stocked bookshop, looking at titles, taking up a volume here and there, and turning over the pages." That is nowhere more true than at Hay-on-Wye, the biggest secondhand bookshop in the world.

Outsiders have come to Hay and settled to stay, and some have played a part in the town's international recognition, but I will always think of Hay as Richard Booth's town. He led Hay to its one ultimate aim—romancing readers.

TRAVELING SMART

Anticipation is part of the fun of traveling, but along with planning the exciting parts of your trip, there are practical matters to take care of. Making your way through the myriad mundane decisions you have to make can be simplified, and spending the extra time on these details will help ensure having a carefree trip once you're in Britain.

TRAVELING SMART

Traveling Light

In the days when travelers went overseas by steamship and cross-country by train, passengers carried steamer trunks, wardrobe trunks with drawers and hanging space, and even travel furniture made-to-order by the world-famous master-craftsman of luggage, Louis Vuitton. A number of women who traveled solo in the past century carried their own bed linen with them. One, Isabella Bird, also included in her 110 pounds of baggage a folding chair, a rubber bath, her Mexican saddle, books, candles, and a "reasonable" quantity of clothes. But then there were scores of porters to handle baggage on docks and in stations and staffs of bellhops to take over the chores in hotels.

At the same time, other solo travelers knew that traveling smart is traveling light. George Borrow, in his walk through Wales, took only a white linen shirt, a pair of worsted stockings, a razor, and a prayer-book in a small leather satchel with a strap that he could sling over his shoulder. At the end of the 18th century a French cavalry officer walked the length and breadth of Ireland with all his baggage in two silk stockings with the feet cut off. A well-dressed young man, he included a pair of silk stockings, two very fine shirts, and "breeches fine enough to be, when folded, not bigger than a fist." In a third packet he had a pair of dress shoes. All three "bags" were tied in a handkerchief and carried on a stick that had an umbrella attached to it.

Today, in the fast world of air travel, the person who wants to travel carefree more closely resembles Borrow and the young cavalry officer than the wealthy travelers of the past. With porters and bellhops almost nonexistent, we handle our own luggage, and traveling light has been refined to an art. Every travel guide you read will include the author's packing tips, and they will all vary somewhat. However, the one thing they will all agree on is—travel light. Many suggestions will be universal, but some might not fit you personally; we each have different priorities. After more then ten years of traveling solo I have found the following method of packing worked best for me. It is a simple way to go in that, with some restrictions, everything you take is a matter of choice—your choice.

I always take only one carryon bag. I can be out of an airport in minutes, I never have a lost or damaged bag, and I can easily handle my own luggage throughout the trip. The major restriction is in the weight of the carryon. I consider it foolhardy to carry more than twenty pounds. After a number of years of taking an extra camera bag that added weight, I found that I could include that in my carryon and still get by. One year, after I had had major surgery and was limited in what I could carry, my bag, including camera and film, weighed only sixteen pounds. However, I missed things I couldn't take with that little weight.

It sounds like you can take a lot with a twenty-pound limit, but most things are heavier than they seem. When you lay out twenty pounds of clothing, toiletries, camera film, shoes, and sundries, it will all fit into a small carryon bag. If, in deciding what to take with you, you find it weighs a little more than twenty pounds, you might think, "What difference can two or three pounds make?" That will be when you should test a twenty-pound weight. Take a strong shopping bag and fill it with twenty pounds from your kitchen—ten pounds of potatoes, five pounds of sugar, five pounds of flour, or cans—whatever weighs twenty pounds. Now carry it around your house or apartment for about ten minutes. If you have stairs, carry it up and down stairs a few times. You will soon conclude that twenty pounds is a lot more than you'd really like to carry.

When you get ready to begin, start with the suitcase. Remember, the suitcase itself is part of your weight. You can get a sturdy soft-sided bag that weighs less than two pounds, or you can get one that weighs as much as eight pounds. You have to consider not only the weight, but the airline regulations. Usually the carryon limit is a bag with total dimensions of about forty-five inches—that is, the sum of its length, height, and width can be no more than that total. For example, it might be 22" long x 14" high x 9" deep. Check with the airline you will be taking. Some airlines are now measuring the size of your bag, and if it exceeds the allowed dimensions, you must check it. And one airline is now allowing a total of only thirteen pounds, which also means you cannot carry on your bag. In any event, your bag must fit under the seat in front of you or in the overhead bin.

You'll often get the suggestion that two smaller bags are better than one, and that might seem easier to handle. However, if you are traveling by bus and train, you need a free hand to grab the handbars that help in getting on. Another frequent tip is to buy one of the very popular bags with wheels and retractable handles. It would be wonderful pulling your bag along in an airport, but that is the only place I would appreciate it. You can't pull it on Britain's cobbled or brick-lined streets; you can't pull it up and down the many stairs you will encounter; wheels are of no use in getting on and off buses and trains; and a bag with wheels and a handle weighs between five and eleven pounds, which leaves too few pounds for necessities. These are some of the reasons why I don't travel with a bag with wheels.

If you need to buy a new bag, there are a couple of things to look for. First, of course, is the weight. Most bags in the lightweight category will be soft-sided and of sturdy nylon. These carryons often have zipper closures on the top of the bag. Be sure the zipper is U-shaped, so it crosses the full top and extends partway down each side. A bag with a zipper that only crosses the top is hard to pack and to find things in.

When you have a bag that will be easy to travel with, packing it comes next. This is the most difficult part of traveling light. Choosing what to take can pose a problem. You have to consider not only clothes you'll want but what travel accessories you'll really need. *Magellan's* is an excellent catalog containing travel products and information that will help make your choices easy. And what I appreciate most about the catalog is that the weight of almost everything is given. You can get the catalog at no charge.

When it comes to what to take it seems that women have more decisions to make than men. Perhaps the easiest place to begin planning is with clothes. Don't leave this to the last few days. If this is the first time you've traveled with only a carryon, a good way to pick the clothes you'll take is to lay out on the bed what you think you'll want. For years the advice from the experts has been to stick to one or two basic coordinated colors, and that is still the best advice you can get. For example, I like navy and beige basics with berry and white accessories, but you will have your own preferences. I wear navy walking shoes, navy pants, a navy cardigan, and a blouse on the plane; today everyone dresses casually when flying. Everything you wear and take should be chosen with comfort in mind. Another thing professional travelers agree on is to *never* wear new shoes. Your shoes should always be well broken in if you are to enjoy yourself.

Coordinating colors will give you a number of outfits, but it is also important to take only easy-care clothes, and that means drip-dry fabrics.

I like blends and knits best. Wool and polyester pants drip-dry easily but still hold a crease and keep their good looks. However, some of the new 100 percent polyester pants have the same properties. Knits are my favorite travel fabric. I like a two-piece knit dress in a small print that can also mix and match with pants and blouses. I always take a vest because it can do double-duty. It can add a change to outfits and can serve as an extra layer on a chilly day. Clothing that is lightweight, instead of bulky, layers better and takes less room in a suitcase. Even my cardigan is lightweight. I began traveling with a bulky acrylic sweater that I loved. It washed well and if I toweled the water out of it, it dried overnight. But I did always have to wear it on buses and trains, because it took too much room in my bag. Then, in one of the many woolen shops in Britain, I found a fine-gauge washable woolen cardigan made in Scotland. That is the one I travel with now.

A silk turtleneck top and silk long johns or opaque pantyhose are all excellent warmers and can be stuffed in a corner of your bag. I cannot travel with some "double-duty" clothes that are often recommended. I cannot use my raincoat as a bathrobe or a sweatsuit as pajamas, and I need bedroom scuffs instead of shoes to lounge in. Some evenings I like to get ready for bed and read or watch TV in my robe and slippers as I do at home. My personal comfort has to come first, and so should yours.

My coat is a raincoat, but to avoid having to wear it when I'm out walking, I take a nylon windbreaker that fits in a small case. I added eyelets to mine so it breathes. The clothes I take are all for cool weather because I travel off-season. If you decide to travel in April or October, you might make some changes.

My list of clothing for all my trips to Britain has been refined to this:

I wear—
raincoat
pants
blouse
cardigan
walking shoes

I pack—

1 pair pants	2 sets underwear
2 blouses	1 nylon pajamas
1 knit top	a lightweight knit robe
1 vest	a pair of bedroom scuffs
two-piece knit dress	a nylon windbreaker

1 T-shirt to layer   2 dress scarves
1 silk turtleneck   1 head scarf
1 opaque pantyhose   1 pair medium-heeled dress shoes
2 regular pantyhose

My camera and all the film I'll need also go in my suitcase. My SLR camera and the films usually weigh about four pounds. If you take a lightweight camera and only a few rolls of film you will save some weight in your bag. If I have room, I like to take another mix-and-match skirt. In the plastic bag where the scuffs go, I put in a card that says "slippers" so I won't use the bag for other clothes. With everything on this list I have clothes for at least twelve outfits. Wearing my cardigan or adding a scarf makes another change. With this list I can have six lightweight layers on to keep me toasty if a cool front moves in.

If you're going on a walking tour, you'll need broken in hiking boots. I am told that the new boots weigh only about a pound and take little room. You might want to plan the walking tour for your first days in Britain and then mail home the boots or any other extras you needed for your tour. One year I started my trip with a Christmas tour so I had extra dresses, which I mailed home when the tour was over.

Of course, the clothes you take cannot fill your bag, because there are other necessities. If you pack carefully, you can include everything you need without going over twenty pounds. I pack with plastic. I use plastic dry-cleaning bags to separate clothes and help keep them wrinkle-free and plastic kitchen bags with the zipper-type closings in several sizes. For example, I have a "bathroom" bag. A quart-size bag will hold my toothbrush, small tube of toothpaste, travel-size deodorant, a small bottle filled with bath powder, a small puff, and a tiny bar of soap in a plastic case.

If you plan to stay in B&Bs, you might want to take your own soap, as there is often a communal bar. Instead of wasting weight and room with the large-size plastic soap holders usually sold, you can buy a mini-size plastic case that will hold a motel-size bar of soap. I found my container in a craft shop. It held straight pins and was the exact size for a small bar of soap. Everything I need before dressing is in this bag; I like having it all together wherever I travel and never change this part of my packing.

I also have a "laundry" bag with a small bottle of concentrated laundry detergent, two inflatable hangers, and a twisted-type elastic clothesline. If I suddenly need a spot cleaner I buy a small stick-type there. I carry a plastic-lined cloth makeup bag with liquid makeup, lotions, etc.—all transferred to the small plastic bottles that hotel amenities or sample cosmetics come in. It also has nail polish remover that comes in small individual-use packets, a few small bandage strips, a small tube of antiseptic cream, and a tiny sewing kit. I also take a small, thin quick-dry washcloth. Most hotels furnish washcloths, but small family hotels and B&Bs often don't.

You'll probably want a travel clock. You can get a small foldup clock that weighs about two ounces. I have a mini-flashlight that I tuck in, just in case. I remove a supply of facial tissue from the box and take that along.

Each traveler will add whatever he or she uses at home—aspirin, antacids, medications, etc. Some might want to take a curling iron, styling brush, or other appliance. Since this method of packing is strictly by choice—your choice—take an appliance if you must, but then remove clothing or something to make up for the weight of the appliance and the adapter and converter required for Britain. That total weight can be almost a pound.

Magellan's catalog has information on foreign electricity and appliances, including those with dual-voltage. You can send for a more detailed description of this from Franzus Company, Inc. Ask for the brochure "Foreign Electricity Is No Deep Dark Secret." Another helpful brochure is "Hazardous Material—Tips for Airline Passengers," which lists some surprising things that are subject to heavy penalties if carried. You can get it from the Federal Aviation Administration (FAA).

When shopping for travel goods, I am never tempted by the lovely matched sets of bags for cosmetics, lingerie, and jewelry, or by the hanging organizers—they take up room and add weight. But if you feel you need this bit of luxury, then take them—but remove something else from your bag that equals the weight. One bag that is valuable is a shoebag of lightweight fabric. If you sew, you can make one to fit your own extra pair of shoes.

There are other miscellaneous items that I always take, some of which I carry in my purse—a pair of small scissors, a flat notebook and pens, a mirror, and a magnifying glass for reading train schedules. On the bottom of my suitcase I lay one plastic dress hanger; some heavy things slip off inflatable hangers when they're wet. I can also dry long pants on it. I take several self-addressed 9" x 12" envelopes to mail home brochures and maps I collect and want to keep. Instead of carrying extra batteries for my clock, watch, or camera, I put new batteries in before I leave home.

There are three other important items I carry everywhere I go. One is a security pouch. There are several kinds you can get—hidden wallets, money belts, leg safes, or bags that hang around your neck. I use the wallet-size pouch that hangs around my neck. I wear it across my body, under my cardigan. With a long thin strap over my right shoulder, the wallet is at my waist on my left side. It holds my passport, airline tickets, traveler's checks, credit cards, and most of my cash. If the wallet is long and slim, it will not be as bulky as it sounds. Anyone could take my purse and I wouldn't lose anything of great value. I keep some cash in my coat or jacket pocket and I don't always have to take my purse if I am out walking.

The second thing I never travel without is my list. I get a new check register from my bank, which is the perfect size—thin and small, it slips into my purse without taking much room. A small notebook without the spiral binding would also work. In my list are:

- my itinerary with dates, hotels, and telephone numbers
- numbers of my traveler's checks
- telephone numbers at home and in Britain to report lost traveler's checks
- telephone numbers of credit card companies in both countries
- telephone numbers of my doctor, dentist, and ophthalmologist
- family members' names, addresses, and telephone numbers
- my bank's telephone number
- my medical insurance company's telephone number
- my airline's telephone number in both countries

Somewhere in here I also write my credit card numbers, not in the correct order, but in a code only I understand. The rest of my check register is blank and I use it for travel notes, train schedules, or information I might like to have.

The third important item I take is a businesssize envelope containing the following:

- photocopy of the first two pages of my passport
- photocopy of my airline tickets
- copy of my prescriptions with both the brand name and the generic

name
- prescription for my eyeglasses
- confirmation of hotel reservations and deposit receipts
- pre-addressed contact labels for cards to send home

I also take an empty envelope for receipts I collect along the way.

Leave a copy of these lists with a family member or friend at home.

Noticeably missing from my lists is an umbrella. On my first trip I took a folding umbrella. I traveled for three months and used it once; it wasn't worth the weight and space it took. I am not usually out in a hard rainfall, but I do carry one of the ugly plastic rainhoods in my pocket when I go out. And I carry gloves in my pocket.

I once read that women should buy the biggest handbag they can find so they can fill it with all the things that won't fit in a suitcase. To me that is nonsense. I don't want the weight on my shoulder or arm any more than I want it in my bag. Some travelers take a second pair of eyeglasses with them. Be sure to take sunglasses if you use them.

Two things I take with me regardless of weight are a family photo for my hotel nightstand and a paperback book. The picture is packed between clothes and the book fits in the outer pocket of my carryon bag. If your pictures are in heavy frames, you can buy a lightweight plastic folding frame with a plastic "glass" and take two photos along.

It seems that men can pack more easily than women as far as the number of things needed. In addition to the clothes worn, two pairs of pants, a sweater, a sports jacket, a couple of wash-and-wear shirts, and maybe one dress shirt should be enough for the trip. Socks, underwear, pajamas, and maybe slippers will not weigh much. An extra pair of shoes will be heavier, and an electric razor, adaptor, and converter will add weight. Except for the women's clothing list, some of the other items mentioned are things men will want to include. And remember—your camera and film are included in the twenty-pound maximum weight.

For both men and women—empty your wallet of everything you won't need. If you plan to drive at all, take your driver's license. I was surprised to be told at a library in Britain that if I had brought my library card with me I could check out books from the town library. If your trip will be a month or longer and you are an avid reader, you might take your card along to see if you could check out books on Britain or some to just read in the evening.

In all my years of traveling I have had a problem only once. At the end of one trip I stayed in a London B&B. On my last full day I packed everything that I wouldn't need again and went out for the day. The next morning before leaving for the airport I packed the remaining things. When I unpacked at home I discovered that a small jewelry bag had been emptied of my chains and earrings. They were costume jewelry, but good pieces, and I was sorry to lose them. In a completely different part of my bag I had put my good magnifying glass in its case, and that was also gone. It was too late to do anything but accept the loss. To file a claim with your insurance company you usually need some proof of loss; it can be a copy of the report made to the hotel and a copy of the police report you filed.

Practical packing like this will not work for you if you plan to attend gala social events, dine in fine restaurants, and stay in luxury hotels. Then you will have to take more clothes and shoes, and you'll have to depend on taxi drivers and hotel employees for assistance.

Whatever you take with you will probably be too much. But if you can limit yourself to one carryon bag that is light enough for you to handle wherever you go, you will have mastered the art of traveling light, and all your future travels can be carefree.

A retired Wisconsin couple, Bud and Mary Peotter of Appleton, have mastered the art. They traveled through nine European countries in two weeks and each had one carryon bag. Mary's weighed seventeen pounds and Bud's weighed nineteen. In an interview Bud explained their enjoyment of the trip with, "It's the luggage, that's the biggest thing," and added, "We didn't think about a thing. We knew we'd get by." Mary told of meeting other travelers who were burdened with too much luggage and of how envious they were of Bud and Mary going their carefree way. Mary didn't even carry a purse; she sewed a large pocket onto the inside of her jacket and kept everything she needed in that. She said, "Maybe older people would do this if they knew we had such a wonderful time." She gave her daughter and son-in-law credit for insisting on the lightweight bags they took. And she agreed with Bud; "It's the luggage, that's the biggest thing."

You can travel light and have a wonderful time.

Hotels, Inns, and Cottages

From the good taverns and inns that Samuel Johnson once referred to as happiness-promoters, it has been a long journey to the hostelries of today. But the hallmark of a good inn in Johnson's day was the same as it is today—warm hospitality.

The B&Bs, inns, and hotels where you'll still find this cordial welcome are those where a guest's comfort and enjoyment are a priority; and in most places of lodging owners have this philosophy. But there are still some places where a traveler is considered a transient who will never return, so there is no reason to consider whether his stay is pleasant or not. After years of working in the travel industry and years of traveling on my own, I have stayed in every kind of accommodation from university dorms to deluxe hotels. A number of times I have made reservations in a hotel for a stay of several nights, but moved to another hotel after only one night. The reason has usually been that the room was shabby or maybe not even clean.

One year I was on a Christmas tour on the Continent and arrived in England by ferry in the late afternoon. Of those on the tour, only two young college students from Singapore and I were staying on the coast for the night. Since they wanted a low-budget hotel and I didn't object to an inexpensive night, we went to a small low-cost hotel on the seafront. The owner-manager was apparently happy to have guests at the end of December and was friendly and solicitous. My very basic room had a TV, a heater, and one lamp. However, the room had only one wall outlet, which meant that I could watch TV, or have the lamp on, or have heat, but I could not use two at the same time. It certainly wasn't a hotel I would choose, but in this case the students made it an enjoyable experience. They offered to walk with me to a nice restaurant, and said they were going to eat at Hardee's. Instead I went with them. We met for breakfast and then took the train out together in the morning. The hotel was typical of many budget hotels.

The quality of accommodations is always important when traveling, but for one traveling alone it is paramount. I agree with John Ruskin, whose philosophy was that

> it's unwise to pay too much, but it's unwise to pay too little. When you pay too much, you lose a little money, that is all. But when you pay too little, you sometimes lose everything, because the thing you bought was incapable of doing the thing that you bought it to do. The common law of business balance prohibits paying a little and getting a lot. It can't be done.

Nowhere is that more true in traveling than in getting your accommodations, especially if you are traveling solo.

It is essential that you have a comfortable, attractive room to end your day in. If you awaken to a gloomy, poorly furnished, possibly even shabby room, your first thought of the day will be, "What am I doing here?" and it will not be easy to start your day with optimism and enthusiasm. If you would like to have a two-week vacation in Britain and stay in budget places, change your plans. Stay for ten days and spend the money the extra four days would have cost on good accommodations. You can find lovely B&Bs that cost half what a hotel will, but it is not easy to make reservations in advance unless someone can recommend a good one to you.

At times I have traveled without reservations so I could be flexible in deciding where to go and how long to stay someplace. Tourist Information Centres have a Book-a-Bed-Ahead plan, which I have used. I have stayed in excellent B&Bs by booking this way, and I have also been sent to places I would never choose myself. On this program you will be asked what your requirements are and how much you want to pay for a room. I always have three minimum requirements. I want a TV in my room because I enjoy certain British programs in the evening and because I watch the early morning news and weather (with a weather forecast I can more easily plan my day). I need a wash basin with hot and cold water in my room if there is no private bath. And I want tea and coffee-making facilities, which most places have.

Several years ago I gave these requirements to a girl who helped me at a TIC. I told her I would pay up to twenty-five pounds if I had a private bath, even though the usual rate was eleven to fifteen pounds in the town I was going to. Because the line was busy to the office she had to call, she suggested that I wander around town for an hour and then come back. When I returned I found that the first girl had gone to lunch and another one had gotten my reservation. She had obviously not paid attention to my three requests. She said there was no TV in the room she had reserved, but I could watch TV with the landlady. The rate was twenty-two pounds per night. When I arrived at the B&B I found that not only was there no TV in my room, but there were no coffee facilities in the room and that the only bathroom in the house was on another floor. The rate for the room was eleven pounds per night, but because I was in a double room I was charged for two. However, it was a spotlessly clean house and the elderly hostess was lovely and gracious, so I stayed for the

There are many kinds of accommodations in Britain. Bradford Old Windmill is one guesthouse that I have stayed in.

two nights I had reserved. She served tea and cookies while we watched TV in her living room. The third day I moved to an old medieval inn in the town center for my last three days. It had everything I had wanted and cost less than the B&B. As with most things, in traveling there are no guarantees.

There are ways that you can stay in better hotels at rates that are lower than the "rack" rates (the high rates you are quoted when you just call for a reservation). Some places offer a senior discount, usually to those over sixty. But in Britain there are package plans called "Breaks." Most hotels have several plans such as "Weekend Breaks" for Friday through Sunday, and "Midweek Breaks" that cover Monday through Thursday. A minimum stay of two nights is always required. The rates vary depending on the month and season. Some breaks include the room and breakfast, and others are for bed, breakfast, and dinner. To get an idea of the savings on these breaks you have to know what the regular room rate is.

For example, a room that I recently checked on charged £75 per night for a single room. That was approximately $115. But if you stay for two nights on a break plan, the rate for a single room with breakfast is £44 or about $67 per night. This hotel is a lovely 17th-century hotel in the Cotswolds and these rates were for stays during the off-season midwinter months. The difference between the regular rate and the rate on a break package is usually substantial in most hotels, during any season.

The difficulty in reserving these break packages is that in many cases you must write to the hotel directly to get the information on them. Travel agents can usually not book them for you, even by mail. When you write to the TIC in a town you plan to visit, ask for information on centrally located accommodations and you will get the addresses and telephone numbers of hotels you might want to consider. Then write to a couple of hotels and ask for a brochure and tariff (rate sheet), including any break packages the hotel offers. A much simpler way to get information on these packages is to get the brochure on breaks from hotel chains if they are available.

One hotel chain that will send you a brochure outlining a number of packages it has is Forte Hotels. Travel agents can make reservations for you on Forte's break packages. The rate is the same for you, and the travel agent will receive a commission from the hotel. Forte's breaks are called *Leisure Breaks,* and you must ask for this particular brochure or you might get another one. Request it by calling (800) 253-0861. I have sometimes found it difficult to get the breaks brochure. It seems that this office receives only a limited number of brochures, but it is well worth getting one if you can request it far enough in advance.

The Forte Hotel chain has several categories of hotels. I always stay in Heritage Inns and Hotels; there are fifty-two of them, and those I have stayed in are truly a part of Britain's heritage. Many are centuries old, with massive beams and huge fireplaces and lounges with a cozy ambience. The Forte Hotels offer the usual midweek and weekend packages, but you can save in addition to these two plans. For example, you can stay Friday and Saturday nights on a Weekend Break and extend your stay over Sunday night with an additional 50 percent off the Sunday break rate. There is also a plan that some of the hotels participate in, in which your entire package is reduced by 20 percent if you stay for five nights. Other money-savings plans are described in the Leisure Breaks brochure, and they all mean that the lovely Heritage Inns and Hotels become truly affordable.

You might even want to splurge and stay in a romantic four-poster bed; you would surely waken in high spirits in a four-poster. Each month different hotels offer special weekends. It might be a "Break for Murder" weekend, where guests help solve a crime, or a classical weekend that includes concerts for music lovers. Visits to gardens and playing bridge are two other specials featured. Forte also has a plan whereby the regular room rate is reduced by 30 percent if you make your reservations thirty days before your arrival date. I usually pick my hotels and then let my travel agent make the reservations for me.

Another directory of breaks that is available is *Best Western's Getaway Breaks*. You can get this brochure by writing to Best Western's office in Kingston upon Thames in England. Your travel agent cannot book these breaks for you; you must contact the hotel directly or call the British reservations telephone number listed in the brochure. You'll find almost 200 hotels on the breaks programs scattered throughout Scotland, Wales, and England. This diverse collection of hotels comprises timbered vine-clad coaching inns, seaside hotels, Regency mansions, a Georgian hunting lodge, and hotels on the shores of placid lakes. Some are old-world inns that date back to the 13th century with log fires, oak beams, and oak paneling that adds warmth. Others, built in the 19th century, have typical Victorian appeal.

The Getaway Breaks are similar to those available in many hotels. Some have a very reduced rate for Sunday night after a Friday and Saturday stay; some are four-night midweek breaks and there are winter specials at further reductions between November and February. Spring and fall specials offer the seventh night free on one-week stays. Best Western has special programs for a variety of interests. There are "Murder Weekends," "Body Beautiful" stays at hotels with spa facilities, and outdoor activities such as riding, ballooning, falconry, and feasting at a medieval banquet in a castle—all of these at selected hotels with the special facilities needed.

Choosing hotels to stay in is a fun part of planning your trip. It's easy picking hotels from the Forte and Best Western directories, which have colored photos of the properties, but you can write to any hotel you read or hear about and get information on that hotel's special packages. Break packages offered by various hotels do change from year to year so details can vary; looking into those available at the time you plan your trip is always worthwhile.

In considering these or other hotels, you can use the British rating system as a guide. There are six classifications that measure the facilities of a hotel. The lowest rating is Listed, which means that the accommodations are clean and comfortable, but services might be limited. From here the ratings are in crowns, starting with one crown and increasing to five crowns for hotels that have a private bath in every room, restaurants and bars that are open late in the evening, and all the amenities found in the best hotels. They do not indicate what the atmosphere or furnishings of the hotel are like or how efficient the service is. These qualities are graded by four levels of ratings that begin with Approved, then Commended, Highly Commended, and finally, at the top, Deluxe. These two methods of rating will give you a basic idea about the hotel.

There are other types of accommodations you might want to consider. The British Tourist Authority has a couple of directories you can send for. One is *Stay at an Inn*. It lists several hundred inns, some with as few as three bedrooms and others with as many as twenty-five. Each inn was chosen for historic, architectural, or literary interest. Many are in countryside locations, a factor you'll have to consider. To get details on any particular inn, write directly to the address in the directory.

The other directory is *Wolsey Lodges*. To get this listing of more than 200 guest homes you can stay in, send $2 and a 6" x 9" self-addressed envelope to the BTA in New York. Wolsey Lodges are patterned after a guest/host setting where you are invited to stay in a privately owned house. The homes are as diverse as the different regions of Britain are. There are rectories, thatched cottages, manor houses, lodges, and grand halls. The Old Rectory in the weaver's cottages in Bradford-on-Avon is a Wolsey Lodge. If you choose to have dinner in these guest houses you usually can, though some hostesses reserve a couple of nights for themselves and do not serve dinner then. I have found that these homes are so popular that even for off-season stays you should make reservations several months before your trip abroad.

If you send for these or other directories, the most important thing to check carefully is the rates. Directories and brochures printed in Britain, as are the four mentioned here, will all have rates shown in British pounds. To figure the dollar rate you will have to convert the pounds to dollars at the rate of exchange in effect at the time. If you write to Britain for reservations, remember to use the British system of writing dates; the day of the month is shown before the month. (March 6, 1997, is written 6/3/97). To avoid any problem with reservations, write out the name of the month. Another consideration in getting accommodations is the location of the hotel. You will usually want to stay in the center of town. Otherwise, you could have a long walk to the TIC, post office, and shops. If you're too far out you might have to depend on taxis to get to town if there is no public transportation.

When you make reservations ask about the hotel's cancellation policy in case your plans change for some reason. To avoid losing your deposit or having charges on your credit card you will have to cancel your reservation before the hotel's deadline.

British hotels use different terms than we do and it is helpful to know some of them. An elevator is a lift. Our first floor is their ground floor; and our second floor is their first floor. A private bath is shown as en suite; and an apartment is a flat.

At some time you will face the major complaint of solo travelers—the single supplement. Some break packages do not charge singles more. If a double room costs £44 per person for a couple (£88), a single room might still be only £44. If I am given a double room, I don't object to paying some single supplement, but if I get a very small single room I do object to an additional charge. I recently checked rates at a hotel at home and was given the rate of $96 for one, two, three, or four persons in one room. One person uses half the bedding that four would use, one-fourth the towels, soap, water, and everything else supplied in the room. I consider such a charge for a single excessive, and I never stay in a hotel that bases its rates strictly on this room basis. I have never encountered rates of this kind in Britain. However, it is possible that solo travelers can be considered less desirable than a couple when a hotel is full. The manager of a small deluxe London hotel was once describing the attention given to guests in his hotel. He explained it by saying, "We even have bathrobes in the singles," as if singles should normally not expect equal treatment.

Another kind of accommodation that can be fun is renting a cottage or apartment (flat). Called "self-catering," these rentals are usually "let" for a week, but, especially in the off-season, many can be rented for only three or four days.

The Landmark Trust, which protects so many historic buildings, has many rentals. You can rent a suite in a Royal Palace, a tower in Caernarfon Castle in Wales, or a stone-roofed grammar school built on a village green in 1556. Or you can take a ferry to the island of Lundy, which rises more than four hundred feet out of the Atlantic, and stay in one of more than twenty places in buildings of the pale-colored granite used there. It might

One year I rented this lovely cottage in an off-the-beaten-path village that had bus service only one day a week.

be a fisherman's cottage set in a sheltered spot on the sea, or an admiralty lookout, or Castle Cottage, built onto the outside of the keep. It was once the old post office. If you order the *Landmark Trust Handbook* that describes all the properties, you will find many you'd like to spend time in.

You might like one of two rentals that are special because of their location—each in the very heart of one of England's near-perfect cities. One is in Bath. It is a two-story apartment in a lovely building on Abbey Square. All the windows in the flat look out on the west front of Bath Abbey. One floor of the apartment has a living room and kitchen, panelled walls, and two fireplaces. Walking in the square and by the Avon River before the city center is awake would be an ideal way to start a day.

The other rental is in one of the most superb spots in all of England— the Cathedral Close in Salisbury. In the attic, up a 17th-century staircase, is the three-room apartment. From the sitting room window you have a painting of the beautiful cathedral with its graceful spire rising to the clouds. As with Monet's series of paintings of Rouen Cathedral, you have Salisbury Cathedral in as many different lights as there are hours of the day. The view out the rear-facing window is of a deep-walled garden that reaches down to the River Avon. The close is another good place for a walk in the still of an early morning.

The National Trust also has many self-catering rentals. When staying in one of these you are contributing to the conservation and preservation work of the Trust. You can choose from a converted stone-built byre, or stable; a ferryman's cottage at an old river landing; a round stone water tower with dormers in a steep conical roof; or a flat in the ancient city of York, near the famous minster and with a beautiful view of it.

You can get directories from both of the trust associations. The *Landmark Trust Handbook* is a catalog-size directory with excellent descriptions of the properties. There is a small map of each one showing the general area of the building and a floor plan of each rental with details such as stairs, fireplaces, and even furniture. You can get the *Landmark Trust Handbook* by calling the United States representative at (802) 254-6868. The cost in 1996 was $19.50. The directory of National Trust rentals is called *Holiday Cottages* and you can get it by writing to the National Trust in England or by calling 0-11-44-1225-791-199 in England and paying for it by credit card. The cost for 1996 was £4.50. *Holiday Cottages* also gives detailed descriptions and illustrations of each property.

There are thousands of other self-catering units throughout Britain, and you can arrange for one through a number of U.S. representatives. Some companies don't have directories or catalogs to send, but will suggest a particular rental after you have told them where you'd like to go and what kind of rental you want. I like to choose my own from a photo and a description of the location. I have rented from British Travel International and like it for several reasons. It has separate catalogs of country cottages in England, Wales, and Scotland. It also publishes a quarterly newsprint brochure called *British and European Traveler* with up-to-date information on events, transportation, and the accommodations it handles. The catalog of *English Country Cottages* has information on more than 2,500 cottages in 400 pages; *Welsh Country Cottages* has 64 pages of details on rentals; and *Scottish Country Cottages* includes 72 pages of information. These catalogs give excellent information about each rental.

If you are traveling by bus and train, there are several things to consider before renting a cottage. One is the town or village where the cottage is located. If the cottage is identified as being near a town, that tells you it is probably in a rural area and there may be no bus service to the location. Another is the cottage's proximity to shopping; at the bottom of each catalog description is the distance to shops and pubs. If it is three miles or even one mile to shops, that could mean that the closest pubs and grocery store are farther than you'd like to walk on a rainy day. Your atlas will show the nearest railway station, and British Travel International can give you some information on local buses.

The rentals in these catalogs are as varied as those offered by the Landmark Trust and National Trust. They include everything from a railway carriage to an oast house, a round tower which has an offset funnel on a cone-shaped roof once used for drying hops. And there is an apartment in a castle built by William the Conqueror in the 11th century. If you have watched the British TV series *To the Manor Born*, you'll remember Audrey's cottage. You can even rent her cottage, called West Lodge. You can call or write for the information on these brochures.

Self-catering rentals in Britain are rated, just as hotels are. The classifications in this case are keys—one to five keys determined by the facilities and equipment in each rental. A cottage with five keys, the highest rating, will have automatic controlled heating, a washer and dryer, bath and shower, telephone, dishwasher, microwave, and refrigerator. All rentals should be clean and comfortable, with a TV and full kitchen regardless of their key rating.

If staying in your own cottage for a few days appeals to you, there are thousands you can consider. You don't have to cook your meals, but it's nice to have a kitchen if you want an evening snack by a fire. It's a choice to think about.

American/British English

George Bernard Shaw said that "England and America are two countries separated by the same language," and once you're in Britain, the differences between American and British English will become obvious.

The first time I asked a restaurant employee where the restroom was, she looked puzzled, but wanting to help, showed me to a room with sofas and chairs where I could rest. It was the hotel lounge. In Britain the restroom or ladies' room, is the toilet or loo. Americans are squeamish about asking for the toilet, but after asking several times, it became easy for me.

In a B&B or small hotel without private baths, you might find a door with a sign that reads "Bathroom." And that is exactly what the room is; it has a bathtub and a chair and often that is all.

We bathe a baby, but the British bath a baby.

Many towns and cities have a "circus," which is a point where several roads converge. Signs of caution are everywhere—Mind the Step, Mind the Head, Mind the Gap—and these signs should never be ignored; they warn of possible danger. If you are to have dinner at half-six, dinner will be at 6:30 P.M. And you will find words like amongst and whilst in your reading.

Here are some of the words you might hear in daily conversations:

BRITISH	AMERICAN
bespoke	custom-tailored
brolly	umbrella
chemist	pharmacy
face flannel	washcloth
flat	apartment
fortnight	two weeks
gaol	jail
holiday	vacation
ironmonger	hardware store
lorry	truck
mackintosh/mac	raincoat
moving house	moving to a new address ("flitting" in Scotland)
off-load	sell, as in property
pavement	sidewalk
post	mail
public school	private school
stone (as in weight)	14 pounds
subway	underground pedestrian passage
surgery	doctor's/dentist's office
tights	pantyhose
torch	flashlight
tube	subway
underground	subway
Wellingtons/Wellies	rubber boots

The one time when you can hardly avoid making errors is in using names of towns and villages. There are really no rules you can use to determine the correct pronunciation of names. Often letters are just omitted, and sometimes letters that aren't in the written word are added in the spoken word. These are just a few:

WRITTEN AS	PRONOUNCED
Alresford	Allsford
Amhuinnsuidhe (House)	A-vinsuey
Beauchamp	Beechum
Cholmondeley (Castle)	Chumley
Colquhoun	Cohoon
Culzean	Klane
Derbyshire	Dar-bishir
Gloucester	Gloster
Hawarden	Harden
High Wycomb	High Wik-em
Keswick	Kezik
Kilconquhar	Kinn-uh-er
Leicester	Lester
Leominster	Lemster
Magdalen (College)	Maudlin
Mousehole	Mow-zel
Salisbury	Sawls-bree
Worcester	Wooster

I have been corrected only once for mispronouncing a name. When I was walking between seaside villages in Scotland and asked a young mother if the street I was on led to the road to Anstruther, she offered to walk partway with me and told me as we walked that the town's name was Anster. Railway ticket agents and bus drivers are apparently used to our precise pronunciation and understand what we mean. Others that I have met have always been courteous and ignored my errors.

On Rails and Backroads

The pleasure of sightseeing in Britain is partly due to the excellent transportation system throughout the country. British Rail (called BritRail in the United States), has 15,000 trains going to 2,400 destinations every day. National Express serves 1,200 towns and cities with daily long-distance buses (called coaches). And local buses extend a spider web of routes linking towns with deep-country villages and opening up remote areas to travelers.

I have heard Britons lash out at railway authorities for the drastic reductions in services. And when I first began traveling in Britain, I read that the rural bus service was infrequent and getting worse. But when I think of the train and local bus service in rural America, and of how non-existent it is in most parts of the country, I know how good British transportation really is. Over the years there have been few towns I could not get to easily. Occasionally I have taken a taxi to a village where buses are on a once-a-week schedule. Even so, considering that I have traveled from northern Scotland to far southwestern England and found good transportation with only a few exceptions, I think British public transportation is among the best I will ever find.

Foreign visitors will discover not only how good the services are but how reasonably priced they are. BritRail offers a number of discount passes for train travel, and National Express also has discount programs for coach travel. Those of us who are over sixty years of age can take advantage of several excellent passes for seniors.

If you contact BritRail Travel International, you can get a brochure on BritRail services and a map showing train routes. The brochure also describes its various passes. The first time I went to Britain I bought a one-month BritRail Pass, but it just didn't work for me. Because I like to stay in one area for anywhere from five days to two weeks, I didn't use the pass enough to pay for the cost. Since that first trip, instead of a Brit-Rail Pass I buy two other kinds of passes that are available only in Britain. The first one is a Senior Railcard. Since it is not sold in the United States, I buy it at the BritRail counter at the airport as soon as I arrive in England. For a very reasonable charge this pass gives me a one-third discount on almost all train services. There are some restrictions that are easy to follow. For example, you cannot always use them during rush hours in certain areas.

The other passes I buy are called Rail Rovers, and each one covers a different region of the country. One Rail Rover pass that I use allows travel in an area that includes Shrewsbury, Chester, and northern Wales. These passes are sold at a very reduced cost and include unlimited train travel for a set number of days. Rail Rovers do not cover all regions of Britain, but if you plan to spend several days in one area be sure to see if this pass is available. If you have a Senior Railcard you will get Rail Rover passes at an additional one-third senior discount. When I buy my senior discount card at either Heathrow or Gatwick airport, I always pick up brochures describing Rail Rovers at the same time.

I like planning my itinerary in advance. In order to do this I need to have details about train schedules to be sure I can easily get to the towns

I plan to visit. To do this advance planning I buy the *British Rail Passenger Timetable*. This timetable lists all the trains in Britain, and although the scheduled times might change, I will know what train service is available and on which routes I might have to change trains. BritRail's British Travel Shop sells the timetable. If I find that there is no train service to a particular place, I still have time to write to the Tourist Information Centre to inquire about local bus service.

It does take some time to get used to reading the train schedules. There are footnotes giving details of schedules that you must check to see if they apply to trains you will take. There are separate schedules for Saturday and for Sunday, when there is limited service. You might be advised to buy the *Thomas Cook European Timetable* instead, and if you plan to travel on the Continent this would be helpful. But if this trip will include only Britain this timetable is of little help. It shows only the main train lines and many towns are not even listed in it. To compare the two books, my old copy of the Thomas Cook timetable includes 75 pages of train service in Britain and my current *British Rail Passenger Timetable* has almost 2,000 pages of schedules. You might even have to use a magnifying glass to read the fine print needed to include all the train schedules in one book.

The twenty-four-hour clock is used in these schedules, but you quickly get used to following the times. For example, 0815 is 8:15 A.M. To convert to P.M. subtract 1200 from times after noon—1415 minus 1200 is 2:15 P.M.; 2005 is 8:05 P.M.

Each time I take a train I try to get a mini-schedule of the route I am taking. Not all stations have these mini-schedules, but many have arrival and departure times posted on monitors or on display boards. I make a note of the few stops before I will get off so I know when we are approaching my stop. Then I can enjoy the ride without having to constantly check the stations we go through. If you have to make a connection and take a second train to reach your destination, you often have to use stairs and an overhead walkway to reach a platform on the other side of the tracks. Everything is set up so simply that there is no problem in changing trains. And, there are always many other passengers who are glad to help you find your way. It is so easy changing trains that I have never missed a connection. If I did, it wouldn't be cause for concern because there will always be another train unless it is late in the day, and I make a practice of always arriving at my destination early in the day to avoid such a problem.

In larger towns and cities, stations have a shop selling coffee, tea, and snacks of various kinds. You can have them in the shop or take them on the train with you. On some trains the seats face each other and four passengers share a table. Britons take their lunch with them, especially on long trips, and so can you. When I stayed in one B&B for three weeks and got to know the landlady well, she packed a train lunch for me—a sandwich, a chicken leg, and a piece of cake. On one train trip a young couple brought their lunch with them and carefully unpacked a bottle of wine and two stemmed wine glasses. Many trains have a buffet car where sandwiches, cakes, and drinks can be bought to take to your seat. Often there is a trolley that wheels snacks and drinks through the train for those who haven't brought a lunch with them.

The trains in Britain have a great variety of cars, from vintage cars that probably should be replaced, to the luxury cars found on the new high-speed trains. It is a real pleasure riding the new trains, but I find some of the doors on the older cars very difficult to use. On some, you must lower a window on the exit door, then reach out and open the door from the outside. This might sound easy but it is not. British women on trains have told me that they cannot open these doors, and I certainly don't try. In fact, I have seen men have a problem with them. If I am the only one getting off at a stop (which is rare), I ask someone on the train to please open the door for me. A train conductor once told me to open the window and then ask someone on the platform to open the door for me. This has never been necessary because, almost always, there were others getting off at my station and I have just followed them off the train.

One thing to watch for is the gap between the platform and the train. This is where you'll see "Mind the Gap" signs. At some stations this gap is wide, and on some trains the step onto the train is high up and narrow. As long as you're aware of these things, you should have no problem getting on and off a train. I toss my bag onto the train before I get on so I can grab a hand-bar and get on easily; I also leave my bag near the exit door when I get off and then just reach in and retrieve it after I am on the platform.

There are several kinds of fares in train travel. A one-way ticket, called a "single," is the most expensive fare. A round-trip, called a "return" ticket, sometimes costs very little more than a one-way fare. There are some inexpensive "day return" tickets and on some return fares you can stay anywhere from five days to three months before using your return ticket. And you can buy a "saver" ticket or a "super-saver" ticket. It's easier to just tell the ticket agent how you're traveling and that you want the lowest fare when you buy a ticket.

Courtesy of BritRail

BritRail's Intercity high-speed trains offer comfort for long-distance trips.

Some discount passes cannot be used during rush hours, service is limited on Sundays and holidays, and there are no trains on Christmas Day. A few times when I've been traveling during heavy rains, service has been cut off because of flooded tracks, but British Rail has always arranged for buses to take passengers to their destinations. Stations in larger towns often have lockers where you can leave your bag if you have an hour or so between connections and want to sightsee in the town while you wait. If there are no lockers, there might be a baggage check-room, called a "left luggage" room, where you can check your bag while you roam.

British Rail has now been privatized, so changes in service and passes, etc. might be made in the future. If you are particularly interested in trains and train travel, you might like to buy another book from BritRail's British Travel Shop. It is an AA book called *See Britain by Train*. With maps and descriptions of more than fifty of the most scenic routes, you might decide to choose some of these areas as a stopping place.

The other long-distance transportation is National Express, the bus service that, with Scottish Citylink Coaches, links all major cities in England, Scotland, and Wales. These inter-city buses are called *coaches*. The National Express office near Victoria Station in London has information on and schedules for all the services offered, but lines at the assistants' desks are so long, even in midwinter, that I have never waited to get answers to my questions. Some TICs have schedules and can also sell tickets for coaches. British Travel International is the sales agent for National Express in the United States and can help you with some coach tickets. Just as BritRail has discount passes, so does National Express. The pass I buy is the Discount Coach Card for seniors over sixty. With this pass you will get thirty percent off all coach tickets. To get the card you need a passport-size photo. I just have a colored photo taken fairly close up so it has my full face when cut to fit and it has been accepted. This card is not sold in the United States, but you can buy it at either Heathrow or Gatwick Airport on arrival. National Express also has good service between airports and to many towns in Britain from either airport. The coaches used are comfortable and you can enjoy the leisurely ride while sightseeing. The cost of taking National Express is less than taking the train, but, of course, it takes longer to go anywhere by bus.

The other type of public transportation that you are likely to use is local buses. I once read that England has better local bus service than any other country in Europe and perhaps in all the world, and I would certainly not argue with that. Riding rural buses is a favorite way of sightseeing. You get a glimpse of life in different parts of the country as you ride. Charming manicured villages with streams and village greens are far removed in lifestyle from industrial or mining towns with dark row houses crowding the streets. Riding through the many different areas of Britain gives you a close-up view of towns and villages.

Local buses take you down the High Streets through the heart of towns, not down the back streets that trains often follow. And they trundle over hills and through valleys on narrow country lanes where you can see the church steeple long before you know a town is up ahead.

These buses are just what you'd expect—usually older, often creaky, but warm and friendly. If a bus you take starts its trip in a larger town, you might find yourself on a double-decker bus where you can ride upstairs and have sweeping views of the countryside. The narrow spiral stairway leading to the upper level is not easy to negotiate on a moving bus so take care. Once up there, you'll find that the ride will be a jolting jarring one, but if that is not a problem you might like to try it on a long ride. It also isn't easy to hurry down the stairs when it's time for you to get off, so you should be down before you reach your stop.

Sometimes these rural rides become almost a social happening. The atmosphere on the rural buses is informal and casual. In the off-season, when the buses are seldom crowded, I have sometimes struck up a conversation with another lone passenger to find that she is a fellow solo traveler. We might both be on our way to a famous landmark and spend the rest of the day together. On country roads, when two buses going in opposite directions meet, the drivers might stop so that their windows are side by side, and make plans for the evening.

The attitude of most rural bus drivers seems to be one of friendly assistance to everyone. Once on a bus to St. Andrews in Scotland a young mother waited at a stop ahead. She had a baby in a carriage and held a toddler by the hand. When we reached her, the driver stopped the bus, got out, picked up the little boy and carried him onto the bus. He held him until the mother picked up the baby, folded up the carriage, and was seated on the bus. It was as if this was an expected service for bus riders. Country ways are slow and easy and neighborly.

In remote areas drivers also double as delivery men. On one country bus I was on, the driver tossed a parcel out the window into a bus shelter and then explained to me that the man would be right out for the package. He would be expecting it. Many local bus companies also have discount passes. For example, Badgerline, the company that serves the area around Bath, Bradford-on-Avon, and down to Salisbury, has a half-price "Go-as-You-Please" ticket for seniors. The low-cost ticket allows unlimited travel on Badgerline buses for the whole day.

You could make a day of circling their route, stopping for an hour or so to see a village, then going on to stop at a museum in another town, and having lunch in yet another town before heading back to your home base. You could absorb a good part of the area in a day on this pass that costs just a few dollars.

I always try to have a bus schedule with me. They are usually easy to get, and if you don't have one you might get one from the driver. It is always important to find out where the bus stops for the return trip. It might be just across the street from where you alight, but it could also be halfway down the block. However, if you don't know where to wait, anyone in town will tell you. If you do miss a return bus, it is nothing to be alarmed about. Just as with trains, there will be another bus unless it is late in the day, but, probably like me, you will have planned to be home before it gets late.

Always there will be someone to help if you have questions. The police can tell you what to do, people in shops will help, as will anyone else you meet. A guide in Rye once told me that if a traveler ever needs anything, he or she should look up the priest or rector or vicar. The smallest towns will have a church that is easy to find.

There are some villages that don't have daily bus service. If you have a reason to visit one of these, you can usually get a taxi from a nearby town. The rates are seldom high and it might be worth the expense to you. In small towns taxis are not a regular service. Sometimes the taxi driver is a housewife who will take you where you want to go. I learned that one day when I waited with two other ladies who became impatient because the bus was late. One suggested calling a "taxi" and said that I could share it with them since we were going to the same place. We walked about a block from the bus stop and the women stopped and knocked on the door of a house. The woman who answered got out her car and took us all to the next town. Since then I have been taken places in a number of family cars by the lady of the house.

If you have thought of renting a car, there are a few things to consider. In Britain you drive on the left side of the road. If you're used to driving a car with an automatic transmission, you might not want to learn to drive one with a stick shift, which is less expensive, at the same time you're driving on the "wrong" side of the road. Some car rental companies have a maximum age limit, so if you are over sixty-five, you should check on any restrictions.

The British are aggressive drivers and seem to ignore speed limits. They career around corners and leave it to pedestrians to get out of the way. Then there are the traffic circles called "roundabouts" that are enough to have a timid driver in tears. If none of these things would bother you, you might want to rent a car for at least a part of your trip. The biggest disadvantage to driving is that it's not easy to read a map, watch for signs, and sightsee while you drive. You can cover much more territory, but you will spend more time alone. However, I have met solo travelers who drove and others who used public transportation, and they all have enjoyed their travels. I met an American traveler who always rented a car and drove to her first destination, then used trains and buses to get around. She didn't use the car again until she was ready to move to another part of the country. However you decide to get around, your time will be filled with seeing, and doing, and getting all the pleasure you can in the time you have.

Dollars and Pounds

The subject of foreign currency can be intimidating to so
in a foreign country for the first time. British currency i
in *Your Vacation Planner* that you get from the BTA. Mc....,
based on the pound sterling (£), and you will need pounds for everything you spend money on in Britain. There are as many ways to get British pounds as there are to get dollars here. You can buy traveler's checks
in U.S. dollars and have them converted to pounds at a British bank; you
can use credit cards for many expenses; and you'll find ATMs (Automatic Teller Machines) in most towns.

One of the most confusing things about foreign currency is that its
value fluctuates daily. For example: One August a few years ago, one
British pound cost $1.94; in October of that year the pound was worth
$1.62; and two months later, in December, the published rate for a pound
was $1.51. That means that 100 pounds bought in August cost $194, and
in December 100 pounds cost $151, a considerable difference if you were
buying $1,000 worth of British pounds. For the past few years the pound
has hovered around $1.55 to $1.68.

When you look up foreign currency values in the newspaper you will
find the rates shown in two different ways. For example, a listing under
the pound might read "Foreign currency in dollars" .65—that is, one dollar equals 65 British pence. This doesn't really mean much to me. I want
to be able to quickly tell how much something I buy will cost in U.S. dollars—how much a hotel, or train ticket, or lunch will actually cost me.
The second way of listing the value in the newspaper shows the value of
a pound in U.S. dollars. The value might be shown as $1.60 for one
pound. Then I know that if something costs 100 pounds, I will pay $160
for it, and I can estimate up or down from there. These two ways of
showing the value of the British pound will work out to something like
these approximate amounts:

Foreign currency in dollars (one dollar equals)	Dollar in foreign currency (one pound costs)
.50	$2.00
.55	1.82
.60	1.66
.65	1.54
.70	1.42

ɔ find the cost for one pound when only the figures in column 1 are ven, divide $1.00 by the amount shown—$1.00 divided by .65 equals $1.54.

There are several ways you can pay for purchases in Britain. Once the most common way used was to bring traveler's checks in U.S. dollars and exchange them at a bank in Britain for pounds as needed. Although we now have other ways of paying for things, traveler's checks are still of value. Often American banks with "senior" clubs offer traveler's checks to members for no fee, but you will pay a fee to convert them to pounds when you're in Britain. Try to cash them at banks in Britain, where the exchange rate is almost always better than in a hotel, shop, or restaurant. There are also Bureaux de Change where you can cash traveler's checks, but again, usually at a poorer rate of exchange.

British banks post the daily exchange rate on currency boards either outside the bank or in the lobby. These boards also show the value of many other foreign currencies, so if you're cashing traveler's checks you will look for U.S. dollars traveler's checks under the "We Buy" column. In many towns there are several banks near each other and you can compare the rate each one offers. In checking several banks in one town, I found rates that varied from $1.52 to $1.61 per pound. But to complicate things even more, each bank will charge a fee for a transaction. On this particular day these fees ranged from £2 to £5. The main value in using traveler's checks is the security you have with them. You don't have to carry large amounts of cash, and if traveler's checks are lost they will be replaced. However, if you choose to cash these every few days in order to not have a lot of cash, you will be paying a lot for high fees in the long run. Some companies sell traveler's checks for no fee to convert them if you go to one of their offices in Britain. However, because I am often in rural areas and these companies seldom have a nearby office, I still have to pay a fee to change these traveler's checks at a bank.

It is important to keep your receipts with the serial numbers of the traveler's checks you've cashed separate from the checks themselves so that if some are lost or stolen you will know which ones are gone and you can have them replaced. When you buy your traveler's checks, get the telephone numbers you would call if you had to contact the company either at home or on your trip. You can also buy traveler's checks in British pounds before leaving home, but the fees are often very high.

Today ATMs are widely used for getting foreign currency. Britain has thousands of ATMs throughout the country, including some at Heathrow and Gatwick Airports. Ask at your bank what fee is charged for transactions at foreign ATMs and what your daily limit for withdrawals is. Be sure you have enough money in your account to cover your expected needs. You can get a directory of the locations of ATMs for your particular card from your bank and either copy the pages that apply to your trip or tear out the pages showing locations in Great Britain. Usually charges on your account will be at the best rate available for consumers. Keep the receipt from each transaction you make so you can check your statement at home when you are billed.

The third way to use money on your trip is, of course, with credit cards. Visa, Mastercard (Access in Britain), and American Express are all widely accepted cards. If you use credit cards to pay for purchases, hotels, and so on, the exchange rate the credit card company uses to convert pounds to dollars is usually the most favorable one. However, it is usually costly to get cash with a regular credit card. You will not only be charged a fee, but you may be charged finance charges beginning with the day you get the cash. Check with your credit card company about charges and also find out if there is a limit to the amount of cash advances you can get on your card. Get the telephone numbers you would call both at home and in Britain for the cards you will use.

For more information on foreign currency there are some helpful brochures you can send for. Ruesch International, which deals with foreign money, will send a copy of *Foreign Currencies and Travelers Checks and Foreign Exchange Tips for the Traveler* if you send a business-size self-addressed, stamped envelope to its office in Washington, D.C. The company also has offices in New York, Atlanta, Chicago, Los Angeles, and Boston. The Consumer Information Center (U.S. Government) has a brochure called *Using Credit Cards Overseas* that is also helpful.

It is not always easy to figure out foreign currency far in advance of your trip because of the fluctuation in its value. Also, banks and credit card companies sometimes change the way they charge for using ATMs and credit cards, so you will want to check with them before you go.

While it pays to have a basic understanding of British currency and how to get it, it should not become such a concern that it causes anxiety while you're traveling. The reason to have some knowledge of it is to save money while you're there. I usually prepay some of my hotel charges, either as a deposit or payment in full if I'm on a break package. Expenses such as the cost of courses or any activity you arrange ahead of time are usually paid in full before you leave home. For the additional expenses I will have after I get to Britain I take some traveler's checks in U.S. dollars, my ATM card, and the credit cards I will use. With these in hand, I can get money as I go along and just relax and enjoy what I came to see and do.

Tours and Travel Agents

One distinct part of traveling smart is making the planning easy. If you decide that solo travel in Britain is in your future, planning the trip will almost always follow certain steps. Before you can know where in Britain you'd like to go, you have to learn something about the country. That begins with your research—reading books and sending for the specific information you want. Special interests you have or activities you'd like to participate in will mark some areas as places you'll want to visit. While you're making choices you can begin to follow airfares. It's not too soon to get some idea of fares and rules by checking with the airlines and following newspaper ads. When you begin to set a tentative itinerary and have some knowledge of airfare costs, and some thoughts about the type of accommodation you'd like, it might be time to talk with a travel professional—a travel agent.

A good travel agent will truly make your planning easy. She/he can untangle the airfares and rules you have become acquainted with. If you have to make a connection in another city to get your overseas flight, an agent can help with the best flights. An agent can also help you with hotels, travel insurance, and a passport if you need one. If you already work with a travel agency, maybe one of the agents has traveled in Britain or is a specialist in the country. That would probably be the agent to get help from. If you don't have a travel agent, spend a little time finding the right one.

There are several things you can do to find a good agent. A recommendation from friends is one of the best ways to find one. If you have to look for one on your own, there are a few things to look for. You can check your telephone directory for listings of travel agencies in your area.

Many agencies belong to the American Society of Travel Agents (ASTA), the largest travel trade organization in the world. ASTA, founded in 1931, has certain professional requirements an agency must meet to qualify for membership. Some agencies listed in the telephone directory show the ASTA logo in their ads. Call a couple of agencies and ask some questions. Is anyone in the office a CTC (Certified Travel Counselor)? In order to become a CTC, an agent must have five years of travel industry experience and must complete a comprehensive series of courses that can involve up to two years of study. It shows a dedication to travel work—to staying in the business over the long term. Being a CTC is an excellent credential for an agent to have. You might also ask if anyone in the office you're calling is a Destination Specialist in Great Britain. That designation indicates that an agent has gained expertise in the country through special study.

Many top travel agencies do not belong to ASTA, and there are first-rate agents who are not CTCs, but both of these show a commitment to professionalism. In looking for a travel agency to work with, you might pick a couple and stop in to talk with an agent. Don't expect a half-hour consultation. Agencies can't afford to spend much time on "shoppers," but they will be interested in a prospective new client.

If you're planning your solo trip to Britain you will have a good idea of what you want before you go to an agency. You can briefly describe the trip you're planning and tell the agent that you already know where you want to go in Britain, what kind of accommodations you've decided on, and that you will want help with your airline tickets and any other reservations she/he can handle. Some of the hotels you've chosen may include break packages that you have to reserve directly with the hotel in Britain, but there is still much that an agent can help you with.

Travel agencies' income has always come from commissions paid by the airlines, tour companies, hotels, and so on. In the past, few agencies charged clients fees for services. However, some of the commissions travel agencies receive were reduced recently, and many agencies now charge some fee depending on the plans they help you with. The kind of trip you are planning would normally be an FIT (Foreign Independent Travel), and would require much time-consuming work for a travel agent. However, you will have set most of your itinerary and the agent will not have to do the research this kind of trip would normally involve.

Talking with an agent for the time it takes to explain what you need will give you a good idea of whether this travel agent is the one for you. If you find one who is knowledgeable about Britain you might get valuable help in areas you haven't looked into.

If you have a home computer you might be able to get information on airfares, hotels, etc., but I prefer being helped on a personal basis. And there are many travel clubs associated with magazines, credit cards, TV programs, and associations for seniors. They normally have toll-free telephone numbers where you can get the information you need. Of course, they will want to make the reservations for you. Some clubs offer outstanding service, often through a topnotch travel agency, but, again, I like to work face-to-face with a professional travel agent of my choice. And after all, a travel agency is the only central one-stop place where you can buy every particular of your trip. If in searching for a travel agent you want to work with, you run across one who suggests that since this is your first trip to Britain you should take a tour—*run!* That agent has no idea of what you're talking about. She/he doesn't understand your desire to discover on your own, to meet the British and spend time with them if the occasion arises, and to join the growing group of solo travelers and to maybe meet some of them.

There are times when you might want to join a group tour. On my first trip to Britain alone, I went for three months, and on the first week I took a tour of Britain to get an overview of the country. You might find a three- to five-day tour that would be a good mid-trip break. If you are focusing on literary Britain, you might like a tour that centers on Dickens, or on the work of another British author you're interested in. Or you might just like a few days exploring a different part of Britain with a tour group,

If you find a tour that fits into your trip, check on the tour company with your travel agent. A good agent knows which companies are reliable and offer good value, and can also find out what consumer protection plans the company belongs to. If the company has any problems that might affect your trip, you will want to be protected. Paying for a tour with your credit card offers you some protection against possible loss. As with all contracts you enter into, read the fine print, especially on the pages called Terms and Conditions. This is where your responsibilities and the tour company's duties to its passengers are outlined. This is particulary important on tours of a week or longer.

Be aware of some of the disadvantages of group tours before committing yourself to one. Check to see if all meals are included; if the hotels used are budget or deluxe, or in between; if the "visits" to historic sights are drive-bys or if you can spend time there. On many tours your bags must be outside the door at about 6:30 A.M., which means you must be up and ready to go by that time. Does the tour move so often that you never spend two nights in the same place? When a tour moves through the country too fast, you often arrive in a town so late that you miss seeing almost everything. It happened to me on a visit to York. We arrived so late in the day that the museum we were to visit was closed, and the guided walk through the historic part of York began after dark. It didn't affect my trip because York was on my itinerary to visit later and I would be able to sightsee there for several days, but if that had been my only opportunity to see York I would have been very disappointed. I needed time to wander through the old streets and to see the museums we missed on the tour.

A disadvantage can be that after a long day of riding, your bones can begin to ache before you finally get to a hotel. The overwhelming disadvantage to spending my entire trip on a tour is that a tour insulates me from the experiences I came to find. There's no time for me to leisurely absorb some beauty I unexpectedly come across, and there is no opportunity for me to talk with British people and learn about them.

Once on the Isle of Skye I sat having cider in a hotel lounge when an older man walked in, almost unsteadily, and sagged into the chair next to me. I knew there were tour groups staying in the hotel and said to him as he sighed, "That sounds like a tired tour member." He slowly shook his head and said, "This is no vacation." As his tired wife joined him I thought that this couple would probably never take another tour; they obviously wanted to travel, but had picked a fast-paced tour that did not fit them. Maybe they would have enjoyed setting their own unhurried pace and not covering so much in a short time.

One real advantage of taking a good tour is that most tour leaders are knowledgeable and can give you information you won't get anywhere else. And you might enjoy meeting the other tour members.

All travel should be an enriching experience. There are tours I would like to take in the future, but they will always be a supplement to my own personally planned travel.

Staying Healthy—Staying Safe

Once you get to Britain you will want to be free to enjoy traveling. That means being worry-free, and you can take care of any anxieties you might have before you leave home. The two areas that might cause concern are health and safety. You can prepare for these in the same way you take care at home.

First, your health. Trust the professionals—your doctor and your dentist. Talk with them about your trip. They can give you advice that fits only you. Be sure to get copies of any prescriptions you have, and that includes eyeglasses. If you've had a special medical problem, you might want a brief report on it from your doctor. If you have two pairs of eyeglasses, tuck the second one in your suitcase. Medical care in Britain compares favorably with ours and if needed you should be well taken care of. Britain has a National Health Service, but it covers free medical care only in case of an emergency. You would be expected to pay for any other services yourself.

After you get a clean bill of health from the professionals, you can prepare for your in-flight comfort. Long flights can cause a number of temporary problems—swollen feet and ankles and jet lag are a couple that can be bothersome. You can work to alleviate both of these. First—and most important—be rested before the day you leave. If you're packed early and have taken care of everything at home in advance, you will be able to have a day or two free before you leave and you won't begin your trip carrying stress as excess baggage.

When you get your seat assignment, consider an aisle seat. It might be tempting to get a window seat so you can see the country you cross, but most of the flight will probably be at night so there will be little to see. Once at the airport, while you wait for the flight to be called, walk around and stretch some. You don't need extra time sitting in addition to the hours you'll spend sitting on the plane.

The first thing I do when I am seated on the plane is take off my shoes and put on soled socks for the flight. I carry them in a plastic bag in the outer pocket of my carryon. If you normally have a problem with your feet swelling, check with your doctor about that. You won't want to take your shoes off if you will have trouble getting them on again.

Whether or not you wear socks, exercise your feet and ankles often. Get up several times and walk up and down the aisles. Occasionally sit tall in your seat and shrug your shoulders; flex your hands and exercise in any way you can. Although the flights are usually at night—with dinner, a movie, and an early breakfast—there isn't much time to sleep. But nap if you can.

All the experts give these same tips for flying long distances: wear comfortable clothes, avoid drinking much alcohol or coffee, drink water frequently, eat lightly, and exercise during the flight. All good advice. The major problem most travelers seem to have is jet lag. For some reason, I haven't been bothered with jet lag, but it is said to cause headaches, nausea, and confusion, and to cloud one's judgment.

Research has been done on jet lag for years. Studies on combating jet lag have included the use of light and the use of hormones, but so far there is no real prevention or proven cure. The last remedy I read about is taking a stroll and stopping for coffee and a roll immediately after you arrive at your destination and before you begin traveling. Having two cups of coffee was said to alleviate symptoms.

You can send for two well-known brochures on jet lag. One is *Defeating Jet Lag* from Forsyth Travel Library, Inc. and the other is the *Argonne Anti-Jet-Lag-Diet* from the Argonne National Laboratory. You might like to try one of them. Other brochures that might be of interest to you are *Ears, Altitude, and Airplane Travel* from the American Academy of Otolaryngology and *Travel Tips for People with Arthritis* from the Arthritis Foundation.

As for traveling safely, follow the commonsense rules you practice at home. You should not walk alone in a strange place at night. Lock your hotel door. Women should carry their purse close to their body, and men should not carry their wallet in their back pocket. Use common sense with strangers. When you set your bag down at the airport or in a hotel lobby, put it between your feet so you can feel it. Be careful using ATMs—be sure no one is close enough to see your transaction. Watch your belongings in crowded areas.

Again, rely on the professionals. Two brochures on safety, at home and away, are of interest. *A Safe Trip Abroad* is a booklet you can get from the Superintendent of Documents in Washington, D.C. It costs $1 and includes a listing of other pamphlets you can order. The American Hotel and Motel Association will send a list called Traveler Safety Tips if you send a self-addressed, stamped envelope to its office in Washington, D.C.

There are no guarantees when it comes to health or safety, either at home or in Britain. The risks abroad are the same as those at home. Most experts advise not walking around looking at a map—you might look like an easy-prey tourist. But I'm a "map person." I like knowing where I am and what's ahead so I can't follow that rule; however, I do use common sense, and I don't usually use maps in big cities where thieves might be on the lookout for someone.

You can't enjoy yourself if you're being anxious about everything, but you can use precautions and the common sense you use at home.

Restaurants, Pubs, and Picnics

For anyone traveling solo for the first time, one of the most daunting experiences is dining alone. I avoid elegant candlelit restaurants in the evening because most other diners seem to be in pairs, and that can emphasize one's aloneness. With that exception I can eat alone as easily as I can browse in a library alone.

Although I want to enjoy the local dishes, food is low on my list of reasons to travel. I treat eating out as casually as I treat traveling through the country. Being served in a restaurant is only one of several choices you have at mealtime. The hearty English breakfast usually included with accommodation is almost equal to our breakfast and lunch combined. Snacks and lunches are easy to plan. You can stop in a butcher shop, bakery, and fruit shop and make up a picnic lunch. Or you can have a pub snack or stop in a cafe or tearoom for lunch. In many towns you'll have a choice of places to buy "takeaway" food to eat on a bench in a park or by the sea.

When I am staying in a hotel on a "break" package, dinner in the hotel is often included and on those days I have a light lunch. With the full breakfast served in most places I need only one other meal and maybe a snack. Sometimes I have one of the delicious lunches served in museums and cathedrals or in other special sightseeing spots, and want just a bite in the evening. Then I might stop in a market for something to take back to my hotel room.

I like British food. Every region has specialties for which it has become known—Welsh lamb and Welsh rarebit, roast beef and Yorkshire pudding, Aberdeen Angus steaks and Scottish river salmon. And then there are the famous regional cheeses—cheddar, Cheshire, and Stilton are just a few. The southwest is probably best known for Cornish and Devon cream teas—tea and warm scones with strawberry jam and rich clotted cream served on elegant English china. Everywhere in Britain you will be enticed by delectable desserts—flans, tarts, cakes, puddings, shortbreads, and every imaginable pastry. And the long-forgotten real whipped cream tops off many of these delights. Vegetarians will be pleased with the many dishes prepared just for them.

Many British words for food and dining differ from ours. Some that you will run into are:

BRITISH	AMERICAN
afters	dessert
banger	sausage
bap	hamburger bun
bill	check
biscuits (sweet)	cookie
chips	French fries
clotted cream	very thick sweet cream
crisps	potato chips
courgettes	zucchini
gammon	ham
gateau	fancy cake
greengrocer	fruit/vegetable store
joint	roast
mash	mashed potato
maize	corn
scone	biscuits with currants
serviette	napkin
shandy	beer with lemonade
shepherd's pie	ground meat/mashed potato pie
starters	hors d'oeuvres
sweet	dessert
swede	turnip

An English breakfast is a cheery way to start a day and is something you will remember. Although it varies from place to place, you will often have all of the following to choose from: fruit, juice, hot or cold cereal, muesli, eggs, sausage, bacon, grilled tomatoes or mushrooms, kippers, baked beans, and fried bread, or toast with jam.

There are a few differences between British and American food. Bacon is much like Canadian bacon (our bacon is called streaky bacon); toast is always cold; bread is always brown or white; and coffee is always black or white. And I found most sausage to have a high content of cereal, though I understand that "proper" sausage is making a comeback. There is no bottomless cup of coffee, and water is not served with your meal. In one restaurant where I asked for a glass of water it was brought in a stemmed glass and placed on a doily. I find that most British sandwiches are skimpy compared with ours. They are often not much more than a tea sandwich with one thin slice of meat and a leaf of lettuce. Soup can be

Stopping in a friendly British pub can become an enjoyable habit.

excellent or watery with very little in it. Restaurants display their menu outside with prices listed, so you can look before you stop.

A pub is a comfortable, easy place for a leisurely snack if you go just after the lunch rush. If a pub has two bars, a Public Bar and a Saloon Bar, or Lounge, the Saloon Bar is the better one. Pubs are usually self-service, with no tipping required. You order your food and drink at the bar. Some pubs have a wide selection of food, including soup, meat pies, jacket (baked) potatoes with peas, sandwiches, and the ploughman's lunch—bread and cheese with some bits of pickle, onion, or tomato.

If you find a friendly pub with good food in the town you're staying in you'll enjoy stopping there. If a pint of ale doesn't interest you, try a sweet cider, mild-sounding, but with a high alcoholic content. Or you might try a shandy—a drink with half bitter and half lemonade, or if that is too sweet, you might try a bitter with a lemonade top. Pubs used to close in the afternoon, but a recent change has allowed them to be open from 11 A.M. to 11 P.M. on weekdays, with shorter hours on Sundays. In quiet rural areas some pubs still close in the afternoon.

Because I have irregular eating habits my meals are often scattered throughout the day. On some days I might have several snacks instead of a full meal, depending on where I am and what I'm doing. Gourmets who place importance on dining can find restaurant guides, such as the red *Michelin* guides, that rate restaurants and cuisine. With the variety of dining options, no one will have a problem being satisfied.

Miscellaneous Notes

Airports and Airlines

The word *travel* comes from the word travail, which means "torment" and "painfully difficult," and nowhere is this more clear than in an airport. Most of us who fly frequently agree that the most stressful part of traveling begins when we enter the airport and doesn't end until we have left the airport at our destination. It's as if we lose control of our lives during this entire period.

With a mandatory check-in of two hours before an international flight, there is what seems an interminable wait before we're on our way. Many travelers fill this time with reading or with people-watching. But do move around, go through the shops, or walk through the terminal occasionally. When you check in you should have both your passport and a photo ID (such as a driver's license) handy. You'll need both when you hand in your ticket. Once you arrive at the London airports, Gatwick or Heathrow, your trip really begins. Transportation into London from Gatwick is excellent. The Gatwick Express train goes directly to London's Victoria Station. From Heathrow you can take the tube to Piccadilly Station, but one of the many bus services might be easier for one going to London alone for the first time. If your first stop is in Southwest or Western England or in Wales, there is good service from either airport to Reading, where you can change trains and then go on to your first destination. *Your Vacation Planner* from the BTA gives more information, and your travel agent can get details for you. The BritRail office in New York can also check trains for you. A nice feature at both airports is that free luggage carts are available for travelers.

One of the best brochures published by any government agency is *Fly-Rights: called A Consumer Guide to Air Travel*. The fifty-eight-page brochure includes tips on baggage, health, safety, how to complain, and more. You can get it by sending $1.75 to Dept. 133-B at the Consumer Information Center.

Passports

A priority in making travel plans is getting your passport. You can apply for one at about 1,200 U.S. post offices. If your local post office doesn't accept passport applications, it can direct you to the nearest passport office. If you do need a passport, apply for one as soon as you begin making travel plans. If you already have one, check to be sure it will still be valid throughout your entire trip. Also update the penciled-in information on the "Notice" page to be sure your address and that of the "Person to Contact" are correct. Normally you will have no reason to contact our embassy in Britain, but if you should lose your passport or want to contact the embassy, you should know where it is located. In Britain the U.S. Embassy is at 24/31 Grosvenor Square in London, and the U.S. Consulate is at 3 Regent Terrace in Edinburgh, Scotland.

Insurance

Travel insurance is something you should think about before finalizing your plans. You may or may not need or want insurance, but if you do, you should be aware of what is available and what the costs and restrictions are. There are many kinds of travel insurance—medical, baggage, trip cancellation, accident, and more.

Before you decide what you need, check on what you already have. For example, Medicare does not cover medical costs in Britain, but if you have a supplemental medical policy, it might pay for overseas care. If you decide to get medical travel insurance, *read the fine print* in any brochures you get. For years insurance companies had a preexisting condition clause in their policies. In some cases payment could be refused for any illness you'd had a medical consultation for or were taking medication for during the sixty or ninety days prior to your trip. Many companies have now relaxed the preexisting clause, but some still have stringent conditions defining their policies. Check on it.

Your homeowners or renters policy might be all you need for baggage insurance. Check with your insurance company to see what is covered. Cameras, jewelry, and other expensive items are not always covered. However, it is never a good idea to take anything of great value on your trip. As for putting valuables in hotel safes, consider that there could be a maximum amount that a hotel is liable for in case of loss. For example, in the United States each state determines a hotel's liability for loss of anything you put in a hotel's safe, and in some states the amount is so low that it might not cover the value of your items. If you should have to file a claim of any kind, your insurance company might require written proof of your claim. You should get a medical report as well as a bill from any doctor who treats you. For a loss, you should get a written police report plus a letter from a hotel manager if a hotel is involved.

Trip cancellation insurance offers compensation for some costs if your plans change due to an unexpected problem. All policies vary widely and you should know what you're covered for before you leave home. Some policies are so restrictive that it hardly pays to have one. I saw one medical travel insurance policy that would pay a maximum of only $50 for outpatient care. Another company charged higher rates for anyone over seventy years of age. And some policies *are not valid* in all states.

Travel agents usually sell travel insurance policies. Some of your credit cards might include some kind of insurance. Whatever insurance you have or get, do remember to have proof of any claims you need to file. And *always read the fine print* to avoid unhappy surprises.

Shopping

With British goods like fine china, woolens, and antiques on sale everywhere, you will probably be tempted to buy more than you had planned to. A worthwhile brochure outlining regulations on bringing articles back to the United States is *Know Before You Go*. This brochure and a number of others are free and available at forty U.S. Customs offices in the country. If you don't live near an office, write to U.S. Customs in Washington, D.C.

Because of weight and lack of space in my bag, I usually send whatever I buy to either the person the gift is for or to my home. I often have the store where I buy something pack it and mail it for me. In that case I am not charged the 17.5 percent VAT (Value Added Tax), but I pay for the postage. *Your Vacation Planner* explains how to get a refund on the VAT charged for articles you purchase and carry home with you.

Discounts

Something to watch for in your travels is the many discounts for seniors. Special rates often apply to those over sixty. Museums, galleries, historic sites, and many events reduce entrance fees for us. You will find senior rates shown as "Senior," "Concession," or "OAP." *Senior* we understand; *Concession* is a special privilege granted; but *OAP* stands for the unflattering Old Age Pensioner. Whatever it is called, it means there is a savings for seniors, and it is willingly given.

On The Homefront

In order to free your mind of concerns about home while you're gone, there are things you can take care of before you leave. Some suggestions are:

- Pay all bills that will be due while you're away.
- Be sure all of your insurance policies are paid up.
- Stop delivery of newspapers.
- Stop mail delivery or have someone pick up mail daily.
- Arrange for the care of pets and houseplants.
- Arrange for the lawn to be mowed or snow to be shoveled.
- Put expensive jewelry and valuables in your safe deposit box.
- Empty refrigerator of perishables.
- Don't leave a telephone answering message that says you're gone.
- Give a family member or friend a set of house and car keys.
- Leave a copy of the papers you photocopied with that person.
- Set timers for lights and maybe a radio if you have them.

If you'll be gone during an election get an absentee ballot. Take a list of any birthdays that fall while you're gone; getting a card from a foreign country is fun for the person at home. First-class letters from Britain can take a week to be delivered to the States.

At the last minute, disconnect electrical appliances, including the TV; adjust the heat in the house or apartment as necessary; lock all windows and doors, including the garage. It might seem like there is an inordinate amount of advance planning and too many "to-do" lists to bring this trip to fruition, but the end benefits of all these are considerable. You can travel worry-free without the niggling doubts you might have if you had left things undone. After all, the trip you're planning is meant to be care-free and fun.

You'll be able to agree with travel writer Rick Steves, who says, "Travel is freedom—it is recess," and that is what you'll have on your trip—freedom and recess from every day. Preplanning will become an easy way to travel wherever you go in the future. *Britain on Your Own* is written for solo travelers, especially those who have wanted to set off on their own but who have hesitated because it all seemed too overwhelming. However, this plan of making your own choices and following your own interests will also fit some who travel in pairs. Couples who would like to design a leisurely trip around their personal interests will find traveling this way a carefree and enjoyable way to go. And there is no reason why two friends can't map out a trip that fits the desires of each.

In the case of two friends traveling together for the first time, it is wise to make plans that will ensure that you will still be friends when you get back home. Talk over your interests and your living styles. Is one of you an early-to-bed and early-to-rise person and the other a night owl? Does one of you need three meals a day at set times while the other prefers changing mealtimes at will? Does only one of you smoke? In an afternoon spent together at home these differences might not be a problem, but this could change if you're together for a week or two.

There are ways to prevent irritations or squabbles that could ruin your trip. Having "separate" days can be a fun change. After breakfast some day you can each take a day-trip to a different place, and when you meet for dinner you'll have a lot to share. You could plan to have separate rooms at the same hotel once in a while. Or maybe you'd each like your own room every night. There are many ways you can travel together compatibly as long as your goals are the same.

Traveling solo can be a marvelous, enriching experience. The afterglow will remain long after you're back home. As William Wordsworth put it, "The music in my heart I bore / Long after it was heard no more."

Maybe there is a reason, a good reason, why you can't travel at this time, but you can set in your mind what you would do, where you would go, and maybe later—maybe another time—you can take your trip, and you'll be ready.

So design your trip and follow your plans and you will find your own Britain. As the English traveler John Hatt advised,

> Pack your bags and go on your travels before it is too late . . . Our greatest disappointments are nearly always for what we haven't done— not for what we have done.

RESOURCES

AMERICAN ACADEMY OF
OTOLARYNGOLOGY
One Prince Street
Alexandria, VA 22314

AMERICAN HOTEL & MOTEL
ASSOCIATION
1201 New York Avenue, NW
Washington, DC 20005-3917

ARGONNE NATIONAL
LABORATORY
9700 South Cass Avenue
Argonne, IL 60439

ARTHRITIS FOUNDATION
1330 West Peachtree Street
Atlanta, GA 30309

BATAVIA CUSTOM TRAVEL, INC.
Louise Brunn-Maywald, CTC
528 S. Batavia Avenue
Batavia, IL 60510
(800) 231-2930

BEST WESTERN HOTELS
Vine House
143 London Road
Kingston upon Thames
Surrey KT2 6NA
England
011-44-181-541-0050

BRITISH TOURIST AUTHORITY
551 Fifth Avenue, Ste. 701
New York, NY 10176
(800) 462-2748

BRITISH TRAVEL INTERNATIONAL
P.O. Box 299
Elkton, VA 22827
(800) 327-6097

BRITRAIL TRAVEL
INTERNATIONAL
1500 Broadway, 10th Floor
New York, NY 10036
(800) 677-8585

BRITRAIL'S BRITISH TRAVEL
SHOP
551 Fifth Avenue, 7th Floor
New York, NY 10176
(800) 677-8585

CALEDONIAN MACBRAYNE
LTD.
The Ferry Terminal
Gourock, PA19 1QP
Scotland

CONSUMER INFORMATION
CENTER
P.O. Box 100
Pueblo, CO 81009

CORNWALL CREATIVE
ACTIVITY NETWORK
Jackie Usher, Secretary
5 Rose Terrace
Mitchell, Cornwall TR8 5AV
England
COUNTRYWIDE HOLIDAYS
Birch Heys
Cromwell Range
Manchester M14 7DJ
England

ENGLISH WANDERER
see Batavia Custom Travel, Inc.

FEDERAL AVIATION
ADMINISTRATION (FAA)
800 Independence Avenue SW
Washington, DC 20591

FIELD STUDIES COUNCIL
Preston Montford
Montford Bridge
Shrewsbury SY4 1HW
England

FORSYTH TRAVEL LIBRARY,
INC.
9154 W. 57th Street
P.O. Box 2975
Shawnee Mission, KS 66201

FORTE HOTELS
Leisure Breaks Brochure
(800) 253-0861
Reservations (800) 255-5843

FRANZUS COMPANY, INC.
Murtha Industrial Park
P.O. Box 142
Beacon Falls, CT 06403

FRIENDS OF CATHEDRAL
MUSIC
Addington Palace
Croydon, Surrey CR9 5AD
England

GATEWAY EDUCATION AND
ART CENTRE
Chester Street
Shrewsbury SY1 1NB
England

HARRIS TWEED AUTHORITY
6 Garden Road
Stornoway
Isle of Lewis PA87 2QJ
Scotland

HF HOLIDAYS
see Wilson and Lake International

HOLIDAY COTTAGES
see National Trust Holiday Cottages

INTERNATIONAL TRAVEL NEWS
520 Calvados Avenue
Sacramento, CA 95815
(800) 486-4968

LANDMARK TRUST HANDBOOK
R.R. 1, Box 510
Brattleboro, VT 05301
(802) 254-6868

LINKS MANAGEMENT
COMMITTEE
Reservation Manager
St. Andrews, Fife KY16 9SF
Scotland

MAGELLAN'S
Box 5485
Santa Barbara, CA 93150

NATIONAL INSTITUTE OF
ADULT CONTINUING
EDUCATION (NIACE)
21 De Montfort Street
Leicester LE1 7GE
England

NATIONAL TRUST HOLIDAY
COTTAGES
Caithness, P.O. Box 536
Melksham, Wiltshire SN12 8SX
England
011-44-01225-791-199

OVERSEAS MARKETING
DEPARTMENT
(for choir information)
Wales Tourist Board
Brunel House
2 Fitzalan Road
Cardiff CF2 1UY
Wales

ROYAL AUTOMOBILE CLUB
RAC Motor Sports Association
Motor Sports House
Riverside Park
Colnbrook, Slough SL3 0HG
England

ROYAL SHAKESPEARE
COMPANY
Royal Shakespeare Theatre
Stratford-upon-Avon
Warwickshire CV37 6BB
England

RUESCH INTERNATIONAL
700 Eleventh Street NW
Washington, DC 20001

ST. ANDREW'S & N.E. FIFE
TOURIST BOARD
70 Market Street
St. Andrews, Fife KY16 9NU
Scotland

ST. DENIOL'S LIBRARY
The Revd. Peter J. Jagger
Warden and Chief Librarian
Hawarden, Clywd CH5 3DF
Wales

SUPERINTENDENT OF
DOCUMENTS
U.S. Government Printing Office
Washington, DC 20402

U.S. CUSTOMS
P.O. Box 7407
Washington, DC 20044

WESTERN ISLES TOURIST BOARD
26 Cromwell Street
Stornoway
Isle of Lewis PA87 2DD
Scotland

WILLOW WREN CRUISING
HOLIDAYS
see Wilson and Lake International

WILSON AND LAKE
INTERNATIONAL
468 B Street, Suite #3
Ashland, OR 97520
(800) 227-5550

WORDSWORTH WINTER SCHOOL
Dove Cottage
Grasmere, Cumbria LA22 9SH
England

INDEX

A

AA Big Road Atlas---Britain, 24
AA Book of British Towns, 26
AA Book of British Villages, 26
AA Illustrated Guide to Britain, 26
Abbey
   Churchyard, 135
   Foregate, 151
Aber Ia, 176
Accommodations. *See* Hotels, Inns and Cottages
Acland, Sir Thomas, 103
Administrative Counties and Regions of Britain (map), 25
Airfares
   blackout dates, 30
   seasons of, 30
Airports and airlines, 236-237
All Saints Church, 103
Allerford, 101-102
Ambleside, 105
American Academy of Otolaryngology, 243
American Hotel and Motel Assn., 243
Antiques, 50
Areas of Outstanding Natural beauty (AONB), 69
Argonne
   * *Anti-Jet-Lag-Diet*, 233
   National Laboratory, 243
Arnold, Matthew, 107
Art, 39-42, 138-139
Arthritis Foundation, 243
Arun, River, 62
Arundel, 62
Ashford Tunnel, 55
Ashley, Laura, 42
Atlas, 24
Austen, Jane, 37, 135, 136
Automated Teller Machines (ATM), 226-117
Automobile(s), 48. *See also* Royal;
Association of Great Britain, 26
Avill River, 96
Avon, River, 128, 135, 142, 146
Ayot St. Lawrence, 45

B

Bach, 43
Barton
   Bridge, 131
   Farm, 131-132
   Steps, 129
Baruch, Bernard, 20
Batavia Custom Travel, Inc., 71, 243
Bath (Aquae Sulis), 44, 46, 116, 134-138
   Abbey, 135
Battle of Hastings, 35
Battle of Stow, 118
Before you go, 240
Benedictine Abbey of St. Peter and St. Paul, 151
Berwyn Mountains, 159
Best Western Hotels, 243
   * Getaway Breaks, 210
Betws-y-coed, 76
"Bible in stone," 138
Bignor, 62
Binoculars, 41
Birdland, 125
Birmingham, 44
Bishop's Palace, 140
Black Mountains, 185
Blind House, 128
Blossoms Hotel, 156
Bodmin Moor, 38
Booth, Richard, 186-194
Borrow, George, 58, 161, 185, 197
Borrowdale, 105
Bossington, 101
Boswell, James, 156
Bourton-on-the-Water, 124-125
Bowness-on-Windermere, 109-112
Boy bishop, 143
Bradford
   Old Windmill, 133-134
   -on-Avon (Bradeford), 128-147
   -on-Avon Discovery Trail, 128-129
Braithwaite, 105
Brantwood on Coniston Water, 114
Brecon Beacons National Park (South Wales), 53-54, 185
Bridge
   Frank, 43
   House, 109, 177
   Tea Rooms, 132
Bridgegate, 154

Brighton, 43, 48
Brioche buns, 137
Bristol, 44, 46
Britain, 21 (map)
British
  * and European Traveler, 214
  Golf Museum (St Andrews), 50
  * Rail Passenger Timetable, 218-219
  Heritage, 26
  Isles, 21 (map)
  Tourist Authority (BTA), 23, 27, 44,
    47, 49, 211, 243
  Travel Center, 45
  Travel International, 214, 243
BritRail , 104, 217
  British Travel Shop, 23, 26, 219, 243
  Travel International, 214, 243
Brockhole, 112
Brontë, Charlotte and Emily, 37
Browning, Elizabeth Barrett
  and Robert, 161
Browns, 155
Bull Ring, 158
Burn How (hotel), 112
Burne-Jones, Edward, 40
Buses
passes, 218
schedules, 25, 104
travel, 217-224
Butcher Row (Flesh Shambles), 149
Butler, Lady Eleanor, 159
Butler Hill (Langollen), 159

C

Caernarfon, 76, 183
Caledonian MacBrayne Ltd., 42, 243
Cambrian Coast Line (train), 183
Camelot, 47
Campanile, 179
Camus, Albert, 8
Canal cruises, 54-57
Caravan parks, 114
Cardiff, 38
Cardigan Bay, 183
Carlyle, Thomas, 58
Cars. See Motor
Castell Dinas Bran, 159
Castle Combe, 19
Castle Museum (Norwich), 40
Cathedrals, 40-41

Chain Bridge, 140
Chamberlayne, Lord, 118, 121
Chapter House, 140, 142
Charles
  I, King, 28, 96, 118
  Prince, 173
Chaucer, 135
Chawton, 37
Chedworth, 125
Cheltenham, 44, 121, 123, 127
  Gold Cup Week, 123
  Promenade, 123
  racecourse, 123
Chequers, 145
Cheshire, 76, 153, 159
Chester, 36, 153-157
  *Heritage Centre, 156
  maps of, 156
  "* Walls Walk," 154
Chesterton, G.K., 32
Chichester, 44
China, bone, 41
Chipping Campden, 116
Christie, Agatha, 45
Churchill, Winston S., 34, 54
Circus, 135-136
Civil War, 28, 96, 143, 154
Clark Village, 138
Classes. See Education, continuing
Cleeve Abbey (The Ship), 103
Clive, Lord Robert, 136
Clwyd County (Wales), 158
Coaches, 221-224
Cob houses, 100
Coleridge, Samuel Taylor, 105, 107
Conigre Hill, 130
Constable
  country, 39-40
  John, 65, 105, 146
Consumer Guide to Air Travel, A, 237
Consumer Information Center, 227, 243
Conwy, 76
Cooper, A. Heaton, 107
Cor Meibion-Llangollen, 161
Cornwall, 38, 163-175
  Creative Activity Network, 243
Corser, Trevor, 172
Cotman, John Sell, 40
Cotswold(s), 116-127
  Antique Dealers' Association, 120
  getting to, 127

Lions, 116
Warden Office for the Cotswolds
    Area of Outstanding Natural
    Beauty, 127
Cottages. *See* Hotels, Inns and Cottages
Countrywide Holidays, 70-71, 244
County Maps of Old England, 109
Coventry, 44, 48
Coward, Noel, 45, 182
Creative Activity Network (CAN), 65
Credit cards, 227
Criccieth, 59
Crome, John, 40
Cromwell, Oliver, 28, 96, 118, 146
Cumbria, 105

D

de Breos, Matilda, 186
de Craeyer, Gaspar, 118
de Mohun's castle, 95, 97
de Montgomery, Roger, 151
de Quincey, Thomas, 107
de la Bruyere, Marion, 157
Declaration of Independence, 61
Dee
    River, 154, 161
    Valley, 159
Defeating Jet Lag, 233
Defoe. Daniel, 117, 137, 153
Delius, Frederick, 43
Derbyshire, 90
Designing your solo trip, 20-33.
    See also British Tourist Authority;
    BritRail; British Travel Shop; Hub;
    Solo traveling;
Devon, 163
Dickens, Charles, 38, 111, 135, 146, 149
Dickler River, 121
Didbrook, 116
Digbeth Street, 117, 118
Documents for travel, 203
Dollars and pounds, 225-228
Domesday Book , 61, 97, 118, 120, 128
    dating of events, 27-28
Domingo, Placido, 160
Dorchester, 38
Dove Cottage, 107
Dovedale, 116
Dozmary Pool, 47
du Maurier, Daphne, 38

Dulas Brook, 185
Dunster
    Priory, 96
    village, 95-104
Dutch Barton, 128
Dwyfor, River, 60

E

Early-closing day, 83
Early Man Gallery, 144
Ears, Altitude and Airplane Travel, 233
East Anglian counties, 39-40
Eastgate, 154-155
Edinburgh, 22-23, 44, 45, 112
    University of, 44
Education, continuing, 60-68, 74-79, 152
Edward, King
    II, 146
    IV, 157
Edwardian village shop, 125
Edwards & Edwards, 46
Eisteddfod, 44
Elgar, Edward, 43
English
    Channel, 138
    Civil War, and dating of events, 27-28
    * *Country Cottages*, 214
    Wanderer, 71, 244
Esthwaite Water, 113
ETARC, 161
Events. *See Forthcoming Events*
Exmoor National Park, 95, 100, 103
Eye, River, 122

F

Feathers (inn), 158
Federal Aviation Admin. (FAA), 202, 244
Field Studies Council, (FSC), 65, 244
Fielding, Henry, 135, 145
Fiennes, Celia, 135
Fittleworth, 61, 62
Flatford Mill, 40, 65
Fly-Rights, 237
Ford, Henry, 125
*Foreign Currencies and Travelers Checks
    and Foreign Exchange Tips for the
    Traveler*, 227
Forsyth Travel Library, Inc., 244
Forte Hotels, 209-210, 244
Forthcoming Events, 23

Fosse Way, 119, 123, 126
Fox Talbot Museum of Photography, 141-142. *See also* Talbot.
Franzus Company, Inc., 202, 244
Frenchman's Creek, 38
Friends of Cathedral Music, 44, 244
Friston, 43

G

Gainsborough, Thomas, 39-40, 105, 136
Gallox Bridge, 98
Gardens, 46-47
  of Remembrance, 97
Garrack Hotel, 174-175
Gate House, 177
Gateway Education and Art Centre, 244
George
  David Lloyd, 60
  Inn, 142, 146
Ghosts, 46
Gilbert, W. S. (Gilbert and Sullivan), 42-43, 145
Gingerbread Shop, 106-107
Gissing, George, 138
Gladstone Pottery Museum, 41
Gladstone, William Ewart, 74, 77, 78
Glasgow, 42, 45
Glastonbury , 128
  Abbey, 47, 131
Gloucestershire, 116
Glyndwr, Owain, 58
Glyndyfrdwy, 160
Girtin, Thomas, 40
Gold Rill Country House, 114-115
Golden Ball pub, 121
Golf, 50
Grapevine Hotel, 127
Grasmere Lake, 114
Gray, Thomas, 105
Green, George and Sarah, 108, 113
Greenfield Village (Michigan), 125-126
Grope Lane, 149
Grosvenor, Melville Bell, 116
Gruffydd, Llywelyn ap, 58
Guide to the Lakes (Wordsworth), 108
Guided Walks in the Cotswolds, 127

H

H F Holidays, 70, 244
Hadrian's Wall, 34-35

Hain Walk, 171
Hand Hotel, 161
Handel, 43, 145
Hardy, Thomas, 37-38, 43
Harlech, 183
Harnham
  Gate, 145, 146
  Old Mill, 147
  road, 147
  village, 147
Harris
  island, 42
  Tweed (Clo Mor), 41-42
  Tweed Authority, 42, 244
Hathaway, Anne's, cottage, 45
Haverthwaite Station, 111-112
Hawarden (Haordine), 76, 78
Hawkshead, 105, 112-113
Haydn, Franz Joseph, 43, 136
Hay-on-Wye (Y Gelli Ganddryl), 185-194
  Butter Market, 186
  Cheese Market, 186
Hayward, Samuel, 152
"Hazardous Material—Tips for Airline Passengers," 202
Health during travel, 231-233
Heath, Edward, 145
Hedgerows, 101-102
Heelis, William, 113
Helford, 38
Henry IV, 151
Hepworth, Dame Barbara, 169, 172
Hereford Cathedral, 40-41
Heritage Coast, 69, 164
Heron, Patrick (window), 173
High
  Cross, 151
  Gate, 145, 146
  Street, 123, 146
Higher Town, 100
Hiking, 69-73. *See also* Walking
Hill Top Farm, 113
Hillary, Sir Edmund, 58
Hole Int' Wall, 111
Holiday Cottages, 214, 244
Holiday travel, 30
Holmes, Oliver Wendell, 13, 20
Holst, Gustav, 43-44
  Museum, 123
Holy Trinity Church, 131
Holyhead, 159

Horseracing, 123
Hospitality, 18-19
Hotel
    lounge, 18
    savings, 30
Hotels, inns and cottages, 206-214
    directories for, 211-212
    rates in, 212
    ratings of, 211
Hotspur, 151
Houseman, A. E., 43, 158
Howson, J. S., 155
Hudson, W. H., 168
Hutchison, Mary, 107

I

Ice Estuary. *See* Aber Ia
In the Footsteps of Brother Cadfael, 151
Industrial Revolution and canals, 54
Inns. *See* Hotels, Inns and Cottages.
Insurance, 238-238
International
    Musical Eisteddfod, 160
    Travel News, 26-27, 244
Inverness, 42
Ireland, John, 43
Islamic houris frieze, 118
Island, 168-169
Itinerary, planning, 218-224

J

James, P.D., 92
Jeffreys, Judge, 133
Jewelery. *See* Valuables
Johnson, Samuel, 17, 156, 206
Jones
    Maureen, 160
    Rees, 158

K

Keith Prowse, 46
Kelley, Ann *(Born and Bred)*, 166-167, 174
Kennet and Avon Canal, 131
Keswick, 112, 114
Keyt, Captain Hastings, 118
Kilvert, Rev. Francis, 191-192
Kilverts (hotel), 193
King
    Arthur, 47

Charles I, 28, 96, 118
    Tower, 154
Edward
    II, 146
    IV, 157
    fortresses, 35
John, 186
Oliver (bishop), 135
Richard of Hay, 190
Know Before You Go, 239

L

Lacock, 141-142
Lady Well
    cottage, 130-131
    Spring, 130
Lake District, 40, 105-115
    tips for walking, 108
    weather in, 108
Landmark Trust, 29
    Handbook, 213-214, 244
Land's End, 164
Langdale, 108
Language, difference in usage, 215-17, 235
Lawrence, D. H., 175
Leach, Bernard, 172
Learning vacations. *See* Education,
    continuing
Legends and Myths, 47-48
Lewis
    Castle College, 42
    island, 42
Lind, Jenny, 153
Links Management Committee, 244
Lion (inn), 149-150, 152-153
Literature, 37-39
    Austen, Jane, 37
    Bronte, Charlotte and Emily, 37
    Dickens, Charles, 38
    du Maurier, Daphne, 38
    Hardy, Thomas, 37-38
Little Venice of the Cotswolds, 124
Livingstone, David, 136
Llandudno, 76
Llangollen, 154 , 158-162
    International Musical Eisteddfod, 160
    The Ladies of *, 159
Llanystumdwy, 60
Llewellyn, Richard, 38
Lleyn Peninsula, 183

Llywelyn, Robin, 182
Loch Lomond, 47
Lockson's Guide to Antiques in
	Britain, 50
London, 23, 50,
	Arts card (free), 45
	ghosts, 46
	to Brighton Veteran Car Run, 48
	West End, 44
Lower
	Broadheath, 43
	Slaughter, 121-122
	Swell, 118, 121
Ludlow (town and castle), 153, 156-159
	Broad Street, 157-158
Luggage, 197-199, 205
Luttrell Arms (a Forte Hotel), 95, 103
Lyme Regis, 38

M

Maentwrog, 60
Magellan's, 202, 244
Manor Hotel, 122
Mappa Mundi, 40
Maps, 21, 25, 34, 41, 43, 44, 47, 53, 58,
	74-79, 138, 156, 158
Marcher Barons, 156, 185
Margate, 46
Market, 83, 145
	Hall, 150
	Square, 146
Maugersbury, 118, 120-121
Maugham, W. Somerset, 194
Max Gate, 38
Mayflower, 36
Mendelssohn, 43
Menuhin, Yehudi, 43
Merlyn, 47
Mikes, George, 31
Milton-under-Wychwood, 116
Minehead, 69, 99, 103
Minerva, Goddess, 135
Minfford, 183
Minton, 41
Misericords, 41, 139, 154
Mitre House, 145
Mon and Brec canal, 53-54
Money. See Dollars and pounds.
Montpellier Walk, 123
Moreton-in-Marsh, 123, 127

Morris, William, 42
Morton, H.V., 15, 19
Motor Museum, 125
Mountain Goat Tours and Holidays, 114
Mount's Bay, 164
Mousehole, 164
Mozart, 43
Museum, 40, 41, 48, 49, 50, 123, 125,
	137, 141-142, 151, 156,
	British Road Transport, of, 48
	Photography, of, 49
Music, 42-44
Myths. See Legends and Myths

N

Nadder, River, 147
Nash, Richard "Beau," 136
National
	Express, 221
	Hunt Festival, 123
	Institute of Adult Continuing
		Education (NIACE), 63-65, 245
	Motor Museum, 48
	Museum of Photography, Film and
		Television, 49
	Trust, 29, 96, 97, 105, 141
	Trust Holiday Cottages, 245
Near Sawrey, 113
Nelson, Sarah, 107
New
	Inn, 146
	Sarum, 147
Newlyn, 166, 172
Newquay, 171
Newtown, 130, 133
Nicholls, Austin, 118-119
Nicholson, Ben, 172
North Gate, 145
Northgate, 154
Northleach Church, 120
Norwich, John I, 29
Norwich School, 40
Nottinghamshire, 47
Nunnery, The, 96

O

Oates Travel, 175
Off-season travel, 20, 30-32, 99 124, 127, 138
Offa's dyke, 34-35, 76, 162
Old

Dee Bridge, 154
House, 146
New Inn, 124
Rectory, 61, 63
Stocks Hotel, 126
Oolite limestone, 116
Oshima, Seiji, 173
Other Place (theater), 45
Outer Hebrides, 41
Overlord Embroidery, 36-37
Overseas Marketing Department of the
    Wales Tourist Board, 44, 161, 245
Oxenholme, 114-115
Oxford, 44, 123
Oxfordshire, 116

P

Paganini, Nicolo, 153
Painswick, 116
Paisley (Scotland), 42
Pantomime, 46
Pargeter, Edith (Ellis Peters) *(Brother Cadfael Chronicles)*, 151
Passports, 238
Pavarotti, Luciano, 160-161
Penrhyndeudraeth, 182
Penrith, 112, 115
Penwith, 163
Penzance, 164
Percy, Sir Henry, 151
Perfumery exhibition, 125
Photography, 48-49
Picnics. *See* Restaurants, pubs and picnics.
Plas Newydd, 159
Plas Tan-y-Bwlch, 60, 177
Poet's Bar, 115
Ponsonby, Sarah, 159
Poole Harbor, 69
Poore, Bishop Richard, 142, 145
Popjoy, Restaurant, 136
Porlock, 101
Porthmeor
    Bay, 174
    Beach, 164
    Hill, 169
Porthminster Beach, 164
Portmeirion, 60, 176-184
    Battery Rock, 179
    Campanile, 179
    Dome, 179
    Gloriette, 179
    Hercules (Hall of), 180
    Number Six Shop, 181
    Pantheon, 179, 182
    Telford's Tower, 179
    Town Hall, 180
    Triumphal Arch, 181
    Wilds, the, (Y Gwyllt), 181
"Portmeirion: The Place and Its
    Meaning," 181
Portsmouth, 38
Postal International Reply Coupon, 27
Potter, Beatrix, 111, 113
    Gallery, 113
Potteries, 41, 125
Poultry Cross, 145
Priestley, J. B., 117
Priory Steps, 133-134
Pubs, 17-18. *See also* Restaurants, pubs
    and picnics.
    signs on, 17
Pugin, Augustus, 147
Pulteney Bridge, 135
Pump Room, 135, 138
Pwllheli, 183

Q

Quay Town, 99
Queen Victoria's Golden Jubilee, 123
Queen's Head (pub), 113

R

Rails
    and backroads, 217-224
    passes, 218-219
Railway model, 125
Red Lion Gazette, 115
Red Lion Hotel, 115, 142, 145, 146
Reservations, 207-215
Restaurants, pubs and picnics, 234-236
Rhondda Valley, 38
Richard III, 157
Robin Hood, 47-48
    Tales of * Center, 48
Rodborough Fort, 19
Roman Baths, 135
Roosevelt, Eleanor, 20
Rose and Crown Hotel, 146-147
Rose Cottage, 125-126
Rosemary Steps, 129

Rothay River, 105
Round Table (King Arthur's), 47
Rows, The, 154-155
Rowton Moor, 154
Royal
    Automobile Club (RAC), 48, 245
    Crescent, 135-136
    Doulton, 41
    National Eisteddfod, 44
    National Lifeboat Institution
        (RNLI), 166
    Shakespeare Company (RSC), 45, 245
    Shakespeare Theater, 45, 65
    Victoria Park, 136
    Well, 123, 127
Royalist Hotel, 117
Ruabon, 161
Ruesch Intl., 245
Ruskin, John, 114
Russell, Bertrand, 182
Rutherfurd, Edward (Sarum), 147
Rydal Mount, 107, 108

S

Safe Trip Abroad, A, 233
Safety, personal, 231-233
Saint
    Alkmund's church, 150
    Andrews & N. E. Fife Tourist Board, 50, 245
    Ann's Gate (Salisbury), 145
    Chad's church, 150
    Deiniol's Library, 74, 77-79, 245
    Edward's church, 118
    Edward's Hall, 117
    Erth, 175
    George's church, 96-97
    Ia, 168
    Ives, 163-175
        Head, 164
        Island, 168
        Museum on Wheal Dream, 169
        Road, 171-172
        Tate, 173
        Wharf, 168
    Julian's church, 150
    Mary Tory, 131
    Mary's church, 150
    Michael's church, 100
    Nicholas's Chapel, 168
    Oswald's, 106

Peter's church, 122
Salisbury
    Cathedral, 48-49, 142-143
    gates to close, 145
    history of, 142
    Sarum, 142-144
    urban planning, 145
Sally Lunn's Refreshment House and
    Museum, 137
Santayana, George, 81
Sarum. See Salisbury
Saxon Church of St. Laurence, 131
Schedules, transportation, 219
Scissor-arches, 139
Scotland, 21 (map), 34, 41-43
Scott
    Samuel, 157-158
    Walter, Sir, 107, 161
Scottish
    * Country Cottages, 214
    Highlands, 40
Scribbling Horse, 132
Seasons of best travel. See Off-season
Selworthy, 101-102
Severn River, 43, 148, 150
Shaftesbury Abbey, 132
Shambles, 132
Sharington, Sir William, 141
Shaw, George Bernard, 45, 181
Sherborne, Abbots of, 144
Sherwood Forest, 47
Shopping, 132, 239-241
Shottery, 45
Shrewsbury, 28, 148-162
    "* Quest," 151
    "* Wonder," 152
Shropshire, 148, 159
    Regimental Museum, 151
    Union Canal, 160
Shuts, 149
Sickert, W. R., 172
Sign of the Angel, 142
Skidden Hill, 170
Slaughter, Lower and Upper, 121-122
Sloop Inn, 168, 170
Smeaton's Pier, 168-169
Snowdonia (Eryri) National Park, 58,
154, 176, 177, 183
Snowshill, 116
Solo traveling. See also Designing your
    solo trip; "Tips for the Solo Traveler"

and age, 20
comforts in, 15
designing your own, 20-33
Somerset, 69, 104
South Wiltshire Museum, 144
Southern National (bus), 104
Southey, Robert, 105, 107, 135, 171
Special Interests: Holidays and Short Breaks in Britain, 67
Special interests, 34-51. *See also* Education, continuing.
antiques, 50
art, 39-42
automobiles, 48
gardens, 46-47
golf, 50
history, 34-37
legend and myth, 47-48
literature, 37-39
music, 42-44
photography, 48-49
theater, 44-46
Spode, Josiah, 41
Staffa (Western Scotland), 43
Stay at an Inn, 211
Steinbeck, John, 182
Stoddard, John L., 36
Stoke-on-Trent, 41, 180
Stonehenge Gallery, 144
Stour River valley, 39-40
Stow
circle walk, 121
Lodge Hotel, 126
-on-the-Wold, (Edwardstow) 116-127
Stratford-upon-Avon, 45, 61
Street, 138
Stroud, 19
Sudbury, 39
Suffolk County, 39-40
Superintendent of Documents, 245
Sussex, 61
Swan
Hotel, 36 (Lavenham), 133 (Bradford), 186 (Hay-on-Wye)
Inn, 62
Theater, 45
Swell, Lower and Upper, 121

T

Talbot
Matilda, 141
Olive, 141
William Henry Fox, 49
Talybont, 56
Tamar River, 163
Tate Gallery, 173
Tatchell, Frank, 22
Teme, River, 156
Tennyson, 161
Thackeray, William, 135
Theater, 44-46. *See also* Edwards & Edwards; Keith Prowse
repertory, 147
Royal, 136, 175
tickets, 45-46
Thirsk, 38
Thoreau, Henry David, 51
Time To Learn (directory), 63-65
Tin mining, 163, 170-171
Tintagel, 47
"Tips for the Solo Traveler," 26-27. *See also* Traveling Smart
Tourist Information Centers in Britain (TIC), 27, 83, 95, 109, 123, 127, 128, 135, 138, 146, 147, 152, 154, 156, 219
Tourist(s)
attitude, 90-91
season
and restrictions, 30
and weather, 31-32
Tours and travel agents, 228-231
Towns End, 107
Trains, steam, 111-112
Transportation, 217-224
discount passes, 221
schedules, 219
super-saver ticket, 220
Travel
agents. *See* Tours and travel agents
documents, 203-204
light, 33, 197-205
reading for, 204
smart, 197-241
* *Tips for People with Arthritis*, 233
Traveler's checks, 226
Tregenna Castle, 172
Tremadog Bay, 59, 176, 183
Trewyn Studio, 172

Trowbridge, 134
Turner, J. M. W., 40, 105, 159, 172

U

Unicorn Hotel, 126
United Kingdom, 21 (map)
University of Cardiff, 150
Upper
　Slaughter, 121-122
　Swell, 118, 121
Using Credit Cards Overseas, 227
Usk, River, 55

V

Vale of Festiniog, 176
Valuables, 238-239
Vangelis, 43
Vicars' Close, 140
Village
　Gardens, 97
　Life Exhibition, 125

W

Wagner, 43
Wales (Cymru), 21 (map), 34, 44, 47,
　53, 58, 74-79, 138, 158. See also Welsh
　Marches
　North, 40
Wallis, Alfred, 172
Walking
　clubs and tour groups, 70, 152, 155
　Lake district, the, 108
　solo, 69, 73, 99, 101, 123, 147, 151
Walton, Izaak, 145
Warren (street), 170
Watch House, 178
Watergate, 154
Waterhead, 109-110, 112
Weather, 31-32
Weaving, 41-42
Webber, Andrew Lloyd, 43
Wedgwood, 144
Well-dressing, 90
Wells
　Cathedral, 138-141
　　clock, 140
　H. G., 182
Welsh Marches, 148, 150, 161
Wessex, 147

West Dorset (old Wessex), 37-38
Western Isles Tourist Board, 42, 245
William
　Duke of Normandy, 35-36
　the I, 150
　the IV, 153
Williams
　Clough, Sir, 176-184
　*-Ellis, Susan, 180
　Michael, 164
　R. Vaughan, 43
Willow Wren Cruising Holidays, 54, 245
Willy Lott's cottage, 40
Wilson and Lake International, 57, 70, 245
Windermere, Lake, 109, 112, 114-115
Windrush, 116, 124-125
Winfrith Health, 43
Wishing Steps, 154
Wolsey Lodges, 211
Wool. See also Yarn Market
　churches, 116
　English, 116
Worcester, 43
Wordsworth,
　Dorothy, 115
　William 105-108, 114, 161
　Winter School, 245
World Heritage site, 144
Wright, Frank Lloyd, 61, 182
Wye. See also Hay-on-Wye
　River, 185
　Valley, 40
Wyle Cop, 149, 152

Y

Yarn Market, The, 95-96. See also Wool
Yew tree (s), 86, 106
York, 28, 35
Yorkshire, 38
Your Guide to Britain's Gardens, 47
Your Vacation Planner, 23, 27, 29, 225,
　237, 239